A WEALTH OF KNOWLEDGE

Roll up your sleeves and put on your poker face, because the all-new *Winner's Guide to Casino Poker* will prepare you to take on the pros. Whether you're looking for general tips or expert secrets, this book will give you thorough lessons and better strategies for . . .

- ♠ Seven-Card Stud
- ♦ Hi-Lo Split—8 or Better
- ♥ Texas Hold 'Em
- ♣ Omaha—8 or Better Hi-Lo
- ♠ Crazy Pineapple—8 or Better Hi-Lo
- ♦ Draw Poker—Loball Ace to 5
- ♥ Jackpots
- ♣ Home or Private Games

Also includes information on ranking hands, fundamentals of winning at poker, managing your bankroll, the art of bluffing, a glossary of poker terms, and much more!

Also by Edwin Silberstang: *The Winner's Guide to Casino Gambling.*

"A must read for every player."
        —Len Miller, *Gambling Times Magazine*

THE WINNER'S GUIDE TO CASINO POKER

Edwin Silberstang

A SIGNET BOOK

SIGNET
Published by New American Library, a division of
Penguin Group (USA) Inc., 375 Hudson Street,
New York, New York 10014, U.S.A.
Penguin Books Ltd, 80 Strand,
London WC2R 0RL, England
Penguin Books Australia Ltd, 250 Camberwell Road,
Camberwell, Victoria 3124, Australia
Penguin Books Canada Ltd, 10 Alcorn Avenue,
Toronto, Ontario, Canada M4V 3B2
Penguin Books (N.Z.) Ltd, Cnr Rosedale and Airborne Roads,
Albany, Auckland 1310, New Zealand

Penguin Books Ltd, Registered Offices:
80 Strand, London WC2R 0RL, England

Published by Signet, an imprint of New American Library,
a division of Penguin Group (USA) Inc.

First Printing, April 2000
10 9 8 7 6 5 4 3

Copyright © Edwin Silberstang, 2000
All rights reserved

 REGISTERED TRADEMARK—MARCA REGISTRADA

Printed in the United States of America

For My Mother,
Fay Silberstang

Contents

If you know the enemy and know yourself, you need not fear the result of a hundred battles. If you know yourself but not the enemy, for every victory gained you will also suffer a defeat. If you know neither the enemy nor yourself, you will succumb in every battle.

—Sun Tzu, *The Art of War*

I

Introduction to Poker

Poker is a fascinating game, because success at the game is not dependent on any single component. It's always good to be lucky, but luck alone will not take home the money in the long run. Two other components are necessary, skill and psychology, and the foremost is skill. The winners at poker know that skill is of vital importance, while the losers bemoan their bad luck.

What exactly is skill when applied to poker? It's a simple question, but the answer is rather complex. There are many elements involved in playing out a hand of poker. For one thing, you're facing opponents who also want to win the money, and you must gauge the strength of their hands against your own hand. You must also build up a pot so that if you win, you win a great deal of money. I mention money often because that's the reason to play poker—to make money.

If you want to play poker to kill time, to amuse yourself, or to lose money and consider it recreational spending, then you're playing poker for the wrong reasons. To repeat, there is only one reason to play this game and that is to make money.

Now, I have mentioned that skill in poker is an amalgam of several elements. Gauging the strength of your hand and the opponents' hands is important, as is the building up of a pot. But there are many other factors to be considered.

What cards should you play in the first place?

Should you raise or call immediately? Do you want few or many opponents in the game against you on this particular hand? What are the odds of winning? What money does the pot offer you for a bet or raise? Should you fold your hand when you feel that you are beaten?

These are but a few of the considerations that make up the skill factor in poker. Another important element is psychology, and this sets poker apart from practically all other games. In chess, which is a game of pure skill, psychology plays an insignificant part. It is the skill of the player that counts. At the other extreme, in a game like roulette, which is pure luck, psychology plays no role either. You can't psych out the dealer or croupier. He takes that little white ball and spins it, and it lands on a number. Nothing you do will change the result. You can stare angrily at him, or smile or whatever, but that ball isn't going to be affected.

However, in poker, psychology plays a crucial role. A player brings to his or her game his or her emotions and feelings. Any poker player brings a lot of baggage to the table, and it is possible to take advantage of another player's weakness and fear, or even his or her bravado. In poker, it isn't always the best hand that takes in the money. An inferior hand can win, if the player of that hand bluffs out the player holding the better hand. This element of psychology must be mastered in order for you to be a winning poker player.

By studying and mastering the material in this book relating to the psychology of poker players, you will be able to take advantage of other players' weaknesses and strengths. You will also be able to interpret their moves and gestures at the table, so as to give yourself a decided advantage.

Although the games covered in this book are those offered by casinos and clubs, the advice given should help any player, whether or not he plays in a club or at home. There are a number of differences between the home and casino game, and these differences will be fully covered. Learning to play the club games can't help but make you a stronger player at private games.

In casinos or clubs you'll be playing against strangers, which forces you to be alert and observant, to get a feel for their strengths and weaknesses. But by the time you finish this book, you'll be well prepared for any game you enter. The good thing about casinos and clubs is that games are offered practically round the clock and at all levels of play. With the proliferation of gambling in general, close to thirty states now allow legal poker in their jurisdictions. And there will be more and more states coming aboard, with the increase in Native American gaming, and with riverboat and other kinds of casinos constantly springing up the length and breadth of America. If you become a skilled poker player, there will be plenty of opportunities to test your mettle and to make money in this fascinating game.

Although most readers may be familiar with poker, I don't want to assume anything. This book will cover everything pertinent to the game, from the ranking of hands to advanced winning strategies. I'll also cover all poker terms in the extensive glossary at the end of the book. My goal is to make you a winner, and everything in this book will be written toward that end. Thus, when you enter a casino poker room or card club, you'll be prepared to win, and have a decided advantage over the other players in whatever game you decide to play. You'll be a winner.

Ranking of Poker Hands

The vast majority of readers already are familiar with these rankings, but they are inserted for those who come to the game as beginners, and for those who might understand high rankings but are unfamiliar with low hands. This is especially true for games like **Omaha 8 or Better**, where both high and low hands share the pot.

High Hands

These are the standard winning hands in most forms of poker, such as **Seven-Card Stud** and **Texas Hold 'Em**. In our discussion of these hands, we assume that they are the best hands and will win the pot. For example, when two players hold a flush, but another holds a full house, the hand holding the full house would win, as we shall see. Therefore, when we examine flush hands to determine the winner we assume no other player holds superior cards. One of the two flush hands will win the pot, depending on the holding.

Five of a Kind

This occurs only in certain games where a **joker**, or **bug**, is used as a wild card. In all other high games, such as Seven-Card Stud and Texas Hold 'Em, there is no way to get a five-of-a-kind hand. An example of such a hand would be:

Royal Flush

When no joker, or bug, can make a five-of-a-kind hand, this is the strongest of all high poker hands. It can be tied but never beaten. It consists of the Ace, King, Queen, Jack, and 10 of the same suit. Suits have no preference, and therefore, a royal flush in clubs is equal to one in spades. The following is an example of a royal flush:

Straight Flush

This powerful hand consists of five cards of the same suit, ranked in consecutive order. Unlike royal flushes, which are all equal, a straight flush's strength depends upon the highest-ranking card shown. For example, a straight flush headed by a 10, called a "10-high flush," will beat one headed by a 9, and a Queen-high straight flush will beat a Jack-high straight flush. The following is an example of a straight flush:

The lowest possible straight flush would be:

This holding would be considered a 5-high straight flush, and any other straight flush higher than a 5 would beat it. If both players have the same high straight flush, such as a straight flush headed by an 8, the pot would be split between them.

In our example of the royal flush, the Ace at the head of the holding made it the highest possible hand. However, an Ace can either be the highest or the lowest card in forming a straight. When it is the highest card, the straight consisting of Ace-King-Queen-Jack-10 beats all other straights headed by a card lower than an Ace.

But an Ace can also be the lowest card of a straight, in which case it has the equivalent value of a 1. An example of this would be a holding of 5-4-3-2-Ace, which is the weakest of all straights in high poker.

As far as low poker games are concerned, where the lowest hand wins the pot, the 5-4-3-2-Ace, known as a **bicycle** or **wheel**, is the best possible low hand. Home game players often consider a low hand which consists of a straight or flush as only a high hand, but in casino and club games, flushes and straights are disregarded in determining a low hand.

Four of a Kind

When all four cards of the same rank form a player's hand, this is a four-of-a-kind hand. The fifth or odd card has no value, since it is the ranking of the four-of-a-kind that determines a winner. If one player has four Jacks and the other four 10s, the four-Jacks hand wins. The highest four-of-a-kind hand is four Aces; the lowest, four 2s. The following is an example of a four-of-a-kind hand:

Full House

This strong hand consists of three identically ranked cards or three of a kind, plus a pair of another rank. An example would be:

The strength of this holding is measured by the ranking of the three identical cards (the 10s in this example). When calling this hand, the player will state he or she holds "10s full of Jacks," or "10s full." It is the **trips** (the three-of-a-kind holding) that determines the value of the hand. Thus, this hand will beat one that has three 9s and two Aces. The pair is not taken into consideration in determining the winner when two full houses are held.

Flush

A flush is when all five cards in the hand are of the same suit. The following is an example of a flush:

The flush's strength is determined by the highest-ranking card in the holding. In the above example, the Jack is the highest-ranking card, and thus this hand is called a "Jack-high flush." It will beat any other flush that is headed by a card ranked below the Jack, and will lose to any other flush headed by a card ranked higher than the Jack, such as a Queen-high flush. If two players have flushes headed by the same ranked card, then the next-highest-ranked card is examined to determine the winner. For example, if another player has a Jack-high flush but his second card is a 9, his hand would be inferior to our example of a Jack-high flush and lose to it.

Straight

A straight consists of five cards in sequential order, of different suits. The highest-ranking straight is headed by an Ace:

The lowest ranking straight is as follows:

The above hand is known as a bicycle or wheel. If more than one player holds a straight, then the highest ranking card in the straight determines the winner. A 10-high straight will beat a 9-high straight. If both players hold identically ranked straights, such as a Jack-high straight, then the pot is split.

Three of a Kind

This poker holding consists of three cards of the same rank plus two odd cards. An example would be:

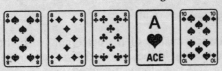

This hand will beat any other three-of-a-kind hand with lower ranking trips and lose to any three-of-a-kind holding higher ranked than 8s. A holding of three identically ranked cards is also known as **a set**. In a community cards game such as Texas Hold 'Em, two or more players may hold three-of-a-kind hands of the same rank, in which case the highest odd card held by a player determines the winner. In our example, the highest odd card is an Ace, which would beat any lower-ranked odd card.

Two Pairs

This hand consists of two separate pairs, plus one odd card. An example would be:

This hand is known as "7s over 3s" and its strength is determined by the higher-ranking pair, in this case the 7s. It would beat any other two-pair holding where the highest-ranking pair was lower than 7s, and would lose to any two-pair hand where the highest-ranking pair was 8s or better. If the higher pairs are tied, the ranking of the lower pairs determines the winner. It is rare to see two players holding the same identical two pairs in most forms of poker, but in Texas Hold 'Em, this may happen more frequently. In that case, the fifth or odd card would determine the winner, based on its ranking.

One Pair

This hand consists of a single pair, with three odd cards. An example would be:

This hand will beat any other hand of one pair where the pair is ranked below the Queens, and will lose to a pair of Aces or Kings. If two players have the identical pair, then the highest odd card determines the winner. If that odd card is identical, the next odd card's rank will determine the winner.

No Pairs

This is the weakest of all high poker holdings. The hand contains five odd cards, not in sequence and of different suits. If two or more players have no pair, then the highest odd card will win. If one player has an Ace and neither opponent has that high a card, the Ace-high hand will win. If two or more players have identically ranked high cards, then we look to the next-highest odd card, and so on, until we determine the winner.

Loball Poker

In those games in which the low hand wins, or in games such as Omaha—8 or Better or **Hi-Lo Split**, where the holder of the best low hand shares the pot with the holder of the best high hand, it is important to know exactly what the strength of your low hand is.

When determining which hand is the best low hand, remember that flushes and straights are disregarded and do not make the hand a high hand when considering its value. The most important aspect of low hands is the highest ranking of the cards in that hand. Unlike high poker, where the highest-ranking card in a flush or straight, for example, must be higher in rank than the opponents' for a player to win, in loball hands, the highest-ranked card in the hand must be *lower* to win the pot.

In high poker, an ace can be the highest card or the lowest card, depending on its best use in making a hand. In loball, however, the ace is always a low card, equivalent to a 1.

Now, let's examine low hands in order of strength.

The Wheel, or Bicycle

This hand is the very best. It can be tied but not beaten. It consists of the smallest straight, Ace through 5. It doesn't matter if it's also a straight flush; flushes and straights do not count against low hands. Here's the best hand; the **nuts** (absolute best). It's the perfect low hand.

Other Low Hands

Unlike high hands, there are no designations or names for each particular low hand. The hands are usually called by the two highest-ranking cards. The next best hand, after the wheel, is the following:

This hand is called a "6-4" to exactly describe the highest-ranking two cards in the holding. It would beat everything other than a wheel.

From a 6-4 we move to a holding of 6-5-4-3-Ace, a "6-5," which will beat another 6-5 consisting of a 6-5-4-3-2. The first 6-5 wins because the Ace in the first hand is lower than the deuce (2) in the second hand. Likewise, a 6-5-4-3-Ace would lose to a 6-5-3-2-Ace. Any "6" hand will beat a 7 holding, and any 7 holding will beat a hand headed by an 8, and so on.

In a number of casinos and clubs, the high-low games such as Omaha are structured "8 or better," which means that any hand 9 or higher doesn't qualify as a low hand. But other games do not have this caveat, and sometimes a hand consisting of a pair will be the low hand, beating out a higher-ranked pair. A single pair beats two pairs, and two pairs beat trips. What we're dealing with here is the exact opposite of high poker.

III

The Fundamentals of Winning Poker

This chapter is going to deal with the principles any poker player must follow in order to be a winner at the game. Study them and follow them; they can only help you.

1. Poker is a constant learning experience.

I don't care how long you've played the game or for what stakes; when you sit down at any game, you'll learn something new. Sometimes you'll get an insight into your opponents' plays, and just as often, you'll gain an insight into yourself.

In order to learn at the table, you must be observant. I see many players who, when out of the hand, simply lose interest in what is going on. But that is the wrong approach to the game. I've watched a friend, world champion Stu Ungar, at the poker tables, playing for extremely high stakes, and it is a learning experience just to watch him play. He observes everything: how the dealer is shuffling the cards, how players put in their chips, what they're saying, how they look at their cards, their expressions, everything.

That's what you should be doing. You're learning about the opposition, and about yourself as well. Are you giving away the strength of your hand by the manner in which you make a bet? Watch the other players and their reactions to your play. Are you forcing them to guess, or do they have some kind of read on you?

And conversely, does the way a player makes his or her bets give away anything that you can use against him?

When I'm up against a strong player, I watch his play carefully. I watch his moves, expecting to learn something new. When I'm bluffed out of a hand, or sucked into a losing play, I go over in my mind the dynamics of what just happened. I don't want to sit there stewing in my juices; instead, I want to come away with knowledge, something I can use against other players, or against the strong player himself. Which brings us to the second principle.

2. Be attentive and involved.

I mentioned that you should be watchful during the play of each hand, even when you're not involved in the betting. To do this, you must have a clear mind. There are various ways to cloud your judgment. You may come to the table with a bad headache. If that's the case, don't play. Don't put yourself at a disadvantage. Get out of the game immediately, take some medicine, and relax. There'll be another game for you. The games go on night and day in the casinos and clubs. Another table, another game.

You can also find yourself depressed or disturbed by some events in your life that have nothing to do with poker, but again, if you sit down with this frame of mind, you're at a disadvantage. Work through whatever is troubling you and sit down only when you feel peace of mind. There's a big difference between a disturbed player and one who is calm . . . and this translates to the difference between winning and losing.

If you come to the table with an illness such as a bad cold or the flu, you're inviting trouble, and the trouble will move rapidly to your bankroll. If you're not up to par physically, don't play. There'll be another game another time. I always liked what my friend Lem Banker said to me: "They play 'The Star Spangled Banner' every day." Lem doesn't play poker; he's a master sports bettor, but the same principle applies. If he doesn't want to get involved on any one day, he knows there'll be a game the next time around.

If you're at the table, the best way to stay alert is to not drink any form of alcohol, not even one beer. The great players don't drink and play, period. I've watched no-limit games at the Mirage, where eight players drank nothing stronger than coffee. Alcohol impairs everyone's judgment, and by doing this, puts you at risk of losing a great deal of money. When you should be cautious, you become foolhardy; when you should be aggressive, you may become a sheep.

Players just love to have a drunk in the game. If he runs unlucky, everyone is going to benefit. The drunk will be in on most hands, hands that no player in his right mind would stay in on. He'll be aggressive, betting weak hands, and often through his actions or words will give away the value of the hand he's playing. He's the sucker, the chump. Why be like him? Who wants to be a sucker or chump in life? Poker is life. It's not removed from life: It's just one aspect of life.

When you sit down, you need a clear head to watch what is going on. I often spot **tells**—that is, gestures or mannerisms that give away the value or strength of the opponent's hand. Is he throwing his chips into the pot aggressively? That's almost a sure sign of a weak hand. Is he, on the other hand, putting his chips in softly, nonaggressively? He might very well have a powerful hand. A player with a strong hand doesn't want to intimidate anyone; he wants to keep opponents in the hand so he can win the biggest possible pot. Is your opponent staring into your face after she's made a bet? That's intimidation. Why would a player with a strong hand want to intimidate an opponent?

Even when I'm out of the hand, I watch to see what all the players are doing. So should you. You'll learn a lot about the players, and this is half the battle in poker. You've got to know the weaknesses and strengths of your opponents. I watch carefully when a player is bluffed out, or refuses to lay down his hand, no matter how strongly others are betting theirs. I want to know which players I can bluff, which I can't. In the long run, this knowledge is going to make money for me.

But it all boils down to being alert at the table, watching every hand being played and each opponent. Go to the table with a clear and rested mind so you can observe everything.

3. Play poker for only one reason— to make money.

This advice sounds simplistic, but you'd be surprised at all the players who go to clubs for other reasons. They want excitement, or they want to get out of the house and play a man's game, or they want the thrill of gambling with money, hoping for a monster win, or they just want to kill some time. Poker shouldn't be a pastime. It is serious business and all the reasons I've mentioned are the wrong ones to play poker.

When you sit down at the poker table, you're there to make money, period. You're staking your bankroll for that purpose alone. You're not there to blow money and think that it's entertainment. It's not. Go to a movie instead, if you want entertainment. It's cheaper and the seats are probably more comfortable.

When you sit down at that poker table, you should be focused on winning money. Don't think negatively, figuring how much you can afford to lose, or when you'll quit a loser. Keep a positive attitude. This is not to say that you'll always be a winner at the poker table. *Nobody is always a winner.* But anyone sitting down and planning to lose, is going to lose. Plan to win.

4. If you're not comfortable with the game, don't play.

I'm not talking about a comfortably cushioned seat. I'm concerned with the ambience of the game. Is it a loose game, with everyone betting and raising on every card, often **capping the bets** (making the maximum number of raises permitted)? You can be playing with good cards, playing intelligently, and yet, to meet all the raises, you're draining your bankroll before you take in a big pot. If this kind of game makes you uncomfortable, then get out. Believe me, it can make anyone uncomfortable. Usually, there are players in there hoping for miracle cards in order to win, while others are going full blast on small or imagined card advantages.

Or you might find, since you'll be playing with strangers, that a couple of players are in collusion, and when they get one or more players in the middle, they raise and reraise, knowing the value of each other's hands. This doesn't happen often, but it can happen. Be alert to this. I remember a game at one of the California clubs in which two players were raising each other. It was **Texas Hold 'Em**, and therefore any player had the right to see the **hole cards** (unseen cards) of anyone who stayed in to the **showdown** (the showing of cards after all bets were in).

I wasn't involved in the pot, but one player was caught in the middle between two wild players who capped the bets on every round of betting. On the showdown, the caller of the last raise was the player in the middle of the raisers, and thus, he had the right to see the hole cards of the final raiser. The raiser turned over a pair of Aces. On the board was another Ace and a pair of fives, giving him a full house, a very powerful one.

The caller conceded, as did the other raiser. I asked to see their hole cards, as was my privilege. The caller, who had been stuck in the middle, turned over a pair of Jacks. Another Jack was out on the board, so he had a full house, Jacks full of 5s, but not strong enough to beat an Aces-full hand. The other raiser turned over a 10 and 6 **unsuited** (not of the same suit), an absolute garbage hand not worth playing in the first place, let alone raising on with a board showing an Ace, a Jack, and a pair of 5s. There was no way he was going to win, let alone be in contention, and yet he kept raising.

"What's going on?" I asked, and other players who were experienced in poker saw what I had seen. They called over the floorman, and wouldn't permit the dealer to remove the cards till the floorman saw the hands. He asked both raisers to leave the table and talk to him privately, and I got out of the game.

I've discussed wild games, but you may find yourself in with **rocks**, players who will only play hands they are assured of winning or have an excellent chance of winning. They'll go out hand after hand, and when they raise you can believe that you're up against a monster holding. This kind of player can make you uncomfortable, because when you're in there with good cards, you're getting no action, unless one of the rocks has a very strong hand. Playing against rocks can be a real struggle, making any player weary.

The best situation is to play against a combination of rocks and wild players with a few steady players thrown in. That's a good mix, enabling you to play at your best and to win some big pots.

In a casino or poker club there are games of all denominations and levels going on. Generally speaking, the stronger the player, the bigger the game he'll play. This is not always the case, to be sure, but it's a good rule of thumb. A player in a $10–$20 game is probably better than one who plays $2–$4 poker. During a game, players drift in and out. Some lose everything and leave; others cash in their winnings and depart.

New players constantly come into the game. If you see a player coming in with bigger chips from another game, you can figure he had bad luck at the other game and is trying to recoup his losses in a smaller game against less skillful players. It may not be so, but you must think of him as a strong player unless what he does at the table tells you otherwise. A player from a bigger game is used to faster action—that is, more raises right from the outset. Be aware of this when such a player comes into the game.

Conversely, a player with smaller-denomination chips may enter the game having scored a good win at a smaller game. Treat him the opposite, as a weaker player, unless he proves you wrong. Players get comfortable at certain levels of play, and can win at those levels, but find the going rough when playing for higher stakes.

Finally, if you're in a game where most of the players seem tough and experienced, and know each other, you might want to find another game to sit in on. Why play against tough players when it's a hard grind? Weaker players, and they number in the millions, are there to be taken. Watch the play of all participants and determine the weaknesses and strengths of the players. This is not as hard as it seems; we'll go into this later in the book, in dealing with individual games.

5. Play only when you feel no anxiety, either financially or emotionally.

What we're discussing here is money. It is perfectly proper to sit down at a poker table feeling a little tense. That mild tension can make you extremely alert, but when it turns darker, into some kind of anxiety, you don't want to be playing.

All this has to do with money. If you can't afford to play poker at a certain limit, then don't play in that game. If the money you're going to possibly lose in the game will hurt you or your family, then don't play. If it's either rent or food money, not poker money, then don't get involved.

Each of us has a comfort zone as far as poker money is concerned. You can have sufficient funds to play, but if your heart starts racing during the game, when a big pot is involved, then perhaps it's best to get out of the game. You don't want to develop high blood pressure under the strain of poker. When you feel comfortable at a game, when you're relaxed and calm, then you're in a good spot.

Try and play in a game you're comfortable in, free from anxiety. If you feel too tense, go to a smaller game. If you're bored, go to a bigger game. There's going to be a game right for you. The same thing holds for the kind of poker you play. If you find **Seven-Card Stud** difficult, having to keep track of the various opponents' hands during the playing out of a game, then try Texas Hold 'Em, where the cards are community cards and easier to follow. Or if you find the action at Texas Hold 'Em is too fast for your comfort zone, then perhaps a different game is in order.

The important thing is to be free of anxiety, that dread feeling that can lead to panic if you see your table bankroll bleed away. Play with money you can afford to lose either financially or emotionally, and you're on your way to becoming a winner.

IV

Bankroll Considerations

Let's assume that you've put money aside for poker, money that won't hurt you financially or emotionally. Just how much do you need to play serious poker? If playing for a long period, you need a "total bankroll"; for a shorter period of time, a lesser bankroll. For one play at the poker tables you need a table bankroll.

In the California clubs and other casinos and clubs around the nation, chips, or **checks**, as the professionals call them, and which terms we'll use interchangeably from now on, come in a variety of denominations and represent the equivalent in cash or money. You'll find $1, $2, $3, $5, $10, and $25 chips, as well as $100 and higher denominations. The poker rooms in the Nevada casinos, which at one time limited the denominations to standard $1, $5, $25, $100, and $500 chips to go with those used at table games such as craps and blackjack, now have added other denominations to make the betting simpler at the poker games.

Tiered Betting

The money you bring to a particular game is pretty much dependent upon the level of play at that game. We're going to discuss games that have a definite two-tier structure, such as $5–$10, $6–$12, $10–$20, and so forth.

What do we mean by a tiered structure, let's say, $5–$10? Assume you sit down at a **Seven-Card Stud** game. There are five betting rounds. The first three are at the lower level of $5; the last three at the higher betting level of $10. When a limit is established by the club or casino, the players must adhere to this limit. In a $10–$20 game, for example, a player can't bet $14 or some other odd amount. He must bet $10 or $20 depending on the round of play.

There are games that have smaller structures, such as a $1–$4 game of Seven-Card Stud. In these games, a player may wager from $1 to $4 on any round at any time. For example, a player may bet $1, and another player may raise $3 to $4, no matter what the round of play. There are games such as $2–$4–$8, with $8 allowed to be bet only on the final round of play, known as **the river**. We recommend avoiding these games. For one thing, the limits are too low for a skillful player, and secondly, the **rake**, or the club or casino's share of each pot, is much too high to make the game really profitable.

Now let's consider how much money you need. We'll start with the table bankroll, the one-session poker bankroll, and work our way up from there.

The Table Bankroll

There are three factors to consider for a table bankroll. The first is the poker game you're going to be playing, the second is the stakes involved in the two-tier betting scheme, and the third is the ante structure.

We'll discuss the two most popular casino and club games, to give you an indication of the correct bankroll for an individual session of poker. **Texas Hold 'Em** has become the most popular of all casino/club poker games, and the stakes are at various limits. You can play $1–$2 all the way up to $300–$600, and beyond that as well.

For purposes of our discussion, I wouldn't recommend playing in a $1–$2 game, or even a $3–$6 game. The reason is simple. You'll be playing against weak players who will be in on every hand. What difference is another buck or two, they figure. There's always a chance of a miracle developing. You can play these games from here to forever and never learn anything new. I therefore recommend a game of at least $5–$10, or better yet, the newly popular $6–$12 games.

$6–$12 is much more of an action game than $5–$10, mainly because of the number of chips involved in each bet. For some reason, the $5–$10 game tends to be a dead game, with a one-chip bet and that bet raised by one more chip, whereas the $6–$12 game requires three $2 chips for a bet and six $2 chips for a raise. There's something inherently more exciting about betting more chips, even if the final denominational value isn't that much more.

If you're in a $6–$12 game, get a **rack** of chips. A rack is a clear plastic container holding five sets of chips, totaling 100 in all. Since the standard chips in the clubs for this game are $2 checks, you'll get a rack of 100 $2 chips, or $200. In a $9–$18 game, you'll get a rack of $3 chips for a total of $300. Keep the rest of your cash in reserve.

The interesting thing about Texas Hold 'Em is that the betting structure is the same, no matter what stakes you play for. There are two "blinds," the small and the big. A blind is a forced bet based on position at the table, and the blinds move around the table in a clockwise position. The blinds are determined by their relation to the **button.** What is the button, first of all? It is a disk that determines the theoretical dealer. There is a house dealer at all times, but position is of crucial importance in Hold 'Em.

In order to level the playing field, the dealer doesn't always first deal the cards to the player to his left and then continue around the table in a clockwise manner. Instead the button moves around the table, and after every deal goes to the player to the left of the previous holder of the button. The cards are dealt first to the player to the button's left, then clockwise around the table, with the holder of the button getting his cards last. This player also acts last in betting, a big advantage to him. The player to his immediate left is the small blind and the player to the small blind's left is the big blind.

In order to promote betting action, the two blinds must make mandatory bets before they receive their cards. Let's say it's a $10–$20 game. The small blind must put out $5 and the big blind, $10. Then the player to the big blind's left must either match the $10 bet (**calling**) or can raise to $20, or if he doesn't care to put out a bet, must fold. In a $100–$200 game, the small blind would be $50 and the big blind $100.

The blinds are in the worst position, because they've already placed bets without knowing the value of their cards. Between them and the button are six or seven other players who can raise and reraise. However, the rule concerning blinds is quite democratic. Each player at the table, assuming there are nine players, will become a small blind and. a big blind once every nine hands. To repeat what we said before, the player to the immediate left of the button is the small blind; to the left of the small blind is the big blind. So when you're playing Texas Hold 'Em, expect to see two mandatory bets out on the table before the cards are dealt.

Generally speaking, the big blind in Texas Hold 'Em is equal to the smallest bet allowed in the betting structure, while the small blind is half of that. In addition to this forced outlay of money, there is an **ante**, or forced wager, to increase the size of the pot, or to give the house its rake. In the California clubs, the ante for the table is generally put in by one player, the button. A button is moved around the table to denote the imaginary dealer, as explained before, since a house dealer handles the cards at all times.

In Nevada casinos such as the Mirage, no ante is required in Texas Hold 'Em games and the rake is limited in the smaller games to just a few dollars. In the larger games, there is an hourly rate charged the players, while in the California clubs the hourly rate applies to games as small as $10–$20. As a general rule, you're going to pay more to play in poker clubs than casinos. I discussed this with both players and executives, and the reason for lower rates in casinos is simple—poker is just a small way to make some money for the casino. The big bucks come from the table games such as baccarat, blackjack, and craps. In the poker clubs outside Nevada, that's all they have going for them, poker games, and thus they have to charge more.

Let's now state just what stakes you need for a poker game. In Seven-Card Stud, I suggest forty times the minimum bet as a reasonable playing stake. Thus, in a $5–$10 game, you should bring $200 to the game. In a $10–$20 game, you'll need $400, and so forth. Since practically all poker casinos and clubs run **table stakes** games, which means that you're limited to betting what you have on the table in front of you, you should always have at least twenty times the minimum bet in front of you. This gives you adequate funds to raise and reraise and to call raises and reraises if you find yourself with a powerful hand that's pretty certain to win, without running out of casino checks. I suggest another twenty times the minimum bet in reserve in case you run low on checks after a particular deal and want to stay in a good game. You just take out cash from your pocket and convert it into casino checks. Now you're adequately funded for the next deal.

Unlike movie poker games, where it seems that if a player is out of cash he can borrow money to stay in the game, if you run out of money in casino/club games, you declare "**all in**," and part of the pot is segregated for additional bets in which you're not involved. Even if you have the best hand, you win only that part of the pot that you put money into. But I advise against being all in; try and have enough money for every bet you can make. It's poor judgment to have the best hand and win but a small fraction of a monster pot.

Seven-Card Stud games are structured so that the

bigger the game, the bigger the ante. In a $5–$10 game the ante is usually 50 cents, while a $10–$20 game requires a $1 ante. This is considered an average ante—10 percent of the minimum bet—but in larger games, the ante can be as high as 25 percent of the minimum bet, so that if you play $100–$200 poker you're putting in $25 before the first card is dealt. Where there is more than an average ante, bring at least fifty times the minimum bet to the table, plus another twenty-five times the minimum bet in reserve.

The two–blind structure, as noted, stays the same in Texas Hold 'Em, so, again, a good rule of thumb in these games is to have available forty times the minimum bet on the table. Thus, in a $5–$10 game you want $200, plus another $100 in reserve. With this much money, you're going to be well prepared to weather a couple of bad streaks at the table and still have enough to win that big pot.

The Total Bankroll

If you're going to play some serious poker for some time, and want to play on some sort of regular basis, you should have a total bankroll of at least ten times your table bankroll. Thus, if you need $300 for a single bankroll, have at least $3,000 as your total bankroll. Nobody wins all the time, and even great players and world champions run into losing streaks. You can, too, but that much in reserve should carry you through. As a rule of thumb, have ten times the table bankroll as your total bankroll.

Cardinal Rule: Always Have Sufficient Capital at the Table

This point has been pretty much covered in our discussion of the table bankroll. Don't be tempted to bring less to the table even if you're permitted to by the house rules. Most casino/club games require a minimum **buy-in**. A buy-in is the amount of money or chips a player has in front of him when he sits down at the table. For example, in the $5–$10 poker games on the Vegas Strip, the minimum buy-in is only $50. I consider that sum insufficient. A player can have only about $10 after a losing hand, and then what is he going to do, go all in? If he does, he'll win a small pot if he's lucky. That's not the way to play poker.

Generally speaking, the minimum buy-ins are about ten times the minimum bet, but I've already suggested having at least forty times the minimum bet plus another twenty times that in reserve. Play like a pro, and fund yourself like a pro. If you see the really big games and the top players in action, they buy extra piles of chips to intimidate the opposition. It's tough to scare out an opponent who has mountains of chips while you're playing around with a paltry few stacks making up a minimum buy-in.

I often think of one hand I was involved in where the pot built up to $1,500 and the best hand was four 8s. Unfortunately, that fool was all in and took the main pot of $100, while Aces and fours won the $1,400 side pot. From that moment on, I vowed never to be in a position of being all in.

How Much You Should Lose in One Session

Let's assume you've come to a $5–$10 Seven-Card Stud game with $200–$300 on the table and another $100 in reserve. But the cards have turned unlucky for you, and after the $200 evaporated you took out the other $100 and got involved in another hand, which you lost. You now have $50 in front of you. What to do? Leave the table. Wait for another game. Never let yourself lose more than you've brought to the game as your table bankroll. The first loss is the cheapest. If you lose $250, you can make that up easily. If you keep stubbornly playing and lose $800, that's a tough loss, and will be tough to make up in three sessions of play. Limit your losses. That's my best advice.

There are writers on poker who disagree with this advice, who feel that you should stay and play as long as the game is good. But the pros I've spoken to get out of games where nothing is going right, as far as the cards are concerned. I have a very good friend who plays $40–$80 stud poker as a pro, and I watched him play against a tough table in the Mirage, where everything went his way. He ended up with a nice four-figure win. I've also seen him play against a bunch of tourists and weakies at the Mirage, for the same stakes, and drop a few thousand. Nothing went right. If he had Aces up, someone had a set (three of a kind). If he had a flush, someone had a bigger flush.

It was a great game as far as the competition went, but he lost confidence in his cards and packed it in. "If things go badly," he told me, "I don't care if I'm playing against chimps; I book the loss and get out of the game." You've probably all had this experience. Some days everything goes wrong, while other times no matter what you do, you're going to win the pot.

As far as losing is concerned, I'd leave when I lost my initial table bankroll and half of the reserves. It's just not your night. Remember, there's another game the next day and the day after that. There's always another game. You want to minimize your losses. A few smaller losses can easily be made up, but a couple of monster losses not only will hurt your bankroll, but possibly will drain away your confidence as a poker player. Don't ever let it reach that point; take your small loss and get away from the table.

Maximizing Your Wins

You must take a different approach to leaving the game when you're booking a winner. Let's assume you're in a $10–$20 Texas Hold 'Em game and you've won a few big pots. You started off with $500 on the table, and now you're counting a win of another $1,000. Do you leave the table? The answer isn't that simple.

There are a number of factors to consider before you make any decision. First of all, is the game a good one? You may have been playing against a bunch of wild, weak players who have pretty much exhausted their resources. They've left and been replaced by some tough players. The weak players remaining in the game have few checks left to gamble with. The game has changed its complexion, going from easy to more difficult. I'd play a hand or two and see if the cards are still coming my way. If I lose the next two hands, I'm out of there.

But let's say that the weak players have bought in for more checks, and have stacks and racks of checks in front of them, just ready to lose. Stay in the game.

The next factor is fatigue. Are you too tired to think clearly? Time to get out. Small mistakes are often fatal in any poker hand.

If you're still alert but want to leave a winner, try a stop-loss approach. Let's assume you're ahead $600 in a $10–$20 game. Separate your chips either physically or mentally, so that $400 is put to one side. You mentally note that you want to leave with at least $400. We'll assume you lose a few hands and now have $420 in winnings. Pack it in.

But let's say that you continue to win. You're ahead $1,200. Put aside $900 in winnings and keep playing. When you get down to that figure or close to it, leave. You've booked a nice win.

What you want to do is leave a winner when you've played for a while and been ahead. It's a lousy feeling to have won $1,000 and watch it all dribble away after another hour or two of playing. When you're ahead, endeavor to leave a winner. That's money in your pocket for the next poker game.

Never take the attitude that the money represented by chips in front of you doesn't really belong to you. Just because you won them doesn't make them belong to anyone else. The worst thing you can think is this: "I'm winning $1,000 and now I'm playing with their money." You're playing with your money, not your opponents'. It's your money, and make sure you leave the table with most of it intact.

Getting Back to Even

Suppose you're involved in a $9–$18 Texas Hold 'Em game and have been playing for three hours. The cards have gone back and forth, and you find yourself behind about $200. You like the game; it's a good combination of wild, weak, and mediocre timid players. So you stay in. Finally, you take two pots running and count your chips. You're now ahead $6, after a few hours of trying to break even. What to do? My advice—leave. Just like draining away winnings, it's bad to break even and then watch it all go down the drain again. Of course, you might keep winning, but you might also have had enough poker for one session.

If you follow my advice in this chapter, you'll book small losses, have a shot at big wins, come out winning after you're ahead, and finally, once you break even, you won't give back anything. I believe these principles will make you a winner in the long run.

V

Essential Winning
Strategies

I'm going to discuss winning strategies that apply to
all games of casino/club poker. In my analysis of individual games, I'll discuss plays and strategies that per-
tain to each particular game, but here, we'll look at a
broad range of winning strategies. If you follow them,
you'll enhance your chance of winning at poker.

1. Aggression is the name of the game.

Poker rewards those who play aggressively, and
punishes the timid. An aggressive player is in there
raising with a playable hand, right from the outset. I
have a good friend, whom I'll call Billy, who came to
Vegas some years ago, leaving a dead-end job in the
East and trying to make a living at poker. He's not
the best educated guy in the world, having left high
school in his junior year, but he knows poker.

When he first came to Vegas, he tried his luck in
the $5–$10 games, and did well. He gradually moved
up, and fifteen years later he's playing $300–$600
against the best players in the country, some of whom
are world-class players. Billy is a **Seven-Card Stud**
player and always has been. That's his game and he
knows it cold. He can read players and he shows no
anxiety at the table. I sat in with him a couple of
times, just watching him play. Both times he was involved in $100–$200 games, and after losing a few
hands and several thousand dollars, he was joking with

me. Whether or not he was bothered by the losses I couldn't tell, and neither could the other players at the table.

Here's his philosophy in a nutshell, in his own words. "I make a decision on **Third Street** [the first three cards initially dealt to players in Seven-Card Stud]. If I'm gonna play the hand, I'm gonna raise any previous bet. I *never* **call**. I'm either in there raising or I'm folding the hand. That's it. There was one exception to this . . . a couple of years back I was dealt **rolled-up** Aces [three aces dealt at the outset]. So I played cute and just called, and everyone folded, saying 'Hey, Billy, you got a set of aces already!' That's the last time I called when I was in a pot.

"Now, doing this gives me a lot of strength. The other players are guessing what I have. If I show a 9 as a **doorcard** [the first open card showing in Seven-Card Stud], they have to do a lot of thinking after I raise. If it's a spade 9, do I have three to a flush? Do I have three to a straight? Do I have a pair of 9s? Trip 9s? Do I have a big pair underneath and the 9 is meaningless?

"They're guessing, which means I have an edge. Now, I could have trip 9s or zilch, but they don't know. I'm in there raising. If I don't want to play the hand, I'm folding. But I'm not always playing with good cards. I could have three **rags** [useless cards] and I'm in there jamming the pot. If I'm reraised, I put in another raise. I'm not going to be a caller." This is Billy's table image. He always protects his image as an aggressive player.

Bobby Baldwin thinks the same way. He'll put in the final raise just so he won't have to call the bet. Bobby Baldwin is a world champion; he knows the value of aggressive play.

I asked Billy about a legendary Seven-Card Stud player. "When I play Johnny [not his real name], he never backs off. You raise him, he comes back at you. The goddamn pot is sky high, he refuses to back off. So, when you're up against Johnny in a pot, you know

you're gonna have to commit a lot of
knows it and you know it. He just runs ov
If you don't have the heart for that kin
you can't play against Johnny. That's
great. He's always challenging you."

While watching Billy in one of the $100–$200 games,
I saw him force out two players with a triple raise.
Then he showed me his hand. He had a pair of 7s.
One of the players had folded an open pair of 8s, and
the other an open pair of 10s. Billy had 7s showing,
and just kept raising. They had to figure him for trip
7s, against two bigger pair. But that's the value of
aggressive play.

This is not to say that you should raise on every
card dealt in the course of a game. There are times
you'll want to check and there are times when it's
prudent to just call a bet. But aggressive play works.
If you can bet, the chances are you can raise, and
raising gives you the advantage.

An aggressive player often takes control of the
game. Everyone is looking to him when it's his turn
to bet. You can see the players literally wince when
he puts in another raise. He upsets the game; he
makes the other players uncomfortable. That's what
you also want to do.

2. Keep your opponents guessing.

In poker, it's a lousy feeling when you have to guess
what your opponent is holding. You're playing **Texas
Hold 'Em** holding two Kings, and there's an Ace on
board. You bet and are raised. Does the other guy
hold the Ace in his hand? You're guessing. You had
bet to see his reaction and now you've gotten it—a
raise. What *is* he holding?

Playing a guessing game is not only aggravating, but
a losing proposition as well. You've got to make your
opponent guess. I think of a hand I was in, holding
two black Kings at Texas Hold 'Em. I had raised in

rly position before the **flop**, and was called by two players. The flop (three cards dealt at once, face up, after the initial bet) held an Ace and two rags. I bet, one player went out, and the other raised me. Now, I was sure he had an Ace, but did he know what I was holding? With two Kings I was tempted to fold, but I wanted him to guess just what I held. I could have raised before the flop with an Ace-King holding. In that case I would have had the Aces also and the top kicker, making him a big underdog.

I reraised him, representing that I had the Ace also with a big kicker. He looked at me, while I kept my eyes slightly averted. Something else he had to guess about. By not intimidating him with eye contact, I was telling him I wanted him to put another bet into that pot. He sat there for a minute, then threw his cards away. I changed the situation at the table. I made him guess.

If you are in a game where you're always guessing, then you're a worried player and you're probably going to end up losing. One of the ways to stop guessing is to play strong cards; another is to play aggressively. We'll discuss these factors further in individual games.

3. Get rid of bad home-game habits.

a. Attempting to Disguise Strong Hands

In home games, players generally wait to see what happens in the course of a hand before raising. They do this for several reasons. Usually home games are filled with what the pros call "garbage poker," games with wild cards, extra draws, and replacement cards. By the time you finish playing one of these hands, you've seen about nine or ten cards. Big hands develop. A straight becomes useless; a flush is so-so. What you need is a full house or stronger hands.

Now, let's say you were dealt the following cards at the outset in one of these wild card games:

The tendency of most home-game players is to just call with a hand like this. First of all, they want to disguise its strength, hoping that another King turns up either in their hand or as a **spit card** (a card dealt open and aside to be used by all the players to strengthen their hands). Second, their Kings may just die against the six other hands all in the game at the same time.

You don't disguise strong hands in casino poker; you raise with them right off the bat. Let's assume you're playing Seven-Card Stud, a $5–$10 game at a casino. The rule is that low card **brings it in**—that is, is forced to make the first bet—for $1. Other players can call the $1 bet or raise to $5, or, of course, fold. Now, before I go further with this hand, I want to explain that *this forced bet is not a blind.* A blind is made before the cards are dealt. There are no blinds in Seven-Card Stud. The lowest card dealt on board at the outset must make a mandatory bet to start the action. The same player may be dealt the lowest card three or four times in a row. I've seen it happen many times. He or she then must make this mandatory bet each time. Since position is determined at random, depending on who has the low card on the first round of betting, and the highest cards for every subsequent round of betting, there is no button or theoretical dealer. And no blinds.

Let's say you are dealt the same hand as above, with the Queen♣ as your door or open card. A deuce of diamonds brings it in for $1, and another player holding a 10 calls the bet, and a third player also calls

with an 8. Now it's your turn, with three players behind you, each holding a smaller card than the Queen.
What do you do?

You raise to $5. By doing this, you're forcing the
players behind you to call a raise, probably with mediocre cards. Let's assume you get them out, and now
the holder of the deuce drops out as well. The two
other players, one holding the 10 and the other the 8,
call your raise. You've narrowed the field considerably. And you have a disguised hand. The opponents
figure you for Queens and if either one gets a Queen
he'll be happy. If you get a King you're absolute
boss here.

If you merely called the $1 bet, you might have let
in a player or two behind you, and the other three
players would also be in the game. You'd have five
players in for the $1 bet and anything could happen.

Here's a rule to remember about poker in general:

> When you have what you believe to be the top
> hand, you want to force other players out and
> narrow the field. When you have a drawing hand
> (a hand that needs improvement to win), you
> want many players in so as to get correct odds
> for your hand.

A pair of Aces at the outset is very strong in either
Seven-Card Stud or Texas Hold 'Em. By themselves
they may be strong enough to win; as the top of two
pairs, they're extremely powerful. Their value goes
down, however, the more opponents there are in the
game. If you hold Aces and don't bet them aggressively by raising with them, you might allow some fool
to stay in and get a miracle card or two and beat you.
If you had raised, he probably would have been long
gone. One of the worst things any player can see is
some weak hand **limp in**, because he wasn't raised,
and ends up drawing cards to beat his Aces or other
strong pair.

Conversely, if you hold drawing cards, you want

many players in the game. For example, suppose you hold 10♦ 9♦ as your **pocket cards** (first two cards dealt and hidden). You basically have a drawing hand, hoping to improve to a flush or straight. If the flop comes up 8♠ 7♦ Queen♥, you have four to a straight, but you're still an underdog. There are eight cards that can help you and thirty-nine that won't. Thus, you have eight chances out of forty-seven to win and with two cards to go, you're about a 2.4:1 underdog. If the next card doesn't help you, you're now a 4.8:1 underdog. What you don't want to do is stay in after an initial raise, and face one or two players. It just isn't worthwhile. You're not getting any value for your bets.

b. Not Raising Till You're Absolutely Sure You Have a Winning Hand

In home games, players will not raise till the **river** (the last card dealt out to the hand), because they're not sure that they have the best hand. If you do this in casino/club poker, you'll end up a loser, no ifs, ands, or buts. First of all, you'll be **checking** and **calling** (not betting or just seeing a previous bet). As Doyle Brunson, a great world champion, points out—if you can't beat a player who just checks and calls, you can't beat anyone. Very true. The other bad thing about this strategy, besides not winning big pots, is that players will realize that you'll only raise with the **nuts** (the absolute best cards) and won't call your raise. They'll read you as if you played with exposed cards.

One of the most derogatory names to be called in poker is "**calling station**." A calling station is someone who calls, doesn't raise, and waits and waits to get the very best cards. This kind of player cannot win at poker.

c. Not Betting or Raising on the River

There are players who, with the absolute best hand, won't bet it, or if it is bet, won't raise. They rationalize that they're nice people, and don't want to take advantage of a player with losing cards. Of course, they'll be raised when another player has the best hand. Poker is not a "nice" game. It is a game of aggression and power. If someone plays weakly, he'll be hurt. Often the difference between winning and losing is getting an extra bet or two in the pot when you have the nuts. It's what separates the great from the good players, and the good from the bad. Make sure you get as many bets in as you can when you have the best hand, especially at the river.

d. Being Ashamed to Fold with a Scare Card

This is another bad habit left over from home games. A player in Seven-Card Stud is dealt a 4♣ 7♥ Ace♠. The Ace is the doorcard. It's also a "**scare card**," because it's the best card in poker, and is scary to the opponents. However, this player is holding garbage, a hand not worth playing. In a home game he's ashamed to fold his cards because of comments by friends that he's a **rock** (a player who plays only the best cards at all times).

But really, who cares what anyone says about your play? You should be playing poker to win, not to please your opponents. If your hand is junk, get rid of the cards, even if an ace shows. Believe me, in a casino or club, no one is going to comment about what you do. Preserve your bankroll and don't play garbage hands because you feel uneasy about folding an open King or Ace.

---

4. Don't give away free cards.

A **free card** can be defined as a betting round in which no bets are made, so that, in essence, everyone in the game gets a free card. Don't you allow this to happen. If you have a hand that's strong and worth betting, bet it. If the hand is checked to you, bet it.

Occasionally you'll be **check-raised** (a player will raise after he checks). This is allowed in all casino/club games. But for the other 90 percent of the time, the player checking wants a free card. He's hoping you'll be checking also.

Two things can happen when you bet after one or more players check. First of all, they'll be calling you with inferior hands. If they had strong hands, they'd be betting. Second, you can win the pot right then and there, with everyone folding. Nothing bad can happen, except the check-raise, and if someone check-raises you, you have to figure that player for a very powerful hand. If you know his habits at the table and believe him, don't call his raise; give him the pot.

Conversely, you want a free card when you're the underdog with a drawing hand. In that case, if everyone checks to you, you can check also and see the free card, but only if your hand is inferior and needs improvement. There are a number of ways to get a free card. Raising at the outset is a good way, especially if you're in **late position** (one of the last to act). On the next card, everyone may check to you, and if you haven't been helped, you check along. That's another advantage of playing aggressively.

5. Learn to read other players.

By reading other players, I mean knowing the value of their hands by their actions or gestures. Here, psychology plays a part. Just the other day I was on the phone with a pro from Las Vegas, a dear friend of mine. I discussed a time some years back when he and I, along with Billy, whom I've mentioned before, were sitting in Billy's living room watching the show *Jeopardy!* It's a show that's watched by millions, of course, and you're probably familiar with it. Well, my head is filled with all sorts of facts, most of them useless, and I'm pretty good at the game, often beating the contestants from the privacy of my living room.

On this particular occasion I was easily answering the questions while my friend, whom I'll call Jack, and Billy were pretty much stumped. But when it came time for "Final Jeopardy," when players must answer the final question and can bet as much as they want, Billy guessed exactly what each of the three contestants would wager, down to about $100. He had already, in the course of the game, *read the players*. That's why he's such a great poker player. That's why he's comfortable at a $300–$600 game against some really scary players.

How does anyone get to read opponents correctly? It's certainly not a science, but I'll call it an art. First of all, you have to be observant. That's the primary factor, because if your head is in the clouds during a game, you'll observe nothing. Watch the game at all times as I've suggested before, even when you're not in the hand. Then watch and see how a player bets or raises.

In the smaller games, the weak players generally do the opposite of the strength of their hands. When they're holding weak cards, they're **splashing** their bets—that is, flinging in their checks aggressively. Why intimidate players when you have them beaten? The whole essence of poker is to keep weaker hands in the game so you can win more money.

Or they bet out of turn, or raise out of turn. When players do this and I'm up against them, I invariably reraise. I know they're putting on an act, and it won't work on any knowledgeable player. With good hands, players don't show overeagerness to bet, as a rule. Or they say something aggressive when betting, such as "Give up, you're beaten." This is strictly amateurish. Usually, they'll stare right at your face in a very intimidating fashion after putting in their checks, just daring you to call the bet or raise. What are they really doing? If they have the best hand, do they want you to fold your cards so they won't win more money? It's ludicrous.

On the other hand, when they have a monster hand,

they're reluctantly shoving in chips, as if it hurts them to make a bet. I got to know one player who talked trash during a game, and when he shook his head and moaned, I knew he was going to put in a raise. Or he'd say "Dummy is throwing away his money," referring to himself. Yeah, sure. As soon as he said this, I was ready to dump my cards. In other words, the amateur or weak player does the exact opposite of what is expected, or so he thinks. When he has a weak hand, he's aggressive. When he's strong, he bets as though it's a physical effort to get those checks to the middle of the table.

These are also called **tells**, giving away the value of their hands by their moves or gestures. Players, in order to entice you into a bet or raise, will often look away from your face down to the table itself. Watch for this gesture; it happens often and is a dead giveaway. They generally have a strong hand and don't want to intimidate you or stop you from betting.

As you get into bigger games or play against stronger players, the tells won't be so apparent. They'll be more subtle. More sophisticated players won't be splashing their checks or staring you down. However, they may bet in a certain manner, giving away the value of their hands. Their faces may change expression or they may count their checks when they have a strong hand, and just shove in their checks when they're weak. Or vice-versa. Be alert to any tell you can pick up; it's an invaluable tool that can make you a great deal of money.

Doyle Brunson, two-time world champion at Texas Hold 'Em, was involved a number of years ago in a no-limit game. No limit means just that; you can bet whatever you have in front of you at any time, go **all in**. His opponent had just made a bet in the thousands. Doyle turned over his cards and immediately stared at the opponent, who, first of all, took a good look at Doyle's cards. Then he reacted to their value. How did he react? His face was stony and nothing changed; after all, this was a world-class player. Doyle studied the man, then shoved in his chips, called the bet, and won the pot. Someone asked Doyle what he had seen.

"The guy's face didn't move," the man said.

"No, it didn't, but did you see the pulse on his neck?"

That's why Doyle is a world champion.

It's not only tells and gestures and pulses that give away a player's cards. Great players follow the trail of the money. My friend Jack was describing a recent hand he observed Billy playing in $300–$600 Seven-Card Stud. Billy was low card and had to bring it in with an open 3. He showed Jack his hole cards, a pair of 4s. Everyone folded but one opponent three seats down, who was holding a King, the highest door card on the table. The King raised, and Billy called the raise. If Billy was behind the King, he would have raised or folded, that's his style, but here, forced to play as low card, he merely called.

The next card Billy got was a 9, and his opponent drew a Queen. The King-Queen checked and Billy bet. You don't get free cards from Billy unless he wants a free card also. He was called. On **Fifth Street** (each player holding five cards) Billy got a 4, giving him trips, while his opponent bought a deuce. The opponent, still high, checked, and Billy bet. He was check-raised. Now here was the situation. Billy held a pair of fours in the hole, and a 3♣ 9♦ 4♠ on board. His opponent held two unknown hole cards and a King♠ Queen♥ 2♦ on board.

Billy, faced with the check-raise, reraised, and his opponent called. The next card each received was a rag, helping neither. The opponent bet, Billy raised and was called. On the river, Billy got a 9, filling in his full house, and when his opponent checked, he bet, and then was called. Before the other player showed his hand, Billy whispered to Jack, "He's got trip deuces." And sure enough that's what the other player had.

Later, Jack, amazed by this call of the cards, asked Billy how he knew he was up against this exact hand.

"Well," said Billy, "when he raised with the King, I figured he didn't have a pair of Kings. He might be tempted to just call and **slowplay** [not raise with powerful cards]. That's his style. So I didn't put him on Kings. His money came out when he bought the deuce, and right then I figured, he came in with deuces in the hole and a King as a doorcard. And that's the way I played it. I followed the money."

What Billy did was almost breathtaking in his analysis. That's why guys with money who play casual poker and get involved in big games like this get themselves broken out of games. This is poker at a high level.

Great players not only play their own cards, but they put their opponents on a hand and play accordingly. Billy played as if the other player had deuces in the hole and would have kept raising if the trip deuces had filled into a full house and that hand was bet and raised. That's what you must do in games, put the players on hands and play accordingly. It's not easy, and comes only in time and with long experience.

How do you do this? Again, we go back to observation. Most average players have parameters to their play. They have limits. They'll play only certain hands; will raise with certain cards, and will raise or not raise depending upon their position. For example, in Texas Hold 'Em, a player may only raise in early to middle position holding the three biggest pairs, Aces, Kings, or Queens, or Ace-King. That's it. If you study the play at the table, you can spot the hands players will raise with. In late position they will raise with more hands. So, if you see a tight player raising early on, you have to put him on one of those four hands.

Will he fool you and raise with other cards? Maybe, but it's not a probability. There are weak players who will stay in with anything just to see the flop, taking triple raises to do so. You can pinpoint these players as well. They'll be aggressive with good hands, putting in raises, but will just call raises when they need big help on the flop.

But most players will stay in to see the flop only with fairly good cards. For example, if a player starts to act aggressively with a flop such as 3♠ 5♥ 2♠ and you know him to play fairly good hands, you have to feel he's holding an Ace-4 **suited**, probably in spades. He already has his straight. Of course, he could also have trips, having gone in with a pair of 2s, 3s, or 5s. Not likely from early position, but possible. In any event, you're holding an Ace-King and you're pretty dead in the water. Give it up if you know you're up against a tight player. Two things you don't want to do in poker—be stubborn and chase better hands. These are the surest ways to fracture your bankroll.

Learn just what kind of player you're facing in any hand. This is done through observation. Get a sense of what hands he or she has played. In Texas Hold 'Em, cards are generally exposed at the showdown, and can be forced to be exposed by any player at the table, whether or not he or she is fighting for the pot. If you see a player show a pair of 8s and lose the hand to Kings over Jacks, with a board showing King♣ Jack♠ 9♥ 3♦ 2♦, then you know this player is a chaser and weak.

Likewise, if a player shows 7-6 unsuited (of different suits), and the board shows A♠, 9♠, 8♦, 2♠, 10♣, then you know he's weak—and clueless besides. He's going after the bottom part of a straight, often called the **ignorant end**, a sure money-loser. On top of this, there are three spades out, possibly giving someone a flush. And to top it off, he's playing 7-6 unsuited, a hand having no real value, and one that can only get you in trouble. In this case, he lost to both a flush and a higher straight. The person holding the Jack-10 can also be classified as a weak player. He stayed in to get a **gutshot straight** (needing the middle card to make the straight), an 11:1 shot, against only two other players. On top of it all, he was **drawing dead**. In other words, even if he made the straight, which he did, he had no chance to beat the spades flush.

In the middle of a hand, analyze just what is happening. What are your opponents representing by their play? Are your opponents weak or strong players? What about their position at the table? Are they capable of bluffing, or can they be bluffed out of a hand? Your mind should be alert to all possibilities on any hand. Sometimes you don't have to think at all, when you know you have the absolute **nuts** (the very best hand). But most of the time you have to put your opponents on a few probable hands and play accordingly. That's what the winners do.

---

6. Practice deception.

Because reading other players is such a big part of the game, you want to avoid being read yourself. You certainly don't want to reveal any tells. Change the way you play the same hand in different situations. This is what Doyle Brunson calls shifting gears. For example, if you would raise with a pair of Jacks in late position at Texas Hold 'Em, the next time you have them, don't raise. Don't let your opposition put you on hands.

In Seven-Card Stud, if you hold an Ace as a doorcard, and a 2 brought it in, and was called by a 7 and King, you're in an ideal situation to raise. Your Ace is probably the strongest card held by the players in the hand. You can pretty much raise all the time, because it's expected and no one can really read what you are holding. It could be trip Aces all the way down to an Ace with two rags. But if you hold a pair of Kings with an Ace behind you, you should raise sometimes and sometimes not. Raising a pair of Kings is expected; not raising them is not. Keep your opposition guessing as to the value of your hand. We'll deal with similar examples in individual games.

As to tells, be on the lookout for gestures or mannerisms you are making that reveal the strength of your cards. In one game I was playing every time I had strong cards, I raised, and everyone went out. I knew or guessed I was revealing something, but what? I took a break and went into the men's room, and washed my face and hands and thought about it. Then I realized I was putting in my bet too fast, not hesitating at all.

The next time I had a weak hand I purposely bet on the river, hesitating a bit after my opponent checked. Sure as shooting, he called my bet. I lost the hand; my smaller pair to his bigger one. But I bided my time, and in a four-way pot, I hesitated with a full house well hidden, called a bet, and took three raises, which made a monster pot. They were stunned to see my full house. After that they were at sea as far as that tell was concerned.

So be careful and alert—alert to your own moves. Are they being studied and read by your opponents? Just as you don't want to play the same cards the same way all the time, you don't want to make the same gestures all the time. If you can't be read, it's a big advantage to you, because you're constantly on the prowl, looking to read the other players.

---

7. Practice self-control.

As I mentioned before, poker is not removed from life; it is an integral part of life, and the strengths and weaknesses you manifest in life apply to poker as well. One of the most important is self-control. Self-control is defined in the dictionary as "control of one's emotions, desires or actions by one's own will." Of course, this definition is subject to interpretation, but the important thing is to keep control of your emotions at the table.

If you can avoid showing anger, frustration, defeatism, and so forth, you're able to exercise self-control. If you play poker often enough, you're going to encounter your share of **bad beats**. A bad beat is a loss when you expected a win—when you were sure of a win, when you were already counting the profits from the pot. For example, you have Aces full, a powerful hand, and you watch as your opponent keeps getting diamonds, first the 7, then the 8, then the 9, and finally the 10, and when he puts in a bet you know you're doomed.

In the days when California clubs were permitted by state law to offer "bad beat jackpots" funded by money cut from each game, a bad beat was any Aces full hand beaten by a stronger hand. Those are tough to lose. But what should you do when you lose such a hand? You may be steaming with frustration, but you have to take control of yourself. Bad beats happen and will happen again. At some point it will all even out, and you'll make someone else at another table in another game the object of a bad beat.

Go to the next hand and play it as if the bad beat didn't happen. It's easy to give this advice and difficult to follow, but you must be able to do it. If you're **steaming** (angry inside) and feel that smoke is coming out of your ears, then get up from the table and take a break. You can't play under these circumstances. It's the ability to shrug off the previous beat and go on and play as if nothing has happened that separates the great from the good players.

Someone once was remarking to me about Chip Reese, generally considered the greatest of all Seven-Card Stud players, that he was this way. We were standing in the Mirage, talking, near a monster Seven-Card Stud game—I believe it was $2,000–$4,000. "You know the terrific thing about Chip," my acquaintance told me, "is that he's always the same at the table. He never gets flustered. He loses a big pot; he's ready for the next pot. You watch him play and you never know if he's ahead or taking a beating. He shrugs off the last pot and is ready for the next one."

A good friend of mine who plays poker for a living doesn't read up on poker odds. He concentrates on books about philosophy, books dealing with self-control and handling of anger. Lack of self-control at certain times is his big weakness and he tries to over-

come it by reading and then trying to practice what
he has read. But it's tough. Once I saw him lose a
gigantic pot, when a player filled in an inside straight
on a hand he had no business playing. My friend got
up without a word to me, his face a mass of anger,
and went for a half-hour walk. When he came back,
he was still grim and proceeded to lose money.

I spoke to several pros about self-control, and they
told me it extends beyond the table and poker games.
"Self-control also means if things are going bad you're
not gambling at the craps tables or taking drugs or
doing something that screws up your health or life.
It's beyond poker. If you don't have control at the
tables, you're liable to extend this to other parts of
your life," one player told me. He had been through
it all—drugs, gambling, being out of shape.

Poker is so interesting as far as human emotions go,
because they're out in the open. You're sitting with
seven or eight strangers and you've just lost a monster
pot. There's nowhere to hide. And they're all watching
you, waiting for some reaction. They know how they'd
react; now they want to see what you do about a
bad beat.

Most of us take defeats in private or one-on-one. If
we lose a job, it's only the boss who's telling us the
bad news. If we screw up a relationship, it's only the
other party who puts it to us. But at the poker table
you're more naked. You not only lose, you lose
money. It's tough to lose money, and often the strangers you lose to seem less intelligent, less cultured. You
feel as if you're losing to a bunch of yoyos. You feel
terrible.

Train yourself to keep that self-control. If you can
forget about the previous hand you lost and play the
next as an independent action, you're on your way to
self-control. Each hand is independent, after all.
There's been a new deal and shuffle, you have different cards, as do your opponents. Concentrate on what
is happening now; forget what just happened the last
hand or two hands ago, or ten hands ago. If you're

brooding about what has happened and can't concentrate, get out of the game. Take a break, or call it a day at the tables.

The important thing is not to alter your play after a bad beat. Don't stay in with cards you wouldn't ordinarily play to get even with the guy who beat you out of that big pot. Don't raise with mediocre cards to get even fast. Play your usual correct and intelligent game. When you change, it's called going **on tilt**. Your opponents will lick their chops as they see you turn from a steady player to a wild gambler. Train yourself to be constant in temperament and don't deviate. That's the way to win at poker.

VI

The Casino/Club Atmosphere

To a poker player, there's nothing more exciting than entering a poker room of a casino, or a card room. The atmosphere is electric, with games at all levels and of all sorts going on. As you walk in, you see dozens and sometimes, depending on the size of the club, hundreds of players in action. They're in all parts of the club, playing all levels of poker. There is usually a roped-off or raised portion of the club or casino where the really big games are.

There may be another section, a large one, for smaller games, and then to one side, an area devoted to medium games. As you walk in, you pass games already in progress. At one table you see a dealer shuffling the cards, with the players' antes on the table. At another table, a game is in progress, and already the table is piled high with checks. Whoever wins the hand is going to win a monster pot. There are various denominations of checks—$2, $3, $5, $10, and $25. As you walk by a roped-off area, you see players bent forward, watching as one player puts in a pile of chips a mile high. This is a no-limit game of **Texas Hold 'Em**, and the checks have a denomination value of $100. Gee, you think, you win that pot and you could buy yourself a new car.

It's heady stuff, all right, and no matter how many times I've been in a club or casino I feel the same expectancy, the same exhilaration. I could start off with a smaller game, say, $10–$20, win several hundred dollars, go to a bigger game, end up in a $30–$60 game, and leave with enough for that car. Anything can happen at a poker table. On the outside you get a salary or some other income and you know what to expect. In the club, who knows what the future holds?

By the time you're in a casino or club, you know two things. One, you know the game you're going to play, and secondly, you know the stakes you're going to play for. Let's assume you want to play Texas Hold 'Em, which has become the most popular of club card games, and you are looking for a $6-$12 game.

In a casino poker room such as the Mirage, you'll see a desk in front, with a casino employee behind it. You go over and say "Six Hold 'Em." You don't have to say you want a $6–$12 game, the "six" is sufficient.

"What's your name?" the employee will ask.

"Ed."

"OK. There's six players ahead of you, but we have three tables going," she'll say as she writes your first name down.

And now you wait. What I like to do in a casino like the Mirage is drift to the back, where the roped-off and elevated section holds some six tables, several of which are big games. At one there may be a $300-$600 **Seven-Card Stud** game going; at another a $150–$300. There may be a $100-$200 Texas Hold 'Em game in progress, while the other tables are hosting $40-$80 and $30-$60 games.

It depends on the night and the action. You might see a really big game, a $2,000–$4,000 game, which I did one night, and watched as it turned into a no-limit game. Packets of bills, $10,000 at a time, were being thrown into the center of the table, along with $5,000 checks. An exciting game to watch, with the top players at the table. There was Johnny Chan, Stu Ungar, Doyle Brunson, Chip Reese—all legends of poker. There were also a couple of millionaires, or maybe billionaires, playing against this all-star lineup. For me, it was better drama than any movie.

As you watch and wait, names are called. "John," you hear, "$10 stud." "Tommy J, $30 Hold 'Em." Finally, after about twenty minutes you hear your name, "Ed, $6 Hold 'Em." I'm using my name, but substitute your own. You go back to the front desk, and the employee points out the table you'll be playing at, or will walk you there.

There's a vacant seat, the four seat. You count seats in clockwise fashion from the dealer's left. The seat to her left is the one seat, then the two seat, and it goes all the way to the ten seat. In Nevada casinos, there are generally ten seats for Hold 'Em games, and only eight seats for stud games. In the California clubs, there are generally nine seats for Hold 'Em players and eight seats for the stud players.

Getting Checks

So you sit down in the four seat, and the dealer calls for chips. You can either go to the cashier in back and get your own checks, or more likely, a chip runner will materialize and take your cash, returning with a rack of chips for the $200 in bills you've given her. Some players tip the runner; others don't. Generally, regulars will take a dollar or two, or one chip from the rack.

Let's suppose that you're not quite ready to play. You want to go to the men's room first. So you tell the desk clerk to "lock it up," and she'll put a little slip with your name on the spot you've taken, the four seat. That seat is now yours, and when you return from the bathroom, you sit down. In Nevada casinos, there's no ante in Hold 'Em games. The dealer takes the casino's rake from the pot itself. So, when you sit down, you're immediately dealt cards. You're in action. If you're not the small or big blind, the two spots to the left of the button, you put nothing into the pot before the deal.

If you're the small blind, you put in $2, and $6 if you're the big blind. The smart thing to do is wait to be dealt cards after the blinds pass you. This way you're not only in great late position to start, a big advantage, but you'll have eight hands to look at before being forced to put in your blinds.

The rack is handed to you by the chip runner and you remove the checks and stack them up in front of you. That's the best form, rather than playing checks out of a rack, which delays the game. There should be nothing on the table in front of you but checks and possibly cash. Suppose you're being dealt a hand before the chip runner returns. The dealer may give you some chips to play with and then take them back when you get your own checks. Or the chip runner might say "$200 behind," designating that you have $200 to play with even if you haven't yet gotten your checks.

Let's say you're in the first hand and call a bet and raise. Then on the flop you fold. The dealer will have segregated chips from the pot in front of you if she hadn't any checks to give you. Then she'll inform the winner of the pot that you owe $12 to him. When your rack comes, you take off $12 and give it to the winner of the pot.

Let's assume that in the course of play you are running out of chips. All games are **table stakes**. This means you're bound by what you have on the table. This isn't the movies, where you reach into your pocket during the course of play and pull out bills or write a check. In a casino like the Mirage, you can play with cash on the table if it's at least a $100 bill. Less than that, and you have to buy additional chips before the next hand is dealt.

If you run out of chips and cash during the course of a hand, then you announce that you're **all in**. This means that the pot is split, with one part holding your bets and the other, bets made after your declaration. The second part doesn't belong to you. You can win only that portion of the pot you contributed to. But I advise never to get into this situation. You don't want to have the best hand and win only a small percentage of the pot. Always have sufficient chips or cash in front of you for any hand.

In clubs the rules are slightly different. I'm going to use the California clubs as an example. When you go into one of these clubs, you'll see many more tables and players than you'll see in a casino. There are hundreds of players at the tables, in all kinds and denominations of games. We'll assume you want to sign up for the $6–$12 Texas Hold 'Em game.

Unlike in a casino poker room, there are various places to sign up for a game. One part may deal with small games, such as $1–$2 to $3–$6. Another part may deal with $5–$10 up to $9–$18. Another area has a board for $10–$20 all the way up to $30–$60, and the last area will have a board for bigger games. You go to the employee who handles the $6–$12 board. You'll notice that it has room for Omaha, Stud, Hold 'Em, and perhaps other games. You tell the employee "$6 Hold 'Em," and he asks for your initials, not your name.

You watch him put up "ES" and now you are free to roam around and watch other games. But because the clubs are so big, you don't want to stray too far. If you're at the other end of the room, you might not hear your initials called, and you'll have to start all over again at the bottom of the board list.

When you do hear your initials called, you'll be directed to a floorman who will point out the table you'll be playing at. As you move toward him, you can say "Lock it up," which means that your seat will be reserved.

We're assuming for this section that you're going to the $6–$12 Hold 'Em game. Seat number nine is vacant; the seat to the right of the dealer. You take out money and ask the dealer for checks. He'll yell out "chips," and a runner will come by and take your cash. If you gave him $200, he'll announce to the dealer, "200 behind," signifying that you're good for that amount.

You can't play the first hand dealt, but you can play after that. If you play, you'll have to put up what is called a **position blind**, a bet equal to the big blind, for your first hand, no matter where you're sitting, unless you actually are the small or big blind. The best advice is this—wait till the **button** passes you before you come into the game. Thus, you start off in next to the best position at the table, after the button, which acts last and is the theoretical dealer. You have seven more hands to play before you have to put in another blind. The dealer will ask you when you sit down if you want to be dealt a hand on the next deal. Tell him you'll wait for the button, and he'll understand, and will put an "out" marker in front of your spot, which will be removed when the button passes you.

In the Nevada casinos, if you're hungry, you can get either a comp or a line pass. Usually comps are harder to come by, unless you're in a really big game, since it's a free meal in the dining or buffet area, but you'll always be able get a line pass, which permits you to avoid the lines that form in the various restaurants in the casino. Just go to an employee and ask for a line pass; you'll be directed to the proper person. In the California clubs (and other clubs) you can get cut-rate meals which can be eaten at the table while playing. A small stand is pushed up beside you, and you'll be served by a waiter. The meals are generally quite cheap. Or you can get a beverage by asking a porter for coffee, tea, or a soft drink. Cocktail waitresses come around in both the casinos and clubs offering liquor and beer, but I advise against drinking any alcoholic beverages while playing.

Casino and Club Rules

There are a number of rules that apply in casinos and clubs. These may vary slightly from casino to casino and club to club, but study them to get an idea of what to expect when playing poker.

Table Stakes

I've already mentioned this. You are limited to the number of checks in front of you as well as cash on the table. During the play of a hand you cannot take more money out of your pocket. Only before a deal can you bring out more money.

All In

If you're out of chips and cash on any hand, you announce that you're "all in," and the pot in which you have a stake will be segregated. You are not allowed to share in any sidepot to which you haven't contributed money, even if you have the very best hand.

Check and Raise

You're allowed to **check and raise**—that is, to raise after you've checked your hand. For example, let's say you're the first to act and you check and someone else bets. When it's your turn you can raise. If someone else has bet and another player raised, you can reraise. There is an exception in practically all casino and club games, where checking is not allowed on the first round of betting. After the first round, in most games, check-raising is permitted.

Live Blinds and Openers

In Texas Hold 'Em derivative games, such as Omaha, the small and big blinds are **live**. This means that either blind can raise or reraise when the bets come around to them. Let's assume that in a $10–$20 game, the big blind has put in $10. Three players call the bet, and now it comes around to him. He can raise at this time or not. Usually blinds who don't want to raise use a hand gesture to indicate that they aren't raising.

In Seven-Card Stud and other stud games, the player who **brings in** the first bet can raise when it comes around to him. For example, in a $10–$20 game in Vegas, the low card brings it in for $1. Let's say that two other players stay in for $1. Now, after their bets, it comes around to the low card. He may raise to $10. His original bet is live.

String Bets

If you've seen the same movies or TV shows I have, the same ridiculous situation comes up over and over again. Someone bets $500 or whatever and the hero hesitates, then puts in the matching bet and says "and I raise you $1,000." Then he collects another $1,000 from his stack and puts it in the middle of the table. Yeah, sure. That's a **string bet** and is absolutely forbidden in clubs and casinos. If you were in a casino in that situation, you gather up $1,500 and bet it all at once. The important thing is to do it in one motion.

Thus, to avoid any appearance of a string bet I suggest you simply say "raise," as you make your bet. Some players don't like to do this because they're afraid their words or inflection will reveal something about the strength of their hand. If you don't want to say anything, make certain that you have enough chips to cover the raise and move the checks forward.

Burn Cards

In most casino and club games, the top card dealt on the first and subsequent rounds of play will be **burned**—that is, slid off the top and put to one side rather than being dealt to the players. This is done to prevent cheating and collusion. The burned cards are out of play.

Muck Pile

The muck pile consists of the burned cards and discards in the course of any game. They go to one side, to what is called the **muck pile**. Once cards go on the muck pile, or *even touch it*, they're out of play and are dead, irretrievable. When you play casino poker, at the **showdown**, after all cards have been dealt and all bets made, it is best to simply turn over your cards in front of you and let the dealer call the winner of the hand. That's his job. If you wrongly imagine you're beaten and fling the cards into the muck pile, they're dead. Even if one of your cards goes there, you have a dead hand. Be careful.

I know a pro who, in a big Seven-Card Stud game, sitting in the three seat, at the far end of the table, was in a pot with the player in the eight seat, at the other end. The pro had called a raise before the show-down, and looking across the table saw his opponent turn over seven red cards. Thinking the other player had a flush, which beat his two pair, he mucked the cards. Then, looking closer, he realized that there were four hearts and three diamonds and no flush. Just a pair of 9s. But it was too late. That mistake cost him $600 and a few headaches.

Cards Speak

In many home games, especially high-low games, the players declare high or low or high-low and are bound by their declaration. But in casinos, the players show their cards and don't declare. The **cards "speak."** No matter what a player thinks he has, when he turns over his cards, the dealer examines them and makes the decision as to who has won the hand. Some desperate players call their hands wrongfully when they turn them over. I've seen this happen. A player with a single pair called "Kings up," while he slowly turned over his cards in a Seven-Card Stud game. His opponent, believing him, mucked his cards. The mucked hand was dead, and it turned out the other guy had only Kings and would have lost to a two-pair hand headed by Jacks.

The floorman was called over by the loser, but the other player claimed he misread his hand and had no intention of cheating the player. The floorman was helpless to do anything—mucked cards are dead. That's why I suggest—just turn over your cards and let the dealer examine them and decide who has the best hand.

Kill

No, don't worry, nobody gets hurt as a result of this word. A loser doesn't have the right to take the winner's life, and a disgruntled player can't off the dealer. A **kill** occurs in certain games where there is a split pot, with high hand winning half and low hand winning the other half. For example, in **Omaha—8 or Better**, the high hand shares the pot with the low hand, provided the low hand is 8 or better—that is, the winner of the low hand must have a formed five-card hand headed by an 8 or lower card, such as an 8-5-4-3-2 or 7-5-4-3-2. Or a hand headed by a 6, or best of all, a **wheel**, a 5-4-3-2-Ace, the best low hand possible.

If a player **scoops the pot**—that is, wins both high and low, or only a high hand wins the whole pot because no one has an 8 or better hand, and the pot is big enough—the kill feature comes into play. A placard is put on the table in front of the winner reading "kill" and the next hand is played for double the ordinary stakes. For instance, if the game is $6–$12, the kill game is $12–$24. If the next hand is split, it goes back to the original $6–$12.

The kill feature is also used in games such as **Loball draw**, in certain clubs. In this game, there are usually three blinds. For example, in a $15–$30 game, there is a blind of $5 by the button, the theoretical dealer, then two additional blinds of $10 and $15. The $10 blind is called the middle blind, and the $15 one, the big blind. When there are additional callers, the club refers to their bets as "strange money"—that is, extra money besides the blinds. If six checks are bet in addition to the blinds, then the next pot is a kill one, with the stakes doubling. These kill features will be discussed in the appropriate games covered in this book.

Buy-Ins

In all club and casino games, a minimum amount of money must be on the table in the form of chips and cash when a player first enters the game. This minimum is called a **buy-in**. It is usually ten times the minimum bet. In any $3–$6 game, the buy-in would be $30. In a $6–$12 game it's $60, and so forth. I recommend that a player go in with much more than the minimum buy-in. For example, though the $6–$12 requires only $60, a wiser choice would be $200.

Once a player loses money at the table, he can stay in without a minimum. As we pointed out before, a player has the right to call "all in" and play for a side or segregated pot, which is another thing I don't advise. Always have enough in front of you to play out a full hand.

The Dealer and the Floorman

All games are now played with a **dealer**, who is an employee of the house, handling the cards. At one time, players used to deal—in the dear old dead days in California when only draw poker was permitted. This led to widespread cheating and collusion. A cheat once showed me a special shuffle, which he claimed allowed him to win a small fortune in the clubs. And nearly got him thrown in jail.

The house dealer now handles the cards exclusively as far as shuffling, dealing, and cutting goes. No one else touches the cards during these moves. Each dealer has two decks to work with. One is in the tray while the other is actively being handled. Players may request a "change of cards," which is done quite often as disgruntled losers figure a different deck will get them better cards.

Players can also call for a **set up**, in which case another house employee brings over two fresh decks of cards, arranged in order from the Ace of clubs through the King of clubs, and so forth for all four suits. Before shuffling these cards, the dealer is obligated to spread them out and make certain that all fifty-two cards are there, in order. Then he turns them and fans the backs to make sure that they're all the same color; that a green-backed card is not mixed in with a deck of brown cards, for instance.

The dealer deals out the cards and should make certain that correct bets are made by each player. If a player raises by putting in additional checks, the dealer should call out "raise" to let other players know this. Also, a really good dealer lets the table know just how many players are in the game, particularly in a game like Texas Hold 'Em. He should call out "three players left," or "heads up" when only two players are fighting for the pot.

The dealer also takes the house cut, or **rake**, from those games in which there is no other collection taken from the players. The dealer also removes the collections from the players in certain games and puts these checks into a **drop box** through a slit, which is usually on the dealer's right. In those games in which a half-hour or hourly rate is charged, the dealer collects this money from the players.

The dealer is usually the arbiter of discrepancies charged by a player, but when he can't give a definitive answer, he calls over the **floorman**. The floorman is a house employee who is in charge of a group of tables or games. If there is a disagreement between players or between a player and the dealer, his word is final.

The Rake and Hourly Rental or Charge

Casinos make their money either by taking money off the table from each hand played, or from an hourly charge to each player, broken down to half-hour rentals.

In some games, one player puts in the collection, and this money is taken out immediately by the dealer before cards are dealt. In most lower-limit Hold 'Em games, the collection is charged to the button. For example, in California clubs, it can be $3 or $4 for a $6–$12 game. Once removed it's gone. If the hand isn't played out fully, it doesn't matter. The house gets its cut first.

In other games, there is no collection, but the dealer removes a number of checks from the game during the course of play, and sometimes at the outset, depending upon the club or casino and its rules. For example, in the $20–$40 **Hi-Lo Split** game in Vegas, there's no rental charge, but the dealer removes $3 if there's a full game. In the clubs, there is a half-hour fee of $8 or $9.

In other games, there's an hourly charge to all players, collected every half-hour. The rate varies from club to club. In Southern California poker clubs, the Commerce Club charges $1 more than its competition such as Crystal Park or the Hollywood Casino. The Nevada casino poker rooms charge much less than do the California clubs. That's because, as mentioned before, the clubs depend upon poker for their money, while the Nevada casinos have their table games as well as slots to bring in the moolah. To give an example—at the Commerce Club you are charged $9 a half-hour playing $30–$60 stud. At the Mirage in Las Vegas, the rental fee is $5 per half-hour for a $40–$80 game.

Also, in the Nevada casinos, hourly charges are only for bigger games. In the California and other clubs, $10–$20 games will have an hourly charge, while in most Nevada casinos, the hourly charge may kick in in games of $20–$40 and even higher.

All games you'll play in will require some sort of payment, either by rake, rental, collection, or ante. If you are unsure of which game to play, you might find it cheaper to play a $10–$20 game in a club paying an hourly fee, rather than a $9–$18 game paying a collection.

Toking or Tipping the Dealer

Toking is the same as tipping; it's the term pros use, just as they use "checks" instead of "chips." The usual practice in most small and mid-range games is to toke the dealer after a win. For example, in $10–$20 stud game, a player usually throws over $1 to the dealer after winning a pot. The same amount is also given to the dealer in a $3–$6 stud game. Toking is not mandatory, nor are there limits, low or high, as to the toke. It depends upon the dealer and the player, and the relationship between the two.

A pro I know who plays in the $30–$60 Seven-Card Stud games, both in the Nevada casinos and California clubs, tells me he tips $1 after winning a pot, and sometimes $2 if it's a really big pot. But with some dealers he refuses to toke at all. He feels that they cost him pots. One dealer sloppily flashed one of his hole cards and denied doing it; another was slow in calling the value of an opponent's hand and so the pro mucked the winning hand. "They owe me," he said to me, "and after I owe them a grand in tokes, I'll start tipping them again."

A dealer can be rude and overbearing or make you uncomfortable in some way. In that case, forget about tokes. I was in a game where I constantly was dealt garbage and folded hand after hand. The dealer, a woman, commented on this. "Boy, you don't play many hands," she said aloud. That remark could get her fired if I complained to a floorman. A dealer's job is to be neutral, to shuffle, deal, and make sure the pot is right. She has no business commenting on what a player does at the table, whether he stays in or goes out often.

In smaller games, like $2–$4, dealers expect 50 cents, in bigger games $1 and sometimes $2. There are players who will tip the dealer $5 or more in a $5–$10 game, but I don't advise doing this. You don't win that many pots, and to give away that kind of money is like giving away an extra bet. Go with the flow; it's easy to see what the average toke is at any game you're in. If you feel it's too high, then tip less. Toke the sum that is comfortable for you.

The strange thing about toking is this—the bigger the game, the smaller the proportional toke, till you get to $100–$200 games, and there are no tokes at all. A woman dealer in Vegas told me what her idea of hell was: "Dealing $100–$200 stud. You get nothing, and you have to be super alert because of the size of the pots. The players are rude, and you leave after your shift with nothing." She preferred the small games, which had the best tippers.

I was playing Texas Hold 'Em at the Bicycle Club in Bell Gardens, California, and another player sitting next to me happened to be a dealer at a different Southern California club. We got to talking and he told me he had dealt a no-limit Texas Hold 'Em game the week before. In the game were two former world champions. Now, no-limit means what it implies, there is no limit to what a player can bet.

"So listen to this," the dealer told me. "I shove an $80,000 pot over to this guy, this world champion, and he takes a $5 check and throws it over to me. I'm about to say 'thank you,' but he says 'break it,' and gives me a buck."

"What did you do?"

"What could I do? Dealing is my living, so I swallowed my tongue. That cheap . . ."

The life of a dealer is not easy. Toke him or her when you win a pot. They depend upon tokes for most of their income.

Raise Limits

In casino/club games, there is a limit on raises, usually three or four on each round of betting. This is to prevent collusion and cheating, where two operatives playing as a team, nail another player between them, and don't stop raising till they bleed all his money. In Vegas casinos the limit to raises can either be three or four; in the clubs it's usually three. However, when only two players remain in the game, unlimited raises are allowed, since then there can no longer be collusion.

VII

Seven-Card Stud

In our discussion of **Seven-Card Stud**, we will only discuss the high game, in which the best-ranked hand wins the pot. There is a version of Seven-Card Stud called Razz in which the low hand wins, but the game is rarely found in casinos or clubs. There's no sense studying a game that is nonexistent for the most part. A variation of Seven-Card Stud is **Hi-Lo Split**, which is a real action game, with both high and low hands splitting the pot, provided that the low hand is 8 or better. This game will be discussed in the next chapter.

At one time Seven-Card Stud was the most popular of all the casino games, but in recent years **Texas Hold 'Em** is the choice of most card players in both the casinos and the clubs throughout the country. However, Seven-Card Stud still has its adherents and there are always games at all levels of play available, whether one wants to play a $1–$4 or a $300–$600 game, or other games in between.

It is an interesting game, in which skill and psychology play dominant roles. It's easy to learn and tough to master, because there are many complexities surrounding play, and a participant has to remain alert throughout play. When a hand is fully dealt out, there are four open cards and three hidden cards, and those three hidden cards can lead to all sorts of bluffs. Or hidden powerful hands. A player can show 5♣ 2♣ 9♥ Jack♠, which looks like a pile of rags, and yet, in the hole he can hold Ace♣ 3♣ 4♣ for a super-powerful straight flush.

Players must be aware of what cards are out, what cards have been folded, what cards are still live. In addition, of course, the other players' strengths and weaknesses must also be studied. This means, as I have said before, being alert to all aspects of the game during the play of any hand.

How the Game Is Played

I'm sure that most readers know how to play Seven-Card Stud, but for those who don't know the game, and for those who have not played it except in home games, we'll explain the casino/club game.

For purposes of this section, we'll assume you're at a casino on the Las Vegas Strip, such as the Mirage. And we'll further assume you've decided to play in the $10-$20 game in their poker room. The table accommodates eight players plus a house dealer, who doesn't play against the players but is there to handle the cards, deal the game, and make certain that the bets and pot are correct.

We'll assume that when you arrive, a seat is available at the game, and so you sit down and hand your cash to an employee to convert into checks. The game is played with $5 checks, also called redbirds by the pros. To make sure that you're properly funded, you ask for a rack of $5 checks and are given one hundred checks or $500. Now you're ready for action. The dealer sits in the center of one side of the table, and the seats of the table are numbered from one to eight, with one the seat to the dealer's left. He also deals in this clockwise manner, with the player in the one seat getting the first card and the player in the eight seat getting the last card.

Each player puts out $1 as his or her ante prior to the deal. This ante is there to "sweeten the pot," and to promote action. Action is necessary in casino poker games, and the rules of each particular game promote this action, in order to build up pots. Since betting position is determined randomly by what cards are showing, the dealer always deals out the cards in the same manner, from seat one to seat eight.

Each player gets two cards face down, known as **hole** or **pocket cards**, and one card face up, known as the **doorcard**. Already there's $8 in the pot, from the antes. Now, the lowest open card must **bring it in**, or make the first bet. This is forced. If two or more players have identically ranked lowest cards, such as the deuce, then the lowest card is determined by suit. The lowest suit is clubs, followed in rising order by diamonds, hearts, and spades, just as in the popular game of contract bridge.

Let's assume that only one player has a 4♠, the lowest card open. He must bet $2. Let's further assume he's in the five seat. After he makes his forced bet, the player to his left, in the six seat, must call or equal the bet, or raise the bet to $10. If he doesn't want to do either of these things, he goes out by turning over his cards and "folding" his hand. He's now out of play for this entire game.

After the 4♠ has bet, we'll say that the next three players in order, in the six, seven, and eight seats, fold their cards. The player in the first seat, holding an open King♥, now raises to $10. The players in the second and third seats fold, and the player in the fourth seat, with an Ace♦ showing, reraises to $20. The player who brought it in folds, and the King calls the bet. Now only two players remain in the game, playing **heads-up**.

At this point, three cards have been dealt. Poker players refer to **streets** when discussing how many cards they're holding; since the two players remaining hold three cards, this is known as **Third Street**. The dealer now gives each player another card face up. This is **Fourth Street**, also known as **the turn**. From Fourth Street to the end, the last card being known as **Seventh Street** or the **river**, the player holding the higher hand bets first, unlike Third Street, where the lowest card must bring it in.

At this point, player one holds 10♦ 6♥ King♥. Player number four holds 6♣ 2♥ Ace♦. Player four leads. He can either bet or check. If he checks and his opponent bets, he can either fold, call, or check-raise. He bets and player number one calls. On Fourth Street the bet is $10 and multiples of $10, unless there's an open pair. Then a player can bet $10 or $20, at his option. Another player can raise by $20 even if the original bettor only bet $10. This can happen only on Fourth Street.

Each player is dealt another card on Fifth Street. The hands look like this:

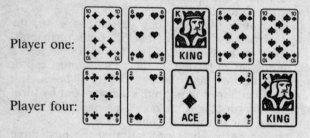

Player one:

Player four:

Player four is still high, and bets. Player one calls the $20 wager. On Fifth, Sixth, and Seventh Streets the betting is at the second tier, or in $20 increments.

On Sixth Street, the hands are as follows:

Player one:

Player four:

Player four now bets $20 and is called. The river card is dealt face down at this point. Both players squeeze their cards, carefully looking at their three down cards.

Player four bets $20 and player one calls. Since player four has been called, he shows his cards first. This is known as the **showdown**, after all cards have been dealt and all bets made.

Player four shows 6♣ 2♥ Ace♦ 2♠ King♦ 6♦ Ace♣. He has two pairs, Aces over 6s. The other player acknowledges being beaten by turning over his cards and not showing his hand, but throwing them into the muck pile. This is his right, and no one can ask to see his hand. He bought a pair of tens and didn't believe that player four had two pair. In the end, whether he got a second pair or not, he was beaten.

Summary of Play

Let's now summarize the rules of play of casino/club Seven-Card Stud.

The Ante Structure

Practically every game in a casino or club requires an ante. In Seven-Card Stud this structure can change according to the betting limits. In $5–$10-and $10–$20 games, the ante is usually 10 percent of the minimum bet; thus, 50 cents for the $5–$10 game, and $1 for the $10–$20 one. This is considered an average ante.

However, in bigger games, the ante structure changes. In many $15–$30 games, the ante is $3, or 20 percent of the minimum bet. By the time you're in a $40–$80 game in Vegas, the ante is $10, or 25 percent. This is considered a high ante. In the California clubs, the $40–$80 game accommodates the players as far as antes are concerned. The $40–$80 can be played with a $5 ante (12½ percent) or the more standard $10 ante (25 percent). The $100–$200 game, with a $25 ante, is also high.

What's the difference? The bigger the ante, the faster the play. By fast play we mean more raises earlier in the game. Here's one way to look at it. If you're in a $10–$20 game, and there's $8 in the pot from the antes plus $2 more from the opening bettor, if you raise to $10, your bet is equal to what is in the pot, $10. You only get even money if no one calls your raise.

In a $100–$200 game, with a $25 ante, although the game is exactly ten times the $10–$20 one, because of the ante structure the raise is more worthwhile. $25 brings it in by low card. There's $200 in the pot from the antes plus $25 for a total of $225. Now, if you raise to $100, you're trying to win $225 outright if no one else calls. It's worthwhile to raise in an attempt to **steal the antes**, or win the pot right then and there.

If you raise to $100, another player, by raising your bet, puts $200 in the pot to win $325. Compare this to the $10–$20 game, where raises on Third Street win only even money. That's one of the reasons the bigger games get many more raises at the outset, and why players who do well in smaller games with medium ante structures have difficulty with bigger antes.

The Deal

The deal is always done in a clockwise fashion, and starts with the player to the dealer's left, player number one, all the way to player number eight. Of course, fewer than eight players can play at one time. The dealer announces whose turn it is to make the first bet, and whether there has been a raise. At the showdown, he determines who has won the pot, and shoves the pot to the winner.

The Streets and Betting Rounds

The first three cards constitute Third Street, with two cards down and one face-up card known as the doorcard. Low card must bring it in, or start the betting. Depending on the game, the first bet is usually from 20 percent to 25 percent of the minimum. Thus, in the $10–$20 game, the first bet is $2. Other players may call this bet or raise to $10. After the raise, other raises are in $10 increments. A player cannot check on this round. If he checks, he is out of the game, and his cards are taken away. He is said to have folded his hand.

The next card dealt is on Fourth Street. It is also an open card. From this street on, the high hand leads the action. The holder of the high hand can check or bet, or check-raise. If he checks, any other player still active can bet, at the minimum $10 level, and all raises are at that level. The only exception is if an open pair is showing. Then the players can bet $10 or $20 at their option. Once a $20 bet or raise is made on Fourth Street, then all other bets must be made at $20 increments.

Fifth and Sixth Streets are also at the higher level of $20. These cards are dealt face up. Seventh Street, or the river, is the last card dealt. It is dealt face down, giving each remaining player in the pot four cards face up and three in the hole.

After the final bet on the river, there is a showdown. The player who made the initial bet or raise and was called by the other players shows his hand first. If he has the best hand, the others can concede and muck their hands. Or if one or more players have better hands, they show them. All seven cards must be shown. The holder of the best hand at this point wins the entire pot.

The Rake or Rental

In the Vegas casino poker rooms, there is either a rake or a rental charged, and the same is true in poker clubs around the country. In the Mirage, for example, for the $10–$20 game, the rake is either 5 percent or $3, whichever is less. In the clubs, for this kind of game, there is usually a rental charged of either $5 or $6 a half-hour.

In the Vegas poker rooms, the rake is removed piecemeal. In the Mirage, for example, $1 is taken off by the dealer when $20 is on the table. Then another dollar when $40 is in the pot. Finally, the third $1 is removed when $100 has been bet. No other money is taken by the house.

Now let's begin our discussion of the strategical principles necessary to win at Seven-Card Stud.

Winning Principles

Third Street Play

We're going to consider two aspects of Third Street play: which cards to stay in with, and how to bet those playable hands.

Because of the nature of the game, low card must bring it in, and therefore, there will be times when you'll find yourself in with absolute garbage because you were low card and nobody raised your initial wager. However, these situations come about rarely, especially in the bigger games, such as $10–$20, where you can expect at least one player to raise the $2 initial wager to $10. In the smaller games, such as a $5–$10 one, about half the time no one will raise on Third Street.

Before the deal no player can be sure of his or her position at the table, and position constantly changes. The low card will be in a poor early position, having made the first bet on Third Street. On Fourth and the later streets, the high hand takes over and leads, and thus is first to act, and is in poor early position.

Position is important in Seven-Card Stud, because you can make plays in late position that you couldn't make in early position. Here's an example. You're in the two seat, and the four seat has low card, a 3♦. He opens for $2 in the $10–$20 game. Everyone folds but the nine seat, who shows an 8♣ and calls the $2 bet. You are showing a King♠ as your doorcard. In this situation the King is a **scare card**, or a scary card, because it is the high card on board at this moment. You can safely raise to $10 no matter what you're holding in the hole. The low card will probably fold, and the 8♣ has a lot to think about. One of his cards, the 8♣, is a rag. Unless he is holding an Ace or has a pair, he'd be wise to fold.

Now, let's change the situation. You are dealt a Queen♠ and seat eight brings it in with a 4♣. Seat number one folds, and you, in seat number two, are in poor early position. Behind you is a King♥ in seat number seven. Now you have to examine your hole cards carefully. Suppose you hold 9♠ 3♣. You've got to fold. Your bad position hurts. Sure, you could raise, representing at least Queens, but if the King calls or raises, you're in a tough spot.

If you have good position and a powerful doorcard, you have an ideal situation to raise against one or two players. The more players in the hand, the weaker your situation. If a 2♠ brought it in, and there were four callers, two of them with **paint** (a Jack, Queen, or King), raising in late position may shake a couple of them out, but if you have junk in the hole and two players call your raise, you're in trouble in the later streets.

Another factor to consider with good position is this. Suppose a 3♦ brought it in, and four players called. In all games, the player bringing it in has the option of raising when the betting gets around to him. Now you're in late position holding the 9♠ Jack♦ and the 8♦ as your doorcard. You can call the initial bet for $2, figuring that the 3♦ won't raise. If he doesn't, then you're hoping for a 10 of any suit to give you four to a straight. Or you might pair one of your cards. If you pair the doorcard and bet out, opponents will be guessing as to whether you already have three of a kind. You're in command. Of course, if you don't improve and there's a bet, you're out of there.

What if, instead of not doing anything, the 3♦ raised to $10? Then you can muck your hand. You took a shot cheaply for $2. Give up the cards. You've got to figure that the raiser has either trips or a big pair in the hole. No sense in chasing him.

At this point we're going to assume that you're not in late position and that you can't really steal the antes, as you could in the first situation we discussed, where you raised with the King♠. What cards will you stay in with? We'll start with the best cards and work our way down in terms of playable hands.

Three of a Kind

A three-of-a-kind hand is your best holding on Third Street. It is also called **trips** or **a set**. The higher ranking the set, the better your hand. Three Aces are the best, then three Kings, going all the way down to three 2s. In most situations, even if you don't improve this holding, you're a big favorite to win.

Let's assume that you were dealt 7s **rolled up**, two 7s in the hole and one as your doorcard. That's the same as calling the three 7s a set. A 2♥ brings it in, a 9♠ calls, and the Queen♦ raises to $10. It's your turn now. If you raise the Queen, he may call the bet, but if he checks and you bet on Fourth Street, he may very well fold, and you'll only win a small pot. So you call the $10 raise. The deuce folds and the 9♠ also calls the raise. You have good three-way action. On Fourth Street, if nobody improves, and the Queen♦ bets, you call again, as does the 9♠. What you're waiting for to show the full value of your hand is Fifth Street, the first of the expensive streets, where the betting limit doubles to $20.

On Fifth Street, the hands look like this:

The threes bet $20 and the second player hesitates. You figure him for a four-straight at this point, with the 5♠ a **blank** (a useless card). He calls the $20 bet finally, and now you raise to $40. You figure that you're up against Queens up and a four-straight. You've gotten them to bet, and now you've trapped them. The Queen isn't going out. He calls your raise. The other player again hesitates. If he has a four-straight, he either holds 7-8-9-10, with your Jack a card that hurts him, or he holds 8-9-10-Jack, and there are two Queens out against him (assuming that the holder of the doorcard Queen has another one), plus your 7. Now he realizes that you may have more than one 7. He thinks and thinks, then folds.

Neither of you improve on Sixth Street. The Queen checks to you and you bet $20. On Seventh Street, you still have trips. The Queen again checks, and you bet. He calls. You show the trips and he concedes the pot. What you've done is **slowplay** the set, to get in two bets on an expensive street.

A good rule of thumb is this: When you are dealt trips, slowplay them, and don't show your true strength until the expensive streets, Fifth and later. Players already in with you are usually committed to seeing the river card, and will stand your late-street raises. You should win with a set, even without improvement. Sometimes you'll get beaten, but you always want a rolled-up hand.

The exception to slowplay is when you are in late position and have a set of Kings or Aces. It is natural to raise with these doorcards, and your opponents won't put you on trips. If you don't raise, you're raising a red flag, and everyone may fold on your first bet or raise on Fourth Street.

Don't be in a hurry, with other trips, to raise on Third Street. You want as many players in as possible. These are extremely powerful cards, and you don't want to put in a raise with three 10s and watch everyone fold their hands.

Premium Pairs—10s Through Aces

If you weren't dealt trips, these pairs are the best cards to hold on Third Street. Unlike trips, however, they probably won't stand up without improvement in a multiway pot with several opponents. So what you want to do is eliminate players immediately and narrow the field.

However, you can't raise with complete impunity. You must be aware of your position and the cards behind you. For example, suppose seat one brought it in with a 2♣, seats two and three folded. Seat four called with a King, and you, in seat five, hold the following cards: Jack♣ 9♥ Jack♠.

The spade Jack is your doorcard. The highest card behind you is a Queen. Go ahead and raise. If you're reraised by the Queen, then you call the raise. Don't reraise. If you're not reraised, you'll probably eliminate the deuce and either the King or Queen. You have to figure that the King is not paired; otherwise an intelligent player would have raised.

On Fourth Street, either the King or Queen will have the lead. You can decide whether to fold if the Queen bets out after raising you on Third Street. If your raise has held up, they'll check to you. Go ahead and bet. Keep betting strongly. Just as you wanted players eliminated on Third Street, you want the same thing on Fourth Street.

Often, with the best pair, you're up against "drawing hands," hands that need improvement to win, such as a four-flush or four straight. What you can't do is give them a free card by not betting on Fourth Street. A player may have three to a flush and a small pair on Fourth Street, and if you give him a free card, he can catch the fourth card to his flush. Now he's back in business. You've got to make drawing hands pay for the privilege of drawing. Don't give away a free card by not betting.

An ideal situation for any poker player is to hold a pair of Aces on Third Street. If they're concealed, even better. But if one is a doorcard that's not bad either. Your goal is to raise, and if raised, reraise. Get players out. Go heads-up against one player if possible. That's your ideal scenario.

If you hold two Aces and have raised and been called by a few players, including one holding a King, and you've not improved on Fifth Street, while the Queen has bought two running 5s, you are probably an underdog here. If the Queen bets out, representing two pairs, you have to eliminate the other players. Put in a raise here. You'll probably knock out the drawing hands, who now have to call a raise, and possibly two or three raises. And the Queen now has to figure you for Aces up, and won't reraise. If he does reraise, you may be looking at a full house, or trips. With just Aces, you may be wise to give it up.

If you're not reraised, you now wait for Sixth Street. If it is a blank and doesn't help you, you can get yourself a free card. The Queen will probably check to you, and you can check also. You now look at the river card. If you have paired any of your other cards, you're probably boss. If it's checked to you, you can bet. If the Queen bets you can call or raise, depending on how live his cards are. You'll at least call with a good chance of winning the pot.

To summarize premium pairs:

Premium pairs should be raised immediately on Third Street. They're stronger if concealed but good either concealed or with one as the doorcard. Any time you have 10s or better, think of raising. The only exception is when you are in early position and there are two bigger cards out against you. Suppose you hold Jacks and there's a King and an Ace behind you. Then you should just call, and see what they do. If either player raises, it may be a **position raise**, with the player taking advantage of his scare card and his position. Go ahead and just call the raise. But don't start the raising yourself with two or more bigger cards behind you.

However, if two players each show a King, then you can raise with your Jacks. The chances are that the Kings negate each other and neither player has a premium pair. Another situation that is beneficial is when you hold a concealed premium pair, such as Aces, with a 10 as your doorcard. Raising in any position forces the other players to believe you have 10s, rather than the concealed Aces. One hand I remember fondly is when I held buried Queens with a Jack as a doorcard. I bought another Queen on Fourth Street, and got plenty of action, especially when another player on Fifth Street was dealt a Jack. I paired a 9 on the river and with my full house won a tremendous pot.

Other Pairs—9s Down to Deuces

The chance of getting any pair is the same as getting any other pair, but the value of bigger pairs is of course much greater. By themselves, these smaller pairs rarely stand up; they need help, namely a second pair. Or they may turn into a set or even a full house.

When you've been dealt a pair, the most important factor to consider is the **sidecard**. The sidecard is the odd card that comes with the pair. For example, say you are dealt 6♥ 6♦ 2♠. Are these cards playable? If you can **limp in**—that is, see the opening bet without a raise—you might see if you get another 6 on Fourth Street, but even this is a dangerous move. More money is lost playing small pairs with a weak **kicker** (sidecard). Here's why.

Suppose you play the hand and get no help on Fourth Street, and see another bet. Then you pair the deuces, but another player with a 9 gets open 4s. He bets. You have to figure him for two pairs, and his other pair is probably bigger than yours. The trouble with a small pair is that you spend your time chasing bigger hands, and now and then, when you make trips, for example, you may find yourself facing a bigger set.

With a small pair and a weak kicker, muck the hand, especially if anyone has raised. These, as I have said, are chasing cards, and the way to lose at poker is to chase bigger hands. It's going to cost you a lot of money.

I would only play small pairs with a big sidecard.

By big, I mean a card higher than any that is showing on board. For example, if I'm dealt the same 6s with a Jack♠ but there is a Queen, King, or Ace on board, and any of those cards stay in the pot or raise, I'm out of there. If I'm in early position and am unsure of what is going to happen, I fold the hand. In late position, if there's no raise, I might see Fourth Street. No improvement and I'm gone.

When would I stay in? If my kicker is higher than any card showing. If I hold a King, and there's a Queen and Jack on board, I'll stay in. If I pair the King, I figure to have the best hand, and I can also improve on the small pair. Otherwise I feel I'm chasing, and I don't want to do that. I want to be the leader and let the others chase me.

There's something else to consider, and that's your doorcard. If your pair is **split**—that is, one of the two 6s you hold is your doorcard, with your sidecard concealed—you play the hand as we just suggested. If you have a small kicker, muck the hand, especially if there's a raise. If you have a high kicker that's better than any doorcard on Third Street, you can stay in against a raise.

When your pair is concealed and you have the highest card on board at Third Street, you can raise, even in early position, for you represent that you are holding a premium pair, and may very well win the pot then and there. If you don't hold the highest card, but hold a King as your doorcard, along with concealed 7s and an Ace before you either folded or limped in with a call, you can raise, again representing the Kings. The sweetest card to get on the next few streets would be a 7, for no one is putting you on trip 7s.

Sometimes a pair of 9s or even 8s can be considered a premium pair if the board shows no live cards for the other players. Suppose two players have a Jack as their doorcard, and there is no higher card out than the 8s or 9s on Third Street. I'd raise as if these pairs were premium cards. I can figure that I have the best hand at this time.

There are factors to balance with a small pair and a big kicker. If the pair is concealed, and your big sidecard is higher than any card on board, you can raise, representing a pair of big or premium cards. You're not revealing the real value of your hand. But if your pair is split, with the sidecard in the hole and you pair it, again you're concealing the real value of your hand. In the third instance, if your pair is split, and you pair your upcard, other players will figure you for trips and give up their hands. In this instance they are able to read the true value of your hand.

Another thing to think about is whether or not the pairs you hold are **live**. By live I mean that no other card of the same rank shows on Third Street. Suppose you hold a pair of 5s with a Queen as the sidecard. Another 5 is held by an opponent. The hand isn't worth playing. An exception would be if the kicker you hold is an Ace or a King, and it's high card as far as the doorcards are concerned.

Sometimes you'll hold a small pair, say 4s with a King, but another King is showing. I'd muck the hand. You need live cards in Seven-Card Stud for improvement, and you don't want to see the same ranked card as your pair or your kicker. It's tough enough making a set from your pair. If you take all seven cards, it's still only about one chance in ten. There are better situations for you.

Now, being alert is beneficial in this case as well. At a showdown by other players, if you see that a player had gone in with a small pair and a small sidecard, you know he's weak and playing too many hands. Take advantage of this when the right situation arises and you hold a powerful hand. He'll stay in against you, taking your raises, hoping for that pair to turn into a set. When you see a player who's stayed in with a small pair when another card of the same rank had showed in another player's hand on one of the early streets, again you know he's weak.

To summarize small pairs:

Play them cautiously. You need them live with a

big sidecard that's also live. If your sidecard isn't the biggest card on Third Street, and there's a raise by the bigger card, get out. If your pair is concealed and you hold the highest doorcard, you can be aggressive and raise, representing a premium pair. But when you don't hold the biggest kicker on board, and the higher card raised, you're out of there. There are better places for you to put your money. You don't want to chase stronger hands, and often this will be the case if you play small pairs with small kickers. If you're remaining in the game, and don't get any improvement by Fifth Street, and someone else has the lead, you don't want to stay in. Finally, when you have a small pair with a kicker, you have a slightly better hand if two cards are of the same suit. It's a real long shot getting that flush, but it's better than having three starting cards of different suits.

Paying aggressively, if you hold a concealed pair and have the highest doorcard, say a King, and a Queen raises, you can go ahead and reraise representing Kings. Right then and there you're taking control of the game, and you're in the lead. On Fourth Street, if neither of you improves and you bet, you'll probably be called. But on Fifth Street, when the expensive streets begin, if you bet you may win the pot then and there.

Drawing Hands—Three Cards to a Flush

When you hold three cards to a flush, you have a pure drawing hand, and your hope is that you complete the flush. That's your first thought. The second is the quality of your three-flush, what it's headed by (what the highest card or cards of the hand are). For example, if you hold Ace-Queen-6 of diamonds, you have an **out** (another way to win the pot). If you pair the Ace or Queen, you might very well have the best pair, and you could **back door** (get a hand you weren't drawing for) by making two pairs.

On Third Street, holding a three-flush, you'll take a raise and see Fourth Street, no matter what three cards you're holding. But if there's a double raise (two players raising), you want to give up the hand unless it's headed by two big cards such as Ace-King, Ace-Queen, or Ace-Jack.

Another important consideration when holding a three-flush is the quality of your doorcard. If it's a 5, for example, with a concealed Queen and 9 of hearts in the hole, and you're in early position, you might face a double raise behind you and be unable to play the hand. But let's say that the Queen of hearts is your doorcard. And it's the highest card on board. If you raise, it's unlikely you'll be reraised, and you're now representing a hand that you don't really have; namely two Queens. That's good deception.

If you don't have any big cards in your three-flush, you want to get in as cheaply as possible on Third Street, because basically you're trying for the flush without any outs, that is, other ways to win the pot. The more players in, the better. Every time there's a raise, it's getting more expensive for you, and you have a pure draw. If someone earlier has raised, and everyone else has folded, and it's your turn in late position, throw your cards away. You're about a 5-1 underdog with four cards to go, and you're going head-to-head against one player. Staying in is a bad move.

We spoke before about live cards when discussing small pairs. Live cards are also important in drawing hands such as flushes. When you hold three small cards of a flush, if you see one card of your possible flush held by another player, that's all right, but if two of your cards are on the table, then get out. Also dump the hand if you only have one big card, and there's a higher card showing on Third Street. Even if you pair your big card, you may still face a higher pair, and the two cards to your suit that are out reduce your chances of getting that flush considerably. The situation would be different if you held two big cards, because now you could pair either of those cards and make another kind of hand.

A great starting hand is to have three to a straight flush, such as King♠ Queen♠ Jack♠. You want to practice deception with this hand, so it's worth a raise, which represents a premium pair. Even if you raise against a higher doorcard behind you, it's a good move and might win the pot for you then and there. If you're reraised, you call the raise. You have a powerful starting hand with all kinds of possibilities: flushes, straights, and a big pair heading a smaller pair. If you get another spade, it's unlikely that your opponents will put you on a flush draw.

Starting with a three-flush, if you don't get a fourth card to that flush on Fourth Street, you can dump your hand if someone bets into you. Even if you get that fourth card to a flush, you're not a favorite to complete your flush. You're a slight underdog, just below 50 percent. You're not in a bad situation, because you're getting more than even money from the pot. The more players in against you, the better the odds you're getting.

On Fifth Street, if you still have your four-flush, the odds are about 1.8:1 against your completing the flush. If you have several players still in the pot, you'll be getting good odds even if you raise. On Sixth Street that raise may give you a free card, since everyone might check to you. Now, you're a bigger underdog, about 4:1. You'll want to see that river card as cheaply as possible.

Many players don't really know the strength of a four-flush by Fourth Street and think they're a favorite to get the flush with three cards to come. That's not the case at all, and they should play accordingly. I wouldn't raise on Fourth Street but wait till Fifth Street and only if there are at least two players in against you.

To summarize playing the three-flush:

If you hold three smallish cards, such as 9-6-3 of clubs, then you'll see one, but not two raises. If you're in early position with big cards out against you, and some aggressive players, with that hand you might want to muck it. You pretty much have a pure draw, hoping for the flush, and it won't stand two raises on Third Street. There are better situations to put your money to work.

If you hold two big cards from the Jack up to the Ace as part of your three-flush, then you'll see a double raise and stay in. You have outs, and may pair one of your big cards and have a chance to win that way. Your doorcard is important. If you hold even one big card but it's your doorcard and the highest card on board, you should raise, representing a big pair, and probably stopping a raise behind you. Now, if you get another suited card, no one is putting you on a flush draw.

If you have two or three big cards to a flush, a raise is in order so that your hand can't be read by your opponents. For all they know, you have a big pair, and if you pair your doorcard, the hand will be yours in most cases. And again, if you get that fourth card to the flush on Fourth Street, no one will put you on a flush. If no one has reraised you on Third Street, and you get a blank on Fourth Street, with no other player improving, go on and bet again. Take control even with a drawing hand if you're just getting calls.

However, if you only hold one big card to the three-flush and don't improve on Fourth Street, muck the hand if you face a bet by a card bigger than any you hold. You're going nowhere with this hand.

With a drawing hand, you want to get in as cheaply as possible and against as many players as possible. Going for a flush with small cards, if the opposition has thinned out to one player, or even two, is not what you want. If you face a raise in this situation on Third Street, get out cheaply.

If you get that four-flush on Fourth Street, you're still not a favorite, but a slight underdog. As each card is dealt, the odds against your getting that flush increase. It's about 1.8:1 against you on Fifth Street and over 4:1 against you on Sixth Street, with only the river card to come. If there are three players in against you on Fifth Street you can raise, for you're getting good value for your raise. By Sixth Street, you don't want raises, for now you're a big 4:1 dog and you're not getting real value for any raise you put in.

Sometimes you'll pair one of your cards in the three-flush on Fourth Street. You want to pair a big card and play it like a big pair. Pairing a smaller card may only induce you to stay in and get hurt. If you start with Queen-9-5 of diamonds, and pair the 5, you're still nowhere. Muck the hand against a raise.

Finally, you want live cards, and if you find that there are two or more cards of your possible flush out on the board on Third Street, and you don't have two big cards to the flush, fold the hand.

Drawing Hands—Three to a Straight

An interesting anomaly presents itself here. Although a straight is weaker than a flush, the odds against getting a flush starting with three cards to a suit are a little over 5:1, but getting a straight with three cards in consecutive order is a 5.7:1 proposition, and yet a holder of a straight will have to pay off a flush.

When you have three to a straight—that is, an **open-ended** one, where you can get cards on either end to complete the straight—the higher the cards, of course, the better the possibilities. A Jack-Queen-King is much stronger than a 3-4-5. Also, if possible, you want two of those cards to be suited. It's not a necessity, but it helps. On Third Street, you can see one raise with a three-card straight of at least 8-9-10, but to see two raises, I'd prefer holding the Jack-Queen-King. In fact, I don't like any three-straight unless I have it headed by at least a Jack. I don't think you can lose much mucking small three-straights against any sort of raise.

Besides the bigger straight, you must look for cards you need that are held by other players. On Third Street, if you hold the 9-10-Jack the most important cards to look for are 8s and Queens, and to a lesser extent the 7s and Kings. After all, if you get an 8 on Fourth Street, then the 7 becomes as important to your hand as the Queen.

Playing for the straight, you want an out, if possible. That's why it's so treacherous to play three small or medium cards (8-9-10) looking for that straight. You've got a pure drawing hand, and if you pair one of you three cards, you're still an underdog. You've got to figure that anyone who raised on Third Street has a big pair, or perhaps a big card or two heading either a flush or straight draw.

If they make their draw and you do also, you're still going to have to pay them off, having the inferior hand. That's why it's so important to have big cards when going for a straight. Jack-Queen-King is optimal, but 10-Jack-Queen is also good. With both those hands, you have an out, pairing one of the big cards. Again, be alert as to what cards are out against you. If there's an Ace on board, and you hold Jack-Queen-King, you can get hurt two ways. One, if you pair any of your cards, you may still be second to a pair of Aces. Two, the Ace is a card you need for your straight, and it's lying dead in another player's hand.

On Fourth Street, if you draw a blank, you've got to think seriously of folding your hand. An exception might be this—a 10 is on board against you and you're holding a King-Queen-Jack, or a Queen-Jack-10. Your 10 diminishes your opponent's chances of getting another 10, and you have either one or two cards to pair that will beat the pair of 10s you feel he has. But if all your cards are lower than a board card, prepare to fold if you face a bet, or worse still, a raise.

If your position is poor on Fourth Street, and there's a bet in this situation to you, with the possibility of a raise behind, then muck the hand. Wait for a better situation. Don't go after the straight with only a three-straight on Fourth Street without the possibility of pairing a bigger card than your opponent is showing.

If you get the fourth to a straight on Fourth Street, then you're about a 1.3:1 underdog to complete the straight with all seven cards dealt. If you don't have your straight by Fifth Street, you're a little over 2:1 dog to get it. And with but one card to come, the river card, you're over a 4.7:1 underdog. You want as many players in against you as possible going for the straight, so you can get good pot odds, more than the odds against your completing the straight. A bad play would be to stay in against one or two players on Third Street, hoping for a straight, without any outs. You want out here. Muck the cards.

Another holding that you might find yourself with is a **gutshot draw** on Fourth Street. This is the same as going for an **inside straight draw**. Here's the situation. You hold 9-10-Jack and get a 7 on Fourth Street. Only an 8 will form your straight. A Queen on Fifth Street doesn't do anything but put you back in your original situation of needing one of two ranked cards for your straight, and you're already on Fifth Street, with only two chances to get the straight, the Jack or 8. If you're in this situation, or if you pair one of your cards, you have to think of folding, especially if facing a Queen, King, or Ace on board. Your hand is still weak, and you're in the expensive streets, facing a possible single or double raise. This a good way to diminish your bankroll, staying in and taking punishment with a gutshot straight draw or a smallish or medium pair.

Finally, you might find yourself holding Ace-King-Queen. This is more like a gutshot straight than an open-ended one. The highest straight you can hold is Ace-King-Queen-Jack-10, but unless you get a Jack, you're not going to complete this straight. This hand is best played for pair possibilities. Stay in on Third Street and hope to pair one of your cards. It's a good raising hand, especially if you are in late position on Third Street and your card is the highest on board.

Let's suppose that you start with a three-straight holding two of a suit, such as 7♥ 8♣ 9♣, and you are dealt a 4♣. Now you have a three-straight, three-flush hand, but already you're on Fourth Street needing two cards to complete either the flush or straight. You're going nowhere. Dump the cards.

To summarize the three-straight drawing hand:

The higher the three-straight, the better off you are. Ideally, you want a Jack-Queen-King to start with. You then have an out; pairing any one of these premium cards and possibly backdooring two pairs or trips, even if you don't get the straight.

To stay in, you want to get the fourth card to the straight on Fourth Street. Even then, you're a 1.3:1 underdog, and with two cards to go (Fifth Street) you increase that to 2.1:1 against. Finally, with one card left, it's a whopping 4.7:1 against your getting that straight. That's why it's important to be alert and see how many cards you need are out. Don't go for a straight with your needed cards dead in other players' hands.

On Fourth Street, if you draw a blank, unless you have three big cards, one of which is higher in rank than any card showing, you should muck your hand. Preferably, you want two bigger cards to draw to in order to pair. Gutshot straights are treacherous, as are three-straight, three-flush hands. Again, if the cards aren't bigger than what's on board, muck them. If you have a medium or smaller straight, draw and pair a card, if that card isn't bigger than anything on board, fold your hand.

Fourth Street Play—The Turn

By the time you've reached Fourth Street, you have one of the playable hands we've discussed. The only exception would be a complete garbage hand held by you because you had to bring it in, and no one raised, so there you are with three junk cards, such as 8♠ 10♥ 4♦. You get another card on Fourth Street, and if you pair the 10 you might be in business. If everyone checks you can come out and bet, figuring you now have the high pair. If you pair the 8 and everyone checks again, you can come out betting. Even if you pair the 4 and bet, you're in good shape. Players fear the pairing of a doorcard, for they equate that with trips.

But if someone bets into you, showing a higher card on board, you're probably beaten even if you pair one of your cards, and on top of that, your sidecards are weak. Don't stand a bet, and certainly don't stand a raise, even if you pair one of your cards.

And if someone on Fourth Street gets an open pair, and you don't improve the garbage hand enough, get out. Suppose you pair the 8♥ but now there's an open pair of Jacks or even 9s. Why chase? You have dismal cards other than the 8s. You've invested a minimum bet on Third Street. Get out as cheaply as possible by folding your hand.

Other than the hands we've mentioned before, there's no reason to see a raise on Third Street to get to Fourth Street, and even if there's not been a raise, there's no reason to see a minimum bet bringing it in. You're throwing away money calling with a hand like 9♣ 5♠ 8♥. You keep calling with these cards and you will keep losing money. If there's no improvement or if you pair any of those cards, you're probably already facing a bigger pair. Even if you're not, the remaining players have 10s, Jacks, or better to draw to, and these pairs will kill your small pair. Even if you somehow make two pairs, you're probably lost because someone has two higher pairs. You have no outs here. Even if one of your cards is a Jack or higher, the other cards are mismatched and there's no real future. You can't depend on pairing one individual card to stay in business. It's just not enough.

Let's assume you've stayed in to Fourth Street with very strong cards, a set of 9s. There are three players in against you, an Ace♠ having raised on Third Street and a Jack♣ and a 10♥ having called. Taking my advice, you've slowplayed the hand. Your doorcard is a 9♥. On Fourth Street, the hands look like this:

The Ace bets, the Jack and 10 call, and you call. You're still on the inexpensive streets, and now you're getting an idea of what your opponents hold. You figure you're up against Aces, a possible flush, and a possible straight.

On Fifth Street, the hands look like this:

Again, the Ace leads, and you figure him for two pairs, Aces over 6s. When the second player calls, you have to figure him for four clubs. He's got to be crazy chasing with a pair of Jacks. Even the third player calls, and now you figure he's holding the 8 and 9 or maybe the Jack and Queen in the hole, giving him a four-straight. You go ahead and raise here. You've trapped the two drawing hands, and the Ace, unless he has trips, will have to respect your raise and simply call, which he does. The other two players call. By forcing them to put in two bets, you've cut their pot odds, plus you've built up a tremendous pot, and you're the favorite to win. You've got to make the drawing hands pay while you're in the lead. It's one of the rules of winning poker.

On Sixth Street, the hands look like this:

The 7s are first and they check. You bet, and are called by all three players. Now you figure, with the **case** (last) 9 out that the 10♥ hand probably started with 10 Jack Queen. There's an outside chance that he has three 10s heading a full house, but you would have heard from him on Sixth Street with a check raise. You still think he's one away from a straight, and is committed to staying in, as is the four flush headed by the Jack♣. Unfortunately for them, they're both **drawing dead**—that is, even if they make their flush or straight they can't win the pot. The Ace may get another Ace to beat you. If he gets a 6, he has a lower full house than you have.

On the river, you bet out. The Ace hesitates, then calls. You know he hasn't improved but feels that, with the size of the pot, he might as well see you. You've made him pay you off. The other two hands fold. They missed their drawing hands. You show your full house and win the pot. The holder of the Ace folds and mucks his cards. That's how strong a rolled-up hand is, for it would have won even without improving to a full house.

With a premium pair, you have a different situation. Instead of slowplaying, you've got to get right in there and raise from the get-go. You've raised with a pair of hidden Kings on Third Street and gotten two callers. On Fourth Street, here's what the hands look like.

The Queen checks, you bet, and the two-heart hand raises! The Queen folds and you think about what has happened. You determine that the hearts are now four hearts, and that hand wants a free card on Sixth Street. You have the high card on board and if you check, and the hearts draw a blank, the holder of that hand will see Fifth Street and Sixth Street for free. He's representing trip 10s but didn't raise previously on Third Street and so you put him on for a drawing hand to a flush. If he had trips, why raise on Fourth Street? Why not wait till Fifth Street, where the bet is twice as much?

If you reraise him, he'll probably call, but you're just a slight favorite here, so you just call his raise, wanting to see the Fifth Street card he gets. It's a rag, so you bet right out. You're about a 1.8:1 favorite, and he's going to call, for the pot's big enough to warrant his bet. On Sixth Street, he gets a blank, and still is stuck with his four-flush. Now he's a 4:1 dog. On the river, you have two pairs, Kings up, and check. If he's made his flush, you're going to lose, but you don't want to pay off two bets. If he has only one pair, he's not going to pay you off, but fold.

After you check, if he bets, then you have to think about the situation. Is he someone capable of a bluff? I'd call and be prepared to pay him off, because he's got to show you a better hand. As it is, he folded, missing his flush draw. If he made the flush, then there's nothing you can do but pay him off. You're not going to win every hand you're in. The river flows both ways, and the river card can be good or bad for you.

With a small pair and a big kicker, if you don't improve on Fourth Street, you can still call a bet, hoping to improve on Fifth Street. After all, Fourth Street is still a cheap street. Let someone else lead the betting, and call. You don't want to bet and find yourself facing one and possibly two raises. With two raises to cover, you might as well muck the hand. What you don't want to do is get trapped between two raises. If you see this developing, you simply fold your cards and wait for another hand.

Your kicker is important in this regard. As long as it's bigger than any other card on board, you can go to Fifth Street. If it's lower, and the higher card leads, then you might have a dismal future with these cards. Fold them. This could happen if you start with split 9s and a Queen. The Queen is high on board on Third Street, and you put in a raise.

On Fourth Street, an opponent gets an Ace and bets. You now have to guess—does he have Aces? He's representing Aces and he's a tough, tight player. In this type of situation you may want to fold the cards. You don't want to be known as a player who can be scared out of a hand by a bet or raise. So every now and then, reraise. Put it to him. In other words, don't bet only one way so you can be read. Now the Ace has to guess what you have. And if he checks on Fifth Street after calling your raise on Fourth Street, and you don't improve, you've gotten yourself a free card. You can see that Sixth Street card for free and decide what to do. But if the Ace bets flat out on Fifth Street, after both of you haven't improved, you're probably facing Aces or Aces up. Time to muck the hand before making an expensive call.

It's a complicated game, and you must be alert not only to the cards but to the players. Try to analyze their moves. What are they thinking? Why is the Ace betting out now? What would happen if you raise? If you're reraised, you're in big, big trouble. Try to figure out what is happening. It's not always easy, but always keep this in mind—you want to maximize your winnings and minimize your losses, not the other way around. Don't keep making fruitless raises trying to force out players that aren't going to go out.

With drawing hands, you want as many players in as possible on Fourth Street, provided you improved your hand by getting that fourth to the straight or flush. Now you're just a small underdog to get that hand you're looking for. On Fifth Street you can put in a raise, with two cards to go to complete your hand. If you do make a flush, for example in five cards, you should raise anyway. Or if everyone checked to you, bet. The other players may or may not believe you, and if you win the pot then and there, fine. You don't want to give free cards away. Anything can happen. A player that might have folded had you bet, may get trips and be back in action.

If you are going for a straight, for instance, and pair your big card, so you have Kings, play the hand on Fourth Street as if it's merely a big pair. Bet it. If your big card was your doorcard, absolutely bet it. The pot might be yours at that moment, as other players fold. Win pots; that's fine. A pair of Kings on Fourth Street might be the leader but may not necessarily win the pot by the river. Put pressure on the other players when you have the lead.

Fifth Street Play

On Fifth Street, you enter the first of the expensive streets. If you have a four-straight or four-flush, you're going to the river with these cards. If there's multiway action, with three or four players against you, you don't mind a raise. You're not even a 2-1 underdog going for the flush, and you're getting 3-1 or 4-1. You have the potential for a huge pot.

If you've started with a set, here's the time to think about putting in a raise or a reraise. Or you could wait till Sixth Street, depending on the situation. If a couple of players have drawing hands, you might as well raise on Fifth Street, forcing them to take less in pot odds, because they're putting more money into the pot. If they reraise, reraise them again. Trips are very powerful, and usually win by themselves. And you are less than 2:1 as far as improvement goes, either to a full house or a four-of-a-kind hand.

Trips are good money makers against two-pair hands, especially those led by an Ace. Here's the situation. You are in against an Ace with an open pair, figuring that he already has two pairs. Another player is also in the game. The Ace has raised on Third

Street and bet out on Fourth Street. The other player seems to hold a drawing hand.

The Ace is first and bets. The Queen hand calls. You figure he is going for a flush in spades and will be there till the river. You should just call here. If no one improves on Sixth Street, the Ace will bet again, having the lead. He can lose the lead only if you or the drawing hand pairs one of your **paint** (picture cards). If the other player pairs his Queen or King, he'll probably check. The King in his hand looks worthless and you still figure him going for that spade flush. If you pair your King or Jack, you're prepared to check so that you can check-raise.

If you check, the Ace is not going to worry about a smaller pair than Aces, giving you Jacks up, and will bet. He'll get a call from the drawing hand, and you can now check-raise. If the middle hand pairs up and bets, you can still raise, still confident of putting him on a flush draw. You're fairly confident because a Queen dropped out on Third Street.

If no one improves, the Ace hand will bet, will get a call, and then you raise. You've trapped the drawing hand, who will probably absorb punishment to try and win with this flush on the river. Here's the situation on Sixth Street:

The Ace is still high and bets, the middle hand calls, and you raise. The Ace hand takes a long look at your cards. Obviously the 7♦ didn't help. The key now seems to be the Jack♣. Undecided about the strength of your hand, he calls your raise, as does the middle hand. On the river you squeeze your cards slowly. You've gotten a 5♦. Not bad. Better in your hand than in the Ace hand. Now the Ace checks, the middle hand also checks, and it's up to you.

You have to figure that the middle hand, if he got a flush, would put in a bet here. You don't show an open pair and probably have a set at best. He's not worried about the Ace hand because he checked as well. If you bet, you can be check-raised, but neither player against you could be sure that you'll bet. Since your previous raise represented trips, if you bet they can't be sure that you haven't "filled up" (made a full house) and it would be foolhardy of them to check raise, unless the Ace made Aces full. But if he did, why didn't he bet? He'd be sure that you'd pay him off, as well as the middle hand if it made the flush.

So you bet. The Ace hand hesitates and calls, and the middle hand folds. You show your trip 6s, the Ace hand disgustedly shows you Aces up, and you win the pot, getting in an extra bet on the river, after carefully thinking about the ramifications of your opponent's checks.

The above example shows why it's so important to use your head in Seven-Card Stud. It's a thinking man's game. You have to carefully retrace the plays, from Third Street on, and try and put your opponents on one hand, if possible, or a couple, from the betting patterns they've shown. You can't always be right, for those two hole cards at the outset can hide a variety of hands, but if you study your opposition and can get an idea of their parameters of play, you can start reading their hands fairly well.

That's why you yourself must use deception and mix up your play. You don't want to be read in the same way. It's like having your cards exposed. Many mediocre players do the same thing over and over again, and they compound these mistakes by having tells, such as aggressive betting when they have weak hands. When playing Seven-Card Stud, watch every hand being played, even when you're out of the game, looking for patterns of play and tells among your opponents.

Sixth Street Play

By Sixth Street, there's enough money in the pot for everyone to see the river card, staying to the end. You can hold three types of hands at this point. First of all, you can have the best hand. If you believe you have the best cards on this street, then you want to get as many bets in as possible. If someone bets into you, you raise. If it's checked to you, you bet.

But there's also the possibility of check-raising. In order to do this, you should be sure that someone will bet behind you. If you've raised on the previous street and been called, the opponents might be happy to check along with you when it's their turn to bet. You don't want this to happen, and you must be fairly certain that a check by you will goad another player to bet, so you can check-raise. If you check and everyone behind you checks, and then bet on the river and everyone folds, you've lost two streets where your bets could have won you some money.

In order to check-raise on Sixth Street, you must be the first to act or just behind the first to act if three of you are left. If you are last to act and everyone has checked to you, all you can do is put in a bet. You'd be in a better situation to check-raise if you didn't raise on Fifth Street. It's a decision you have to make on the previous street.

One aspect of this decision is the strength of your board. If you find you'll be last to act on Sixth Street, you're not going to be able to check-raise. Another is whether or not you raised before on Fifth Street. If you did, and even if you have the lead, a check by you might be welcome to the other players, who all decide to get a free card on the river as we pointed out before. If you didn't raise but merely called a bet, or better still, a raise, now with the best hand, you'll probably get an opportunity to raise the lead bettor.

Not only is the pot big, but the other players have invested a lot of money already on their hand, and feel that they can possibly win with the river card. It's hard to get anyone out on Sixth Street unless your board is so threatening that no one else feels they have a chance to win. An example might be the following hand which you hold. We'll look at it the way your opposition does.

Pairing the doorcard was frightening enough to your opponents, but now they fear that you have a four-of-a-kind hand. If they're drawing for a flush or straight they would feel they're drawing dead, and anyone holding two pairs even headed by an Ace will probably give up this hand. He's close to an 11:1 underdog, and may also be drawing dead if you have four Kings.

Generally, with drawing hands on Sixth Street you might want to merely call. You're a 4:1 or better dog, and you want to see that river card as cheaply as possible. However, there are times, even with a drawing hand, that you might want to raise. One example would be if you held a four-flush headed by a King in the hole, and you paired your King. Your opponent has an open pair smaller than your King showing, say a pair of Queens, along with two hearts on board. You've already seen a Queen in another player's board, and you feel you're up against Queens up. Or maybe not. Maybe he has just two Queens and a four-flush. Having a four-flush yourself and a higher pair, you're an underdog, but not that much if he does have those two pairs.

There's one other factor to consider. If you just call the Queens' bet instead of raising, on the river you might face another bet that you'll have to pay off. After all, he might just have the Queens. Assuming he doesn't reraise you on Sixth Street, if he doesn't improve on the river, he's going to check to you. If you've improved to Kings up or a flush, you bet. If you haven't improved, you check also. If he has two pairs he beats you, but you had put yourself in a spot to get in extra bets—a raise on Sixth Street and a bet on the river—both of which you'd win if you improved your hand.

Seventh Street Play—The River

Most of your decisions on the river will depend on the caliber of one or more opponents. You may be up against a loose sucker, who will fall in love with any hand he has, and will call any bet on the river, afraid that if he doesn't, he'll be bluffed, which other than getting cancer, is his worst fear in life.

On the other hand, you might be up against a **rock**. A rock is a player who will go in only with very strong cards, and will stay in when he feels he has the best cards. Otherwise he's gone. Sometimes, going to a table for your seat after your name or initials are called, you see seven middle-aged conservative men who seem to know each other, glumly looking you over. You've just been thrown not to the wolves, but to the rocks.

Here's what's going to happen. When you have a good hand and stay in, anyone in against you will have a strong hand. When you raise, you'll be called, and eventually raised on the river. You'll have to grind out a win that will leave you limp and worn out. The best thing to do is to immediately request a change of table. Like the loose sucker, you won't be able to bluff these rocks out of a hand, but that's because they probably have better cards than you.

The third category is moderately skillful players. These players will respect strong hands, and can be bluffed. Occasionally, they'll try bluffs themselves, for they mix up their play to create deception.

Finally, there are the weak players, who play too many hands because they love to gamble. They're a cut above the loose suckers, for they know something about odds and correct hands to play, but their gambling undercuts their skill. Sometimes their conversation gives them away: talk of action, of betting on games and horses. You sometimes see them reading the *Racing Form* at the table. In Vegas, they take time away from the table to bet on horse races. Anyone who tries to beat the horses is a gambler; the odds are just too great against them, what with the various cuts the tracks, state, etc., take. They're giving up about 18 percent on each bet. You love to have them at the table against you.

When you have to make decisions on the river, you should know which category or categories your opponents fall into. You'll probably find yourself in a game with all three types. Sometimes the gamblers we mentioned are older men, sometimes young men who love action. The loose suckers are in on practically every hand; they're not hard to spot. The tight, tough players, who are moderately skillful, will give you the most trouble, because sometimes it will be hard to read them. The rocks in the game will become readily apparent.

On Seventh Street when you're in the lead with the best hand on board, you have to study the players in against you. Suppose you're head to head with a loose sucker. You're showing a pair of 8s, but have Queens in the hole. You can just bet out against him. He's showing a pair of 6s, and probably has two pairs, but you know from the cards that are out that your Queens are boss. He'll end up paying you off. But don't try and bluff him. If you're beaten on board, instead of having the best hand showing, and he bets, fold your cards. If he checks, then check after him. If you bet, he'll sure as shooting call.

On the other hand, against a rock, you can make a good move and get in an extra bet. First of all, you must have the best hand. You know he's in with strong cards. Suppose you suspect him of having trips, but smaller trips than you're holding. You check. You can be sure he'll bet, and then you check-raise him. But don't try and run any sort of bluff against him. He'll have strong cards.

The gambler will be on the river with all sorts of drawing cards. He'll go after inside straights, because every once in a while he's hit the perfect middle card. If you hold the best cards at the river, but sense that he's drawing for a flush or straight without any other outs, check. He'll bet if he's made it and check along if he hasn't. Sometimes he'll try a bluff. You have to gauge the situation, but most of the time, if you have a hand of any kind, and his board cards look weak, call his bet.

For example, he's holding:

You have two pairs, 10s over 3s, with 3s showing. His first two cards indicate that he might be drawing for a straight, but he might also have a four-flush. His river card is of course a mystery to you, so you check. He bets. You call. If he made his flush or straight, you pay him off.

Holding two pairs is a no-brainer here. You're going to call. But suppose you hold the following hand:

You raised on Third Street, bet out on the turn and on Fifth Street and were called. On Sixth Street, your opponent led and you called. Now you squeeze your river card, hoping for that second pair, but nada. Nothing but a blank.

Your opponent is showing the following cards:

He is a moderately strong player, but has been losing and turning into a gambler, playing a lot of hands he shouldn't. You check and he bets. What to do? It looks like he has two pairs. He bet out when he got the second 10, but in Seven-Card Stud that's almost an automatic play. Get an open pair and bet if you're on the lead.

He has you guessing, but on Seventh Street, don't

guess in these situations. It pays to call. You'll be paying off hands a lot of the time, but if you win one out of nine hands by calling correctly you're going to be ahead of the game. With bets on every street, the pot is large, even head-to-head.

There's another reason to call. If he has nothing, he's bluffed you out, and you don't want to get a reputation of being someone who can be bluffed. Better to be known as someone who will call any river bet with a decent expectation of winning. On this play, the opponent has two pairs and wins. But there'll be other times when you'll win, even with your one pair.

Some players, especially moderately skillful ones, are easier to bluff. They'll respect a good hand and when you bet out at the river, especially when you show an open pair, they'll believe you have two pairs, and won't pay you off with their single pair. They'll simply fold.

After playing with the same players for a couple of hours, if you're alert enough, you get a sense of how they play. And you can make good use of this on the river. Some players will fold when you bet out with an open pair; others will call with one pair. Some players will bet their one pair or even raise with their one pair. It takes patience to learn what they do, and often the best way to learn is to observe when you're not in the pot. It's cheaper that way and just as rewarding as far as information is concerned.

Occasionally you'll run into this situation. Neither you nor your opponent has a pair showing, but he has a King high board and yours is Queen high. You started with a pair of 10s and a Queen, the Queen being the doorcard. You raised and were called by two players, one of whom folded on Fourth Street when he drew a blank. On Fifth Street, you bet, and were called. On Sixth Street, your opponent paired 3s and checked. You checked behind him. On Seventh Street, instead of looking at his river card, he shuffles the three hole cards and says "Check in the blind." This is a common move made by mediocre players.

When an opponent says this, I feel he's weak and wants to save a bet. By not looking at his card, he figures he's scaring his opponent into checking because who knows what that river card can be? I inevitably bet when this happens. Now he has to look. Ninety percent of the time he calls or folds. If he raises, I give up my hand. I don't think this kind of player is capable of bluffing correctly.

Which brings me to another situation, and this can happen on any street. When a player says "check to the raiser," after I've raised on the previous street, I make a bet without hesitation. Only rank amateurs make this statement, and I figure with any decent hand I'm going to win the pot. What has happened is this—the amateur had bet on Fifth Street showing an Ace; I already had two pairs and saw an ace in another player's board. He bet and I raised. He called. Now he checks by making this statement.

Of course he's checking to the raiser. That's obvious. All he has to do is rap his knuckles on the table indicating a check. Then I think, am I going to be check-raised if I bet? Probably not. Every time that statement is made I've found myself up against weaker cards and weaker opposition.

Some Final Thoughts

Seven-Card Stud is a complex game, as I've mentioned earlier. It's a game where you constantly have to be alert. You're up against from one to seven other players, and on each street you have to note what cards are out, what ones are dead, and what ones are alive. You have to determine the playing strength not only of the cards, but of the players themselves. And those three hidden cards add an extra mystery to the game. It's hard to know when you have the very best hand sometimes. That's why you have to be alert to what is out and what is not.

You must also be aware of Third Street calls and

raises. What does a raise represent? How scary is the doorcard? What does an open pair mean when it's other than the doorcard? Is the player going for a flush or straight, or is he playing a big pair? A lot of this comes with experience, and the best way to gain that experience is by playing the game.

I would suggest playing a smaller game, but not less than $5-!0, which is a good springboard to bigger games. If you can win consistently at this game, move to $10–$20 and then up, to $15–$30 and higher, if possible. But don't move up till you can win at the smaller games. Don't be a gambler, trying to win back losses by playing bigger games. That's financial suicide.

The bigger the game, the better the players and the faster the action. Seven-Card Stud is structured so that more money is in the pot before the first bet in bigger games, encouraging action. This is done by the ante structure.

In the smaller games, the ante is usually 10 percent of the minimum bet, or $1 in a $10 game, 50 cents in a $5–$10 game. There's no reason to steal the antes in these games by raising and reraising, but in a bigger game with a 25 percent ante—that is, 25 percent of the minimum bet—ante stealing is not only more prevalent, it's almost a necessity. Otherwise the antes are going to eat you up. You have to make early moves, raise early. In other words, you have to fastplay.

If you play only when you're comfortable with the game and the stakes, you can think clearly and be more observant. Again, start with smaller games, test your skills and heart, and if you're a winner, move up. That's my best advice.

VIII

Hi-Lo Split—8 or Better

This is **Seven-Card Stud** with one big difference: The low hand, provided it is headed by an 8 or smaller-ranked card, is as valid as the high hand, and splits the pot with the high hand.

For example, suppose one player holds the following hand:

and another player has:

The pot would be split between them if they were the only two players left at the showdown. The high hand, with Queens up, would win half the pot, while the low hand, a 7-6 low, would win the other half. The five best cards in any holding forms the best hand. Five cards can be used for high and a different group of five cards can be used for low. Or in the case of a low straight, or flush, the same cards can be used for high and low. If another player were in and had Jacks up, he would lose. And if another low hand was in with an 8-5, he would also lose.

The best low hand to hold is a wheel, consisting of Ace-2-3-4-5, for flushes and straights do not affect the low value of the hand. The best high, of course, is a royal flush, consisting of Ace-King-Queen-Jack-10 of the same suit.

What happens if two or more players compete for the pot, and there is no valid low hand of 8 or better? Then the best high hand **scoops the pot** (wins the entire pot). What if two or more players compete for low? The lowest hand wins half the pot and the highest hand wins the other half of the pot. Something like the following can result with two players left in the game.

The first hand has a 7-5 low, while the second has a 7-6 low. But the second hand has an Ace-King high hand, while the other player has an Ace-Jack high. The pot is split.

An ideal situation is to hold a low with a flush or straight developing from that low, such as the following:

This player has a 6-5 low and a straight. Remember, straights don't have any effect on the value of a low hand. With a powerful low and a straight for high, this hand has a good chance of scooping the pot.

A low hand whose very lowest cards are extremely low is said to be a **smooth low.** For example, a hand for low that is 8-4-3-2-Ace is an 8 smooth hand. On the other hand, a holding that doesn't have these extremely low cards making up the remainder of the hand is said to be **rough.** An example would be an 8-7–5-4-3. That's a rough 8-7.

The goal of a player is to scoop the pot, and win the entire thing. If he can't do that, his next goal is to win at least half the pot. That is not always possible, and it is a fatal mistake in **Hi-Lo Split** to stay in with mediocre cards figuring that you'll win half the pot anyway. That kind of thinking will cost you a lot of money. Going high-low or going for high or for low, you want to play with good starting hands, and if those hands die or don't develop, you should fold them, rather than delude yourself into thinking, "Shoot, I'll win half the pot anyway," because you won't many times, and it will end up costing you a good chunk of your bankroll.

As in Seven-Card Stud, you'll be seeing a lot of cards open on the board, and you must stay alert to which cards are dead and which alive, and how the various opponents stack up as to playing skill. This game attracts some weak players who think it's a simple game to beat because, like the sucker described above, they think "Shoot, I'll win half the pot anyway." Playing with good cards, playing aggressively, and being aware of what is happening in each game should make you a winner.

How the Game Is Played

The game is played at various limits, but the most popular game found in most clubs and casinos is the $20–$40 game. If this game is too big for your budget or temperament, you can find smaller games from time to time. But for purposes of discussion, we'll deal with the $20–$40 game as played in the California clubs.

In Las Vegas, there usually is no hourly rate for this kind of level, and the dealer takes out $3 for a full game of eight players. In California, the half-hourly rate is either $7 or $8 to play. It's a big-money game and a lot of cash can be won or lost. This is not a game to gamble wildly at. You must play skillfully and sanely.

When playing Hi-Lo Split, the cards speak. What this means is that at the showdown, after all the cards have been dealt and all bets have been made, the players show their cards openly and the dealer then determines which hand wins low and which high, or if there is no low, which hand scoops the pot. Or perhaps one player scoops with a high-low hand. To make the distribution of the checks easier, dealers during the game constantly make two separate and equal piles of checks, ready to distribute a pile to one player and another pile to the other winner.

Home high-low games are usually played as **declare.** Players don't show their cards till they declare, either high or low or high-low. In casinos, cards speak because allowing declarations leads to arguments and fights, and sometimes collusion among players.

Eight players make up a full table. Each player puts in a $3 ante prior to the cards being dealt. The ante is thus 15 percent of the minimum bet, a moderate, not high, ante. Each player is dealt three cards at the outset, two down, called hole cards, and one open, the doorcard. Low card brings it in for $5. Thereafter, a player may raise to complete the bet to $20, but this doesn't count as a real raise, and three more are permitted on Third Street. An Ace is always considered a high card in this respect, even though it can be used as either a high or low card in a player's hand.

If two players have identical low cards, then low card is determined by suit, as follows, from lowest to highest: clubs, diamonds, hearts, and spades. On Third Street the betting is in the lower tier of $20. The same holds true for Fourth Street. Unlike Seven-Card Stud, an open pair doesn't affect the betting structure; it still stays at $20. Fifth Street and the streets thereafter are at the higher end of the tier, in this case $40.

Let's assume that a 2♣ brought it in, a 5♠ called, and an Ace♦ raised to $20. Everyone else folded but the 2♣ and 5♠. The next card dealt is Fourth Street, or the turn. On this and subsequent streets, high card is first to act. If two players have identical high cards, such as Ace-Queen, the player closest to the dealer, counting clockwise, is the first to act. Here are the Fourth Street cards.

The deuces bet, the middle hand folds, and the Ace ♦ raises. The deuces call the raise. On the next card, Fifth Street, we have the following hands:

The deuces check, the Ace bets, the deuces call. On Sixth Street, we have:

Again the Ace bets and is called.

Then the river card is dealt. The Ace bets out, and the deuces call. The cards are turned over.

Neither hand has a low. The three 5s in the second hand make up the best high hand, so, it wins the entire pot. After Sixth Street, the second hand couldn't make a low, but looking at the first hand, he knew that it couldn't make a low either. The Kings and deuces from the turn on knew his hand could only go one way, and since the second hand represented a low hand with the possibility of also having Aces, he stopped raising and just called.

Playable Starting Hands

Many players philosophize that it's best to play low hands, because a low hand can develop into a high hand as well, so that there's a possibility of scooping the pot. But in games in which only a few players remain in contention, often the best high hand wins outright, with no low hand developing. After all, if you start with a high hand, you can't weaken it, but a low hand can develop into a catastrophe.

An example might be:

Now that's a wonderful starting hand for low. But it ended up like this:

That's a hand that can't win either way. Low hands that start off great and then die out are the bane of all Hi-Lo Split players. It's going to happen to anyone who plays the game, and you should expect it as well. To prevent this from happening, you should play your low hands as if you're playing a drawing hand in regular Seven-Card Stud. In other words, if your Fourth Street card is a blank and doesn't help, throw away the cards.

Suppose you have started off as before but your fourth card hurts your low:

Let's assume that you're in against two other players. The first holds:

Now he possibly has four to a low, or perhaps three to a low with a pair of Aces. He's got you beaten low and high. The third player holds:

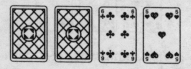

You can be sure he's in with a low hand of four cards, if he's a halfway decent player. Right now you're probably holding the weakest of the low hands, and you need two low cards to complete your low. As for your high hand, you have nothing at all.

On the next card, Fifth Street, the hands look like this. You hold the first one:

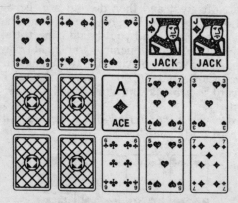

You're getting in deeper and deeper. Your pair of Jacks, even high, may be third to a pair of Aces and a possible straight. You check, the Ace bets, and is raised by the third hand. Now you're in a real bind. There's going to be a raise and reraise here till the bets are capped, and you're in the middle. That's why it's so dangerous when your Fourth Street card isn't helping your low hand. Again, to repeat my suggestion, play the low hand like a drawing hand and if you are badly hurt on the turn, fold your cards. You'll save a lot of money in the long run.

Let's now study some of the best playable starting hands.

Strong Low Starting Hands

Three to a Low Straight Flush

These are ideal starting cards, but you're not going to see them very often. Their power is their scooping ability—a chance for high and low. A good example would be 3♠ 4♠ 5♠.

You're going to play them fast. Two of them will be concealed and no one can put you on this hand. And you have a slew of cards to help you, either high or low or both ways.

A Pair of Aces and a Low Card

Aces are very powerful since they can be used high or low. A pair of Aces gives you a lot of leeway, for you stand a good chance of winning high, and at the same time, if low cards come to you, those aces smooth out any low hand. They should be played fast, for if an Ace is your doorcard, you have some deception with the hand, with opponents unsure of whether you have three good low cards or a pair of Aces.

Three Small Cards to a Flush

This is a strong starting hand, and if one of the cards is an Ace, it is quite powerful. You now have a chance to scoop, with a flush for high and a low hand as well. You should play fast, and put in a raise. Without an Ace, you would be happy to have the smallest possible cards, such as 5-3-2 (4-3-2 would be a possible straight flush hand).

If you have an Ace, and it's the doorcard, your raise will possibly represent Aces, so you have a good hidden low here. Even if you get two additional cards to the same suit, there is an element of deception here, since the other players may think you started with Aces and will disregard the three-to-a-suit showing. For example, if you started with 4♣ 5♣ Ace ♣, the Ace being your doorcard, and you were then dealt 9♣ 6♣, it's uncertain to the opponents whether or not you are going for a flush or simply have a pair of Aces, with one of the open cards possibly giving you a two-pair hand.

In this situation, you probably have the best high hand, and have a shot at a solid winning low hand. You're in an ideal situation and you can raise and reraise and hammer the opponents.

Three Small Cards to a Straight

This is another strong starting hand, and one that should be played fast, so a raise is in order here. The lower the straight the better the hand, and ideally you would want a 4-3-2 or 5-4-3, with chances to make the straight at both ends. An Ace-2-3 is also strong but figures to play for the small end of the pot rather than the high end, because of the limited chances to make a straight. However, if the Aces are paired, it's a hand that can go both ways, and if any of the other **babies** (small cards) are paired, that gives you a potentially good hand going both ways.

An 8-7-6 is a borderline hand because of its limited value as a low hand. If there are a number of small cards out that could help you, this hand should be folded. For example, if you see a couple of Aces, a 2, 3, and 5 on the board.

Another difficulty with that hand is that even if you improve by pairing one of your cards on Fourth Street, you can only go one way. If you get caught between a made low hand and a strong high one, it can end up costing you a lot of money. By made low hand, I mean one already formed, such as a 6-5-4-3-Ace.

A Pair of Low Cards and Another Low Card

A typical hand would be a pair of 5s and a 2. Or a pair of deuces and a 5. Which is better to hold? The higher pair, the 5s, for it gives you a little more leeway going for high. If you're up against another low hand head to head, with no high hands in sight, the 5s may win as high pair. It's a little extra strength for the hand.

If you get a blank on Fourth Street, you've got to think of folding these cards. For example, holding 5-5-2, you are dealt a Jack. There's an Ace out against you as well as a 7-3. You're in no-man's-land. Fold 'em.

Two Low Cards and an Ace

This is a better hand than the previous one, for the Ace is superpowerful in Hi-Low Split. If you pair the Ace, you figure to have the best high hand early on, and if you get another baby, you have a strong starting low hand, one that you should play fast. The Ace in your hand certainly gives you an out for high, and takes away this Ace from any other low hands.

A Low Pair and an Ace

This is a two-way hand, for the low pair and the Ace kicker give you a shot for low or high. If the Ace is high on board and is alive, you want to pair the Ace if everyone else is going for high hands, or is having rough going, with big cards hurting their chances of getting a made low hand. However, if you get a blank on Fourth Street and another one on Fifth Street, I'd give up the hand.

Three Small Cards

Finally, we have just three small cards, neither suited nor in consecutive order. They go up in value depending on three factors. First, it's best if two are suited. Second, if they can form a straight, that's good. And last, the lower the lead card, the better. For example, a 6♥ 3♥ 2♠ is better than a 6♥ 3♦ 2♠ because in the first instance, two cards are suited. For a second example, a 6-5-3 is better than a 7-5-2 because there's a much better chance of making a straight with the first hand. Finally, a 7-3-2 is stronger than an 8-7-3. The 7 is lower than the 8, and the 7 hand is much smoother than the 8 hand.

Strong High Starting Hands

Trips

As in Seven-Card Stud, holding trips gives you a big lead over any other high hand, and should win without improvement. If possible, you want to make both a low and high hand and scoop the pot, but that's a long shot, even starting with a hand like 3♦ 3♠ 3♥. What you hope for is to be able to scoop because no one else makes a completed low hand. In that way, holding three babies to a set gives you an extra edge. Those are three small cards that aren't going to help any low hand competing against you.

I would slowplay them, for you want a lot of action, and on Fifth Street I'd put in my first raise. You want some deception with the hand. If you raise on Third Street with trips, showing a 4♠, for example, and then get a Jack♥ on Fourth Street and keep raising, and on Fifth Street get a 10♦ and raise again, your hand is pretty apparent, and if no one is improving his or her low hand, the pot may be yours when you bet on Fifth Street.

But if you slowplay, and can get in a raise, or better still, a check-raise on Fifth Street, you may trap a couple of players who have missed their lows but have two pairs instead. It's a matter of making more money.

An ideal situation would be holding trips against two or three players going for low. You've got them all in the middle and should build up an enormous pot for yourself.

A High Pair

This is a tricky holding in Hi-Lo Split. If you start with a premium pair, you don't have the same advantage that you would have in Seven-Card Stud, because you'll be up against players who are going for low. A hand like 2♣ 3♦ 4♠ would be thrown away against a Queen that raised in Stud. But in Hi-Lo Split, that's a very strong beginning hand. It can develop into a straight to win both ways and also can develop quickly into a made low hand, if the holder catches two odd low cards, such as a 7 or 5.

So, if you raise with a premium pair, and find yourself going head-to-head against a low doorcard, or worse still, an Ace for a doorcard, you will probably be going for only half the pot, while your opponent is **freerolling**—that is, he has a free shot at the whole pot while you're limited to only half. And if he scoops the pot, it's going to cost you a lot of money. It's a losing proposition to go for only half a pot when you can easily lose the whole thing.

On the other hand, not all starting low hands are completed, and if your opponent is dealt a blank on Fourth and Fifth Street, your premium pair may be enough to win the whole pot.

There's another danger, however, when you start with a high pair. You must make sure that it's the highest hand out there on Third Street. Since you don't have X-ray vision, you must be alert to the action. For example, suppose a 2♦ brought it in, a 5♣ called, and now it's your turn after three players folded. You hold Queen♦ 9♦ Queen♠. In Stud you'd have no hesitation in raising with this hand, even though there's a King♠ behind you.

But the King reraises, you're in a real bind. You're guessing as to whether or not he has Kings, and if he does, you're an underdog to win even half a pot. That's a catastrophe. You can't afford these kinds of situations. So, if you call instead of raise, and wait to see what the King does, it might be more prudent. Suppose the King just calls. Then you can be pretty sure that your Queens are boss and the King hand probably has a smaller pair in the hole, or perhaps a drawing hand, such as a straight or flush.

But the holder of the King♠ is a tough player, and even with a pair of 10s in the hole he figures he has the best high, so if you just call, he'll throw in a raise. You decide to raise, the King calls, and the opening deuce of diamonds reraises. He's still live even though he brought it in originally for $5. The others, including you, call this reraise.

On Fourth Street, the hands look like this:

The King checks, the deuce bets, the 5 calls, and now it's your turn. You raise and the King folds. The deuce calls your raise. You can be sure that both low hands out against you haven't completed their lows in four cards. The 5-3 hand didn't reraise the 8-2, and you decide that the 3 probably paired one of its hole cards.

On Fifth Street, the hands look like this:

You bet, the deuce raises. If he has a completed hand, he's a favorite at this point, even with an 8, over a potentially smoother low hand that is not yet made. The Jack has hurt the middle hand's low, and even if he paired, he's still facing your Queen and Ace, and from the beginning, you've represented a pair of Queens. He folds. You and the deuce hand both get rags on Sixth Street. You check and he bets. On the river, you pair your 4s and check, and the deuce hand checks behind you and shows an 8-6-5-3-2. You split the pot. He was hoping for the 4 so he could scoop the pot. Not being able to beat you for high, there was no sense in his betting.

If he had been dealt an open Ace and kept betting, he would have put you on a difficult call, for his hand, looking low, might have been a high hand led by Aces and another pair. That's the problem with the high pairs.

Obviously, the bigger the pair the better your hand. But if you're dealt a premium pair and there are two higher cards behind you, I'd call the $5 that low card brought it in for, and not call a raise. If you're reraised you may be chasing, and for only half the pot. The best hands to get are the low ones with an ace giving you that out for high. Or a three-flush or three-straight with all low cards.

A Small Pair with a High Kicker—Not an Ace

This hand is very playable in Seven-Card Stud but has limited potential in Hi-Lo Split, even if the kicker is the highest card on board. You're basically going one way, high, but your pair may already be second best. If both of your cards are very live, and you face only a $20 bet on Third Street, I'd see Fourth Street for that one bet. If I don't improve I'm out of there, especially if an Ace shows on board. If there are two raises on Fourth Street, I'd definitely muck the hand.

Three to a Flush

This is a drawing hand, and it's best if all of the cards are 8 or lower. Now you have a chance to scoop the pot by winning both ways. With this kind of hand, say 7-5-3 of spades, you can play it fast and raise. Another low spade would be terrific, and any spade, even paint (Jack, Queen or King), gives you a solid chance at a high hand. And still leaves you with a shot at low if you catch two more low cards. If one of the low cards is a spade, even better.

With this hand you welcome as many players as possible in multiway action.

Not as good is a three-flush with one or more cards above an 8. Here you may be limited to competing for high, and I'd play these cards cautiously. Suppose you start with the Jack-7-5 of spades and get a Queen♦ on Fourth Street. You throw your cards away. You must be helped on the turn to continue playing. If you get a low spade on the turn and now hold Jack-7-5-3, you'll be going to the river with this hand. However, if you get a 3♥ instead of a spade 3, then you're in a bind. You have a two-way hand, chasing both ways. I'd give it up right then and there.

With a three-flush without holding three small cards, you also want multiway action, but don't fall in love with these cards. And don't get in the trap we showed of going both ways, or more properly, chasing both ways. It's going to take a dent out of your bankroll.

Three to a Straight—Medium or High Cards

An example of a medium straight would be 7-8-9 and of a high straight, 10-Jack-Queen. These are definitely one-way hands, and are not recommended playing. The only exception is if you get in cheaply on Third Street, seeing the $5 bet, and you get the fourth-to-a-straight with multiway action. Then you have to think of going to the river. Or if you pair any of your cards in a high straight, and it's top pair on board. Other than these two possibilities, I'd pass on this hand.

Three to a High Straight Flush

Last but quite strong is a hand such as Jack♣ Queen♣ King♣. It's a great drawing hand with all kinds of possibilities. If you are helped on Fourth Street either as a flush or straight, I'd play it fast, hoping for multiway action. But these hands come quite infrequently, and you have the same chance of getting a 3♦ 4♦ 5♦, which is a much stronger starting hand, for it gives you the chance to scoop two ways. With the lower straight flush, play it fast on Third Street. It can take a couple of raises, for it can develop into a scoop hand with a couple of good catches.

Other Third Street Considerations

To reiterate, there are two ways to scoop in Hi-Lo Split. First, you have the best high and low hand in your seven cards, such as a flush and a 6-4 low. Or you have the best high hand, and there are no valid low hands competing with you. For example, you hold trip 9s and no one has a low, and the best high hand is a pair of 10s. The entire pot is yours.

If you are in action against one or more players and you merely have the best low hand, you're only going to take half the pot. If your cards are 7-5-3-2-Ace-Jack-9, anyone holding a pair, no matter how small, if it's the best high hand, will take half the pot.

When playing Hi-Lo Split, it is of the utmost importance that you be aware of the cards on the board. This is your first chance to see them. For example, suppose you hold Jack-9-Jack and there's another Jack on board. This weakens your chances considerably, and you can safely muck the hand. Your Jacks aren't really alive anymore, and any low hand pairing an Ace or any high hand with a concealed higher pair, are overwhelming favorites against you.

With a pair of split Queens, for example, you'd want to see a bunch of small cards on board. If you see a 5, 6, 3, 7, and 8 arrayed against you, with a King that has already folded, then your hand has increased in value considerably. With five different players holding low doorcards, the chances of getting a made low hand has decreased considerably for them. Your high hand might very well be in a position to scoop the pot.

With three low cards to begin with, you have a wonderful starting hand. But again, if there's a 4, 2, 2, 5, and Ace out on board, all cards that could help your 7-3-Ace, you have to proceed cautiously. If you have to face two raises to stay in, you can safely muck this hand. One or two other players may be going for low, or perhaps the holder of the Ace has Aces, or maybe one of the raisers holds trips or a pair of Kings or Queens.

It would be much better for you holding the 7-3-Ace hand if the board showed 7, 3, 3, 7, and Ace. All of these cards are out in other hands, cards that, other than the Ace, can't really help your hand. Your low possibilities are enhanced seeing these cards. You can now fastplay your hand, figuring that any low card dealt to you on Fourth Street will probably help your hand.

Probably more than any other poker game, Hi-Lo Split requires you to keep track of cards out against you, because of the split nature of the game. If you come to this game tired or unable to concentrate for any reason, you're asking for trouble. Don't play under these circumstances. Wait for a different time or a different day.

Fourth Street Play

Having a hand that is quite playable, you find yourself on Fourth Street with a 6♣ 4♠ 2♣, the deuce being your doorcard. On Third Street, your deuce brought it in, a King♠ called as did a 5♥, and an Ace♣ raised. You called the raise, the King folded, and the 5♥ also called the raise.

Here are the hands on Fourth Street:

The Ace bets out. You have a choice of raising or calling. The 8 probably helped the middle player, and he'll call the raise because he knows you don't yet have a complete low hand. So you raise, are called by the middle opponent, and the Ace-King reraises, representing a high hand, probably Aces. You call the raise, waiting for Fifth Street, the expensive street. If you reraise here, you might chase out the middle hand. You don't mind multi-action here, figuring you have the best low and a gutshot chance at a straight, which will allow you to scoop.

Let's look at another situation: You've been dealt Ace♠ 2♠ 8♠. A 4♦ brought it in, was raised by a 4♥, a Jack♦ called the raise, and now it's up to you. You have a great hand to scoop the pot, but your 8 is a bit high against the raiser and possibly the 4♦. But if the 4♦ has a baby in the hole and any other card, and stays in, if he catches good on Fourth Street, he may be added competition for you. So you reraise, figuring he may not call a double raise with his cards. You're right. He folds. The 4♥ calls your raise as does the Jack♦.

On Fourth Street the hands look like this:

You're first, and check. The 4-3 hand bets and the Jack-Queen hand raises. Now what do you do? You muck your hand. The King♥ was a killer card, breaking up both your low and your possible flush. Going now for only half the pot, your situation is not good at all. The 4-3 is probably now four to a low, and you can be sure it's not an 8 heading his low. The prudent move is to dump the hand. If the King had been a spade, you'd definitely stay in till the river, with an outside chance of getting a low as well as a good chance of getting the flush.

One last example: You were dealt Queen♦ Queen♠ 5♥. A 2♦ brought it in, was called by a 10♣, a 9♣ folded, but a 6♥ called. An Ace♠ raised. Now it's your turn. Behind you is an 8♦ and Jack♠. You think about raising and decide to do it, rather than let the Jack in cheaply. And if you can knock out the 10♣ that's good also. It's difficult to call a double and possible triple raise with mediocre cards on Third Street. After you raise, the 8♦ and Jack♠ fold, the 2♦ also folds, but the

6♥ calls the double raise. The Ace reraises. You call. Your hand has some deception. You could represent a very low hand. The 6♥ also calls.

On Fourth Street, the hands look like this:

The Ace checks, and now you feel he had a low hand broken into by the King. You check, the first hand bets. The Ace calls. Now, you don't want to reveal your strength yet, but having two hearts gives you the opportunity for deception. You raise. The first hand, having the best low so far, reraises. The Ace-King is in a bind. He has two big cards plus two babies in the hole. He calls, and you call.

You're hoping that the Ace-King gets a small card or pairs the King or Ace. Now he's forced in. If the first hand gets a needed small card, he'll definitely bet and once more you can check-raise. You really don't want another heart, for it might scare off the Ace-King hand. You figure you have the high hand locked up, and you can scoop the pot if the first hand dies with just four babies.

Fifth Street Play

On Fifth Street, we begin with the expensive streets, double the previous streets' bets. As we are discussing a theoretical $20–$40 game, the bets and raises are now in the $40 range. It's here that you must make a decision as to whether or not to proceed with your hand.

In terms of scooping the pot, most scoops come from the best high hand winning over other high hands, after the low hands failed to complete a five-card holding 8 or lower. Relatively few scoops come from one hand having high and low. And again, we have to remember that a pure low hand will win only half the pot and fall to any mediocre high hand for half the pot.

Saying all this, *we have to avoid the delusion that, going against whatever hand appears to be the opposite of our hand, we'll automatically win half the pot.* This kind of thinking is the downfall of many a Hi-Lo Split player. And on Fifth Street, when we have to call or bet or raise on the higher tier of betting, we should carefully see what we are holding in relation to our opponents, to avoid this situation and any others that will cost us big bucks.

Let's assume you hold the following hand:

You're up against two players:

The 9s bet, and now it's up to you. The two 9s hurt your chances of getting the straight, but you think, "Well, if I get my low, I'm winning half the pot." But are you? On Third Street the King raised, and was reraised by the 6♠. What did that reraise portend? Obviously he doesn't have a high hand, and more probably is holding something like Ace-4 or Ace-3 in the hole. If he's holding Ace-2, then you still have to catch a small card to complete your low hand. You're a dog as far as a straight is concerned, and if you're up against two pairs and trips, you may complete your straight and still be drawing dead.

If the second deuce slowed down the other hand, which may now hold Ace-4-6-2-2, he may still raise with that low holding. He has a shot at trips or Aces up for high. And he has great low possibilities. What do you do? Rather than face a couple more raises, it would be prudent to fold the hand. A good question to ask yourself—would you rather have the other low hand or yours? Definitely the other one. Would you rather have your high hand possibilities or the open pair of 9s and probably Kings? Definitely the other one. You're in against two hands superior to yours, both high and low. There's no future here for you.

By the time you get to the expensive Fifth Street, your hand should allow you the following—either it's got a good chance of scooping or if it can't scoop, it's an outstanding hand going one way. If you have a dynamite high hand, such as trips or a pair of Aces with three other small cards, you've got an outstanding chance of scooping. If no one completes their low, you'll probably have the best high with a set. And with the Aces hand, you've got a chance for a powerful low, and your Aces may hold up for high by themselves.

If you don't have scooping possibilities, then you'd better make sure that you have an overwhelming chance to win half the pot. You can't afford to make big bets and take a couple of raises on each expensive street and end up with nothing. A few of these situations and you'll be tapped out.

Another tough hand would be: 5♥ 7♠ 2♦ 4♠ 5♦. You're up against two other hands:

The Ace raised on Third Street. The 8s bet out on Fourth Street and were raised by the Ace hand, then called by the 8s. You've been calling. Now you look over the situation. For all you know, the Ace hand is already a formed low hand. And the hand with the 8s, whether high or low, shows a bigger pair than your 5s. Looking further over the situation, you notice that no 6s have shown yet (none were on the board in folded hands on Third Street). The Ace hand can have an Ace in the hole, and have a high hand. But he could just as well have a 6-4 as pocket cards.

Your hand is second best for high, and second best for low. If the Ace hand has a 6-5-4-3-Ace low, you're dead in the water. Again, you'd have to ask yourself the question, which low hand would I prefer? And if that is the low, what about high? The 8s are better than the 5s for high. You're out of there. Otherwise you'll be chasing both ways. With the hands you're already facing, there'll be capped raises from now on—and you'll be in the middle.

Sixth Street Play

Sixth Street play is going to be relatively cut and dried. If you have absolutely the best hand (full house at this time, with two opponents going for low), then you'll want to get in as many bets as possible. Since you're probably leading the betting, you'd be better off with a bet, for the opponents may not yet have

made their hands and neither would want to be caught
in the middle of a check-raise. If you check, they may
very well check behind you. If you bet and one of
them raises, then you come in with as many raises as
you can get.

If you're fighting for low against another player, and
you're unsure of whether or not you have the best
hand, you don't want to be caught in the middle
against and an aggressive high hand player. If he
checks to check-raise, check as well. This situation
may occur when you hold:

The other low holding is:

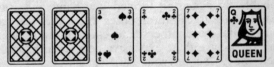

The third hand is:

The trip 10s bet, and now you're tempted to raise,
but you know that the other 7-low hand is going to
the river no matter what happens, and when you both
show down your cards, the lower hand will win half
the pot. There's no way to bluff him out. Even though
you show a very smooth 7 on board, in fact you have
a rough 7-6 low. If you raise, you're going to be called,
and in the end you'll be reraised, and you might find,

after all bets are in, that you lose your half of the pot to a 7-6-4-3-2 or a 7-6-3-2-Ace.

Of course, if your raise could force out the other 7-low hand; then it would be worthwhile, for he'd face your raise, a reraise by the 10s, and your reraise to see the river card. You have to know the player you're up against. You're representing a very smooth hand, but at this point, and with the size of the pot, he might go all the way, no matter what. He still has another card to buy and could end up with a 6 low for all you know.

Finally, you may fold on Sixth Street if the following cards came up. You started with a 7♦ 4♥ 2♣ 3♦ and caught Queen♦ 9♠. That's your complete hand on Sixth Street. One opponent has a high hand, and your competition for low holds * * 6♦ 3♥ 10♣ Ace♠. He caught real good on Sixth Street and you got a blank. The high hand bets and the 6-3-Ace hand raises. Now it would be wise for you to fold your cards. You're probably up against a formed low hand and you're going to have to call three raises to see the river card, which could be another dead card as far as you're concerned. Save these expensive bets. Your hand died when the 9 fell on your cards like a sick pigeon's droppings. Wait for the next hand before investing any more money.

Seventh Street Play

You're at the river. In Hi-Lo Split, you're going to find that the players remaining in the game have thinned out considerably. You'll be up against one or two opponents. If you have a single opponent, he may or may not be going the same direction as you; or he might have a hand that is possibly going both ways. If he's going the other way, you'd prefer to have a high hand. What you already have, you have. It can't get destroyed the way a low hand can by drawing a blank on the river.

For example, suppose you're holding: 8♠ Ace♣ 8♥ 8♦ King♠ Queen♣ Jack♦. If you were going low, those last three draws would have been the kiss of death, but your trip 8s are still intact.

Your opponent holds the following cards:

He may or may not be holding a complete low at this point. You're not too worried about his holding a straight, because the 7-5-2 needs a miraculous 3-4-6 to fill in. And flush is a long shot. You can safely bet here. There's no point in checking. If he makes any kind of high hand, such as two pairs, he'll call you and you'll get in that extra bet.

If the situation were reversed, and you held his cards:

you'd be in a much more precarious position as you squeeze out your river card. Whether your opponent bets or not is immaterial. Either you're going to take half the pot or you're going to hope to have a winning high hand. If he bets and you get a blank, you're not paying him off—you're just folding. If you end up with trip deuces or two pairs, he'll call the bet or possibly raise with the set.

So you squeeze and squeeze, and look at paint! You drew a King—as bad a card as you could hope for. You fold your hand. Even though a player can't go high-low with a high hand, that same high hand can still scoop a lot of pots. If you play the game often

enough, you'd be amazed at all the high hands that
scoop as the low hand draws die at the river.

If you don't get your low, and you have nothing
else, bluffing is not going to do you any good against
a player going for high. He'll call your bet—he wants
half the pot. If you hold the same type of hand as your
opponent, then you can try a bluff, but only against a
fairly good player. A weak player is in love with his
cards; you bet and he'll call. He's also going to be
dreadfully afraid of being bluffed. Let's say you were
in against a fairly tough player. At the river, this is
the situation. You hold:

The 3-6-10 are your hole cards. Your opponent has:

You raised on Third Street and got two calls, including his. On Fourth Street you bet, and he raised, driving out the other player. You reraised, and he called.
On Fifth Street, you bet and were called. On Sixth
Street, still leading, you bet and were called. Now, at
the river you've missed your low, and you have to
figure your opponent for Jacks over 3s. If you made
your low, you'd probably check here and be ready to
split the pot. He can't have a low. But you bet. You
have Aces on board, and possibly Aces up. Your bet
is telling your opponent that is exactly what you have.

A weak player with two pairs is going to call automatically, but in this situation you have your opponent
guessing. He's not going to raise; you figure if he

doesn't have a full house, he's going to respect the fact that you could have trip Aces as well. He should see your bet, for he can afford to lose a lot of river hands if he makes one and scoops the pot.

But this is the only way you can win, by betting. You take a shot. If he calls, you're probably going to lose. If he folds, it's a great bluff. You can only do this against a good player, for this is a thinking man's game.

It's a more difficult game than Seven-Card Stud, and that's why you see so few Hi-Lo Split games available in a casino or club. In various casinos in Las Vegas you rarely see the game played. In the bigger California clubs there may be one or two games going, and that is in a club where twenty or so Seven-Card Stud games are in operation.

Some Final Thoughts

If you decide to play Hi-Lo Split, see if there's a smaller game. Even a $3–$6 game is OK, for you can get the feel of the game. If there are no smaller games, then you have to decide whether you'd be comfortable in a $20–$40 game. Watch these games in a casino or club. Watch the action. See who knows how to play and who the suckers are. If you feel it's an easy game with several weak players in it, you can try it out. Start with only good cards, and don't fall under the delusion of winning half the pot somehow by just going the opposite of your opponents.

A good way to practice is to take a deck of cards and deal out eight hands at a time. Play one of the hands as your own. Make the game an aggressive one without suckers. See how you can handle it. If you get a good feel for the game, and can afford a bigger game, fine. But as we will constantly mention, don't play with money you can't afford to lose emotionally or financially.

And above all, be alert. You have to think about

not only the high hands but also the low holdings. A hand can be deceptive, especially when an Ace shows. See who plays what hands. This is not a game to indiscriminately play hands, hoping for something to develop. The hand must already be developed by Third Street one way or another. Punish those who play practically everything. You can pick your spots to put in raises because you choose your hands carefully. So, be alert, play strong cards. Those are keys to winning.

IX

Texas Hold 'Em

At one time, **Seven-Card Stud** was the most popular of the casino and club games, but in the last decade there has been a phenomenal rise in the popularity of **Texas Hold 'Em,** also known simply as Hold 'Em. The game seems to have originated in Texas, and many of the early great players came from the Lone Star State.

These players are legends now: Texas Jack Straus, Sailor Roberts, Texas Dolly Brunson, Johnny Moss, and Amarillo Slim Preston, all colorful players with great nicknames. When poker players and even the general public talk about a world championship of poker, they are referring to the annual World Series of Poker held at Binion's Horseshoe in Las Vegas, Nevada, where the big moment is the crowning of a World Champion. That World Champion is the winner of the no-limit Texas Hold 'Em tournament.

Other winners now include a group of non-Texans, such as Stu Ungar, Johnny Chan, and Bobby Baldwin, to name a few. They are great poker players who play for enormous stakes, and are feared competitors. But it isn't just these legendary players who have popularized the game. The game itself is intriguing and simple to follow, yet it has a devilish complexity to it.

One reason for its popularity is that it looks deceptively simple. Unlike Seven-Card Stud, the players only have to follow the cards on the board, and the two in their hands. All the cards on board are community cards, belonging to every player. In Seven-Card Stud and **Hi-Lo Split, 8 or Better,** a player must follow each competing hand, remembering what cards have been dealt out and what cards have already been folded. It's much more strenuous mentally than Hold 'Em, where the only cards the player sees are his own and the board.

Nine or ten players are easily accommodated in this game, for each player only receives two cards, with five more on board. There is usually more action in this game, because of the betting structure, and the fact that the board, whose cards belong to all the players as community cards, often improves the potential hands of all the remaining players. It's a great money game.

Another factor giving it an enormous popularity is its inherent betting structure. In Seven-Card Stud, the ante structure changes from game to game, so that the bigger games, with high antes, force action. A $100–$200 Stud game isn't just ten times bigger than a $10–$20 game; the ante is twenty-five times as big. In Hold 'Em, however, there are two forced bets, called the blinds, and these remain constant no matter how big the game is. The **small blind** is almost always one-half the minimum bet of a two-tiered betting structure (for example $10–$20) and the **big blind** is equal to the minimum bet. Thus, in a $10–$20 game, the small blind is $5 and the big blind, $10. In a $100–$200 game, exactly ten times the $10–$20 game, the small blind is ten times $5 or $50 and the big blind is ten times $10, or $100.

Now that we've explained its popularity, let's look at the game itself.

How the Game Is Played

For purposes of this discussion, we'll examine the $10–$20 game. Let's assume we're playing in a poker club such as the Commerce Club, in Commerce, California. You can find all levels of games there, from $1–$2 all the way up to $300–$600 and beyond at times. Though I've never counted the tables, there could be as many as fifty Hold 'Em games going on at one time.

We'll assume that you entered the club and want to play in the $10–$20 Hold 'Em game. You go to the appropriate section (any employee will gladly direct you there) and have your initials put down for the game with a black marker on a white board. Let's further assume that a seat has just opened up and you're directed to the $10–$20 Hold 'Em table.

First, you'll notice that there are nine seats at the table, allowing a maximum of nine players. Seat one is available. That's the seat to the left of the dealer. The seats are numbered clockwise, with the last seat, to the right of the dealer, known as seat nine. This game has no ante; each player pays a fee of $6 per half-hour. In some other clubs, the fee might be a dollar less per half-hour, while in the Vegas casino poker rooms, a rake will be taken from each game, usually $3 or 5 percent of the pot, whichever is less.

Having your seat, you now are ready to play. A chip runner will ask you if you want checks, which you do. You give her $500 in cash and get a rack of $5 chips, one hundred in all. You take the checks out of the rack and place them on the table. Only amateurs and players who don't know any better play out of a rack. It is awkward removing the checks, and delays the game.

If you want to start playing before you get your chips, the chip runner will say "500 behind," indicating that you have $500 in credit to play with before you actually get your checks. You are now in the game. If you lose the next pot, whatever you owe will be noted by the dealer, and when you get your checks you will give that amount to the winner of the previous pot. Of course, if you win the pot, whatever is in there belongs to you.

The Blinds and the Button

As we shall see, position in this game is of the utmost importance, and to indicate the position of the various participants, a button moves around the table in a clockwise manner. Whoever has the button is the theoretical dealer and acts last, an enormous advantage in Hold 'Em. In many games, when a new player enters, there is what is known as a **position blind**—that is, a bet equal to the big blind, made by the incoming player. When that is the case (most often in clubs but not in casinos), it is wise to wait till after the button passes you. You simply say to the dealer: "I'll wait for the button."

At this point, the dealer will put a small disk marked "out" in front of you, indicating that you will not be dealt to. At any time, any player can stop playing temporarily, and the same disk will be put in front of his or her spot.

Now that you're in the game, you see the following—prior to the deal, one player, to the left of the button, puts in $5 as his small blind, and the player to his left puts in $10, the big blind.

The Deal and Betting Rounds

The cards, dealt in a clockwise fashion, first go to the small blind and then around the table. They are dealt face down, one to each player; then, again starting with the small blind, another card, face down, is also dealt. The blinds are known as **live blinds**—that is, when the bets come around to them, they may call, raise, or fold.

Now that each player has two hole or pocket cards, the first round of betting begins. The player to the immediate left of the big blind begins. He can either call, raise, or fold. Checking is not permitted on this round of play. If you check, you're out of the game. If you call, you must equal the big blind by betting $10. If you raise, you make it $20. After all the players have bet, that round of play is over. Let's assume the button is with you at seat number one; the small blind is seat number two; and the big blind, seat number three. Seat number four bets, seat numbers five and six fold, but seat number seven raises to $20. Seats number eight and nine call the raise, as does seat four. You, as the button, fold, as do both blinds. Four players remain in the game.

Next comes the flop. The dealer burns one card off the top of the deck and puts it aside, then puts out three open cards at one time. These are community cards, belonging to all the players in the game. In Hold 'Em, the players must use five cards to form their best hand. They can use both of their pocket cards, or one pocket card, or none—simply **playing the board,** using all five cards that ultimately end up on the board as their best hand. Suppose a player holds Jack♠ Queen♠ and the board is 10♣ Queen♦ King♠ Ace♥ Jack♦. The board is an Ace-high straight. Since no one can have a flush, that's the best possible hand, and whoever remains for the showdown can play the board, rather than a combination of their pocket cards and the board. If two or more players remain in the hand, they split the pot, or "chop chop" as the players say.

Here's the flop in our example game:

After the flop is dealt, another round of betting begins. Since the two blinds have exited the action, as well as seat number three, seat four begins the betting. It still is at the lower tier, $10. Now he can check his hand without going out. He checks, and seat seven, the original raiser, bets. Seat number eight folds but seat number nine raises. Seat number four hesitates, then calls the raise, as does seat seven.

The next card off the top of the deck is burned and

a fourth card is dealt open to the board. This is known as **the turn.** From now on the betting is at the higher $20 level.

The board looks like this:

This is a pretty **ragged board,** since there are four **rags** out there without any high cards. There's a chance at a diamond flush or a straight, but right now, nobody can hold a made flush or straight. It's pretty easy to tell when a straight or flush hasn't been made because each player only holds two cards.

There are now only three players left, contending for the pot. A good dealer will announce how many players remain before dealing each card. It aids the players in determining their moves. Here, there are only three players, but if there were six, the betting could get quite complex, and each player wants to know how many opponents he faces.

Seat four is first to act again. The position never changes from round to round in Hold 'Em as it does in Seven-Card Stud, for example, because each player's cards are hidden, and the value of the hands doesn't matter as far as position is concerned in Hold 'Em. He checks, seat number seven checks, and seat nine checks behind them. Seat nine has made a common strategic move on the flop by raising. Being in last position to bet, he has bought a free card on the turn, the expensive street, and now can see the river card for nothing as well.

The dealer burns the top card and deals the river card. The final board looks like this:

Seat four checks. Seat seven bets $20, and seat nine calls. Seat four folds. Since seat seven was called, he shows his cards. He holds a King♠ Queen♠. Seat nine concedes, but someone at the table asks to see his hole cards. This can be done in Hold 'Em. Anyone at the table, even if he or she isn't competing for the pot, can ask to see a player's hole cards, provided that that player called the last bet or raise. Why? Because in Hold 'Em you never see a player's hole cards otherwise, unless he voluntarily shows them or is called and must show them.

Players are competing against strangers and need this information to get a better idea of how wild, conservative, strong, or weak a player is. Seat nine had already tried to muck his cards, but the dealer retrieves them and shows a 10♦ Queen♦. Up to the river he had the lead, with a pair of 10s and a chance for a diamond flush. He mumbles something about "the damn river," and waits for the next hand to be dealt.

The button moves to seat number two, and seat three puts out the small blind, while seat four puts out the big blind. The first cards are dealt to seat three. On this round, if three players called the big blind, and nobody raised, the small blind would have to put in another $5 to complete his action. He folds instead, and the big blind, which is still live and can raise, doesn't. He simply waves his hand over his cards to indicate he is standing on his big blind bet and not increasing his wager.

Reading Hands

Because there are five cards on board that belong to all players, figuring out who wins and loses, or even what one's best hand is, can at times be difficult. The difficulty sometimes involves the kicker, which is the odd card in a made hand. For example, if you hold Ace–5–2 in Seven-Card Stud and then are dealt another Ace, you have Aces with a 5 kicker, because the 5 is the largest of your side cards. Suppose you finish the hand with only a pair of Aces and a Jack kicker, having been dealt the Jack on Sixth Street. If another player also had Aces, and a 10 or lower kicker, you'd win at the showdown, assuming only the two of you had the best high hand of Aces. If the other Aces had a Queen or King as kicker, you'd lose. You'd be said to have been **outkickered.**

Before I go further into this discussion, it's important to point out that in Hold 'Em, even though a player has been dealt two cards, he doesn't have to use both of his or her cards to form the best hand. He or she may use both cards together with three on board, or one with four on board, or he or she may simply "play the board," without using any cards in his or her hand.

Let's give an example of each situation. In the first, a player with a holding of King♣ King♦ sees the following board: 6♣ Queen♦ 5♠ 5♥ 3♣. Using the pocket Kings, his best hand is two pair, Kings over 5s, with a Queen as an odd card.

In the second instance, a player is holding Ace♦ Queen♥ and sees the following board: 9♥ 3♥ 2♥ 5♠ 10♥. He uses his Queen♥ to form his flush together with the four hearts on the board. His Ace♦ is disregarded for it has no value in forming his best hand.

Finally, a player holds 8♠ 8♥ and the board shows 10♦ Jack♣ King♠ Ace♦ Queen♣. The board holds an Ace high straight, which can't be beaten, since no one can hold a flush or a full house. The player's 8s are useless, but if he plays the board, he is assured of winning the pot, or splitting it with whoever remains in the game at the showdown.

In Seven-Card Stud, with players having separate hands, it's fairly easy to figure out who has won. But in Hold 'Em, with community cards, it gets a tad more difficult. Let's look at two hands—or, more accurately, the pocket cards of two players and the board—and see just what the situation is:

Player A:

Player B:

The Board:

Who is the winner, Player A or Player B? Actually, the pot will be chopped, for it's a tie. Player A has Queens, plus a King, Ace, and 10. Player B has the same hand, since a player can use the board or one or two of his hole cards to form his best hand. Although Player A has a weaker kicker (the 3) than Player B's 9, he uses the Ace, King, and 10 from the board, and disregards the 3 in his hand. He was lucky that a 10♦ came up on the river. If a 6 was dealt, then Player B's 9 kicker would prevail and win.

Here's another kicker situation that often comes up:

Player A:

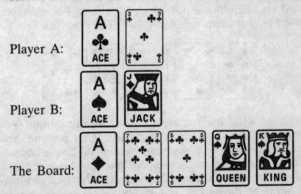

Player B:

The Board:

Player A had a nut flush draw, for if a third club came up on the board, he'd be a winner. He, however, also had a pair of Aces, which he felt might win, or at least tie, since he could use the King and Queen and hopefully the 7 to split the pot, assuming his opponent also had an Ace and didn't have a kicker higher than a 7. But his opponent had a Jack and won. This is the danger of a low kicker along with the Ace. In Hold 'Em it costs players a lot of money.

The Nuts

In Hold 'Em, more than any other poker game, there is a variety of hands that constitute the **nuts,** or the absolute best hand, a hand that can't lose. In Seven-Card Stud, because of the three hidden cards, you may think you have the nuts, only to lose. For example, you hold Aces full and look at an opponent's board. He has 5♦ 6♥ 7♣ Queen♦. You think, "How can he beat me? He has at best a straight or a flush, but not a straight flush, and yet, he keeps raising me!" Then he turns over rolled-up 5s, three of them in the hole—a bad beat (a loss when it seems a player has the hand locked up for a win).

In Texas Hold 'Em, you can be more secure with any number of hands. If it looks like a nut hand, if it quacks and waddles like a nut hand, then it is. For example, your pocket cards are Ace♥ 10♥. The board shows:

"Thank God for the river," you silently intone. You have an Ace-high flush in hearts. Can anyone beat you? No way. No player can have a full house because there is no pair on board. No one can have a higher flush because you have the boss Ace. No one can have a straight flush. The pot is absolutely yours. You've got the nuts, and even better, **the living nuts** as some players refer to this kind of situation.

Dangerous Boards

We've just shown how an Ace-high flush can be the nuts. Now that's not a very powerful hand as poker hands go, but with the right board, it can be the best possible hand. But the board holds community cards, useful to all players, and sometimes what seems the nuts can evaporate into a bad beat.

Suppose you hold: 5♠ 5♦. The board is as follows:

Wham! That fourth 5 came up for you, and you confidently bet, only to be raised. You reraise, and are reraised. Now you look at the board a bit more carefully. What's the fool raising on? A heart flush? Or . . . and then you realize that if he started with a 6♥ 7♥, he has you beaten from here to forever. And many players will start with what are known as **suited connecting cards,** especially in late position.

Any time there's a pair on board, your flush or straight hand might be in jeopardy, for a player could have a full house or better. Without a pair, there can be no full house, because only two pocket cards are held by players. But with a pair, beware!

Say you hold Jack♠ Queen♠. The boards holds:

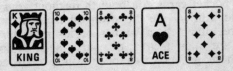

You got the nut straight on the turn. After the Ace fell, no one could beat you with another straight but could tie you, also holding a Jack-Queen. There's no possibility of a flush, no matter what river card comes out. But what you didn't want to see showed itself on the river: The board paired. A player now bets into you. You call just to keep him honest, and he turns over Ace♠ 8♠.

Here's another example of trouble. You start off with Ace♦ Ace♥. Holding two aces in the pocket is your best possible holding. Against one other player you should win over 87 percent of the time. With four players in the game you'll win two-thirds of the time. With five players it drops to below 50 percent. That's why, as you will see, you automatically raise with pocket Aces, to thin out the field.

The board shows:

Three other players are still in the game. You're doomed. There are three cards to a spade flush out there, and anyone holding a Jack or 6–7 has a straight. If there's raising and reraising, even on the turn, you can muck your Aces, as sad as that thought is. You're probably up against both a straight and a flush.

Before the Flop

The pocket cards you hold throughout your career at Hold 'Em will be the strongest factor in whether you are ultimately a winner or loser at the game. There are other factors, of course, such as how you play those pocket cards once you're involved in a hand, but if you consistently play weak junk or garbage or even semi-garbage hands or hands that seem OK but are not money winners, in the long run, you've got to lose.

Above all in Hold 'Em, the most important word

to remember is this—*patience.* You must be *patient,* and not succumb to the temptation to play a hand just because you want to get into the action. If the cards don't warrant it, keep mucking them. And you'll muck a lot of hands before you make a bet, because you're only dealt two cards, and for long periods of time, you may find that you don't have a playable hand. After seeing 7♦ 4♣ or Jack♠ 2♥ or 6♠ 4♦ or King♣ 5♠ and so forth, hand after hand of garbage, you can get restless. In the meantime, you're losing a small blind and big blind every nine hands, as well as either rental money or antes, as the junk keeps coming.

But if you are patient, when the playable hand comes, you'll be ready to compete. And often you're competing against hands held by players who don't have your patience; who want action. You'll clean their clocks.

Which cards do you ultimately play? Well, that depends on two elements: the cards themselves and your position at the table. You can play cards in late position that you'd throw away in early position. Position is the key to card selection. It is a hugely important factor in Hold 'Em. There's a saying that goes as follows: "Play tight in the front and loose in the back." Very true in Hold 'Em.

Let's discuss position before we deal with the playable pocket cards. Once you understand position at the table, it'll make card selection easier.

Position

Position in Hold 'Em cannot be emphasized enough. The later your position at the table, the better off you are. Conversely, early position puts you at a disadvantage. And during any particular game the position never changes. If you're the small blind, for example, on the flop, turn, and river, you're going to be first to act. This means that players behind you can make moves on you, can raise, reraise, or whatever.

In club games you'll be playing a nine-player game,

and in casinos, a ten-player game. Let's assume a nine-player game, in which we divide position into three distinct categories.

Early Position

Early position covers the first three players to act, which are the small blind, the big blind, and the player to the left of the big blind. Before the flop, the small blind and big blind actually are last to act, for they are live blinds, and although their money is already in the pot, they can call, raise, or reraise when the betting gets around to them again.

Theoretically, if you're a small blind or big blind, you're going to get a weak unplayable hand dealt to you merely by random selection. Most hands dealt in Hold 'Em are unplayable. But this isn't always the case. As a small blind, you're putting in half a bet; in a $10–$20 game, it's $5. Assuming no one has raised the big blind, when it's your turn, you can complete the bet by putting in $5 more in checks, or raise to $20 by putting in $15 more in checks. Or you can fold.

What should you do? If you call the previous bets with another $5 wager, then only the big blind behind you can raise. If you went in with junk, and he raises, you wasted $5. If he called, it's still junk you're playing. For example, as the small blind, you are dealt Jack♦ 4♠. Many weak players complete their bet even with garbage like this, hoping for a miracle flop. They're praying for Jack-Jack-4, or 4-4-Jack, and instead, stuck with their hand, they see 2♣ Queen♥ Ace♠. The Queen and Ace are **overcards** (higher cards than your Jack, and even if you get Jacks, someone could already be holding Queens or Aces).

When you're the small blind, accept the fact that you're in early position and only play those hands we will suggest for early position. If you're the big blind, most of the time you'll be looking at junk, such as Queen♠ 8♥, and hoping that no one raises your blind so that you can see the flop for nothing. A big mistake is to think "Well, I've already invested $10; I might as well see the flop for another $10." That's thrown-away money. Sure, once in a blue moon the flop would have really helped you, no matter what garbage you had. But even then, it can be a trap.

I remember a hand where, as big blind, I had Queen♦ 6♠ and was raised. I threw away the hand, only to look at the following flop:

Two rags came out on the turn and river, and while I bemoaned the fact that I didn't stay in, someone turned over Ace♠ Queen♠ and took the pot. In the end, all I would have is a bad beat, with my three Queens beaten by a better kicker.

Save money by not playing junk as a small or big blind. Each two times you don't complete the bet as small blind, you're saving a full bet. Each time you don't call a raise with the big blind, you're saving a full bet. Better to use these checks to see the flop when you have a legitimate playable hand.

The player to the left of the big blind is also in early position, and must adhere to our recommendations for playing hands. He is in a terrible spot, with not only six players behind him, but two live blinds. Also the player to his left, in the fourth betting spot, I consider early position. They're **up front,** and must play tight.

Middle Position

Middle position consists of betting spots four through seven. Here a player has a little more leeway in playing hands, and can bet cards that he would throw away in early position. Why? For one thing, he has already seen two players act if he's in fifth position, and in seventh, four players have acted. If there are raises and reraises before he himself acts, then he has gotten a lot of information and can throw away fairly weak hands. If no one has raised or even called the big blind, he can make his own moves with hands that wouldn't hold up in early position.

Late Position

Late position consists of the button (the best late position) and the player to his right—in other words, players eight and nine in a nine-handed game. With ten players, we would include players eight, nine, and the button as late position seats.

Here, in late position, you can play a maximum of hands. You already know how most players have acted, especially if you're the button and act last. You want a hand that, with the right flop, gives you an opportunity to make some moves on the other players. If you raise in late position, no one really knows the strength of your hand. For all they know, it's a position raise. Or it may be a legitimate raise with powerful cards, such as two Queens or Kings. If you reraise again, they have no idea of what you hold.

Often, with a raise, when the flop comes, everyone will check to you. Then you can decide whether you want a free card, or want to bet. You're in control at this point.

Playable Hands

In designating the hands, I will specify whether cards are suited or unsuited by using an **s.** As an example, Ace King **s** means the cards are the same suit. If Ace King is written alone, it means the cards are unsuited—for example, Ace♥ King♦. Suited hands are always stronger than unsuited hands, because of the added chance of making a flush.

The Strongest Hands
Ace-Ace
King-King
Queen-Queen

Ace-King **s**
Ace-King
Ace-Queen **s**

With these hands, you can raise from any position. Holding Aces or Kings, if you're raised, you can re-raise, again from any position. With Queens, you have to proceed a little more cautiously, since you may be up against Aces or Kings in another hand. Or, if you're facing Ace-King, an Ace or King may come up on the flop, putting you in a chasing position.

The Aces, Kings, and Queens can often win without improvement. There are two purposes to your raise with these cards. First of all, you want more money in the pot. And second, you want to narrow the field, since these cards play better against fewer players.

The other hands are basically drawing hands. Though you might win with an Ace-King, suited or otherwise, more likely than not you'll need some kind of improvement. You want to raise with these hands to get more money in the pot. If you hold Ace♣-King♦, an ideal situation would be to get it down to about three players, and see a flop like this:.

Now you have Aces up, with the top kicker in the King♦. There's no straight or flush draw, though one may develop on the turn.

With the same cards, this is what you don't want to see on the flop:

There are all kinds of hands that will be helped by these cards. An Ace♦ Jack♣ or a Queen♠ Jack♥, or worst of all, a Jack♠ 10♠ and you're beaten. If there is raising and reraising on the flop, it would be wise to muck your Ace-King. The flop hasn't helped you at all. Your one hope is to see a Queen for a straight, but with the two 10s on board, you might be facing a full house. Players tend to play connected cards such as Jack-10 or Queen-Jack more than they will play Queen-10 or Jack-9.

With drawing hands, such as Ace-King suited or unsuited, don't get stubborn. It's easy to get away from these hands if the flop doesn't help, or it seems to be one that will help your opponents. If you hold Aces or Kings, you must try to eliminate players to narrow down the field if you're in early position. Sometimes, in late position, for deceptive purposes, you might **slowplay** these cards but do it rarely. For example, suppose you hold Ace♦ Ace♥ and all but one player has folded. You're in late position. You can just call here, and face this player and the blind.

Or, in a similar situation, a player has called, and another raised, with everyone else folding. You're on the button. You can call here as well, figuring that the blinds will fold. Let's assume they do, and you face two players. The flop comes up:

The caller of the raise checks, the raiser bets, and you call. The first player also calls. On the turn the board looks like this:

There is a straight and flush draw. Again, the first player checks, the raiser bets, and you raise, driving out the first player. You are reraised, so you reraise. You're called. The river comes up like this:

If the raiser has a straight you're beaten, but would he have raised before the flop on a 5-7 or a 5-2? Not likely. He probably has a high pair, and figured when the Ace came out you were representing Aces but didn't have them. Or he has an Ace with a big kicker. That's more logical. By raising on the turn, it is very possible that you had Aces, and there's no reason for the reraise, if your opponent holds a pair of Queens, for example.

On the river, you're checked to, and you bet. Again you're raised. Now you think back to what has happened. You're probably facing Aces up or trips. Or a straight. But it couldn't be a straight, not by logical thinking. You know your opponent is a good player, and he wouldn't be raising pre-flop with garbage. So you put in a reraise. You're called. You show trip Aces and your opponent disgustedly shows you an Ace♠ Jack♠. In late position he raised before the flop, hoping for a good board. He got one, and had high pair on board, and then came the Ace on the turn. It helped him, but gave you the nuts. End of story.

Strong Hands
Jack-Jack
King-Queen **s**
10-10
Ace-Jack **s**
Ace-10 **s**

These are hands that can be played from any position, but whether or not you fastplay them depends on your position and what has occurred before it's your turn to act.

With two Jacks or two 10s, you must expect an overcard on the flop. With the Jacks it will come up over 55 percent of the time, and close to 70 percent of the time with the 10s. Therefore, in a multiway pot, you don't want to raise, because you are in jeopardy of that overcard. On the other hand, if there has been a lot of raising pre-flop, your Jacks or 10s might be very alive, with most players holding cards like Ace-King, Ace-Queen, King-King, and Queen-Queen.

An ideal flop for you if you hold 10s would be:

There will be action from anyone holding a high pair. And others might call. In this situation, you put in a raise right on the flop. Opponents might read you as having a four-flush in spades. The trips are well concealed. Then you don't mind a final board that looks like this:

Your opponents will think that everyone was hurt by this pile of rags, but your trips are very solid here. Sure, there's a straight possible if someone holds Jack-8 or 6-8, but who would be holding these cards after so much raising before the flop?

A King-Queen s can be raised from an early position to test the waters and to drive out any hand holding an Ace with a weak kicker that might decide to limp in and call a bet. Your early position raise is a red flag for them, for if you are holding Ace-King, they are a huge underdog with their Ace-8 or Ace-9. If an Ace comes up on the flop, they'll have no confidence in their hand if you come out betting.

With King♠ Queen♠ you still have a drawing hand, but any good flop and you're in business. For example, if you get an ideal flop like:

you've got the top pair and a four-flush headed by a King. In this situation you want the turn to come up:

Now you're holding the nut flush, and ideally you'd want two opponents in with you, one holding Ace♥ Ace♣ and the other, King♦ Queen♠. The King-Queen hand is drawing dead, for nothing can help him that will beat you. He's praying for another spade or another King, but that won't do him any good against your completed flush, Ace-King high. The Aces need the board to pair in order to win. Any other card other than a King, 6, 3 or Ace and he is doomed to pay you off.

Ace-Jack s and Ace-10 s are drawing cards as well, and if they pair on the board you prefer that the smaller card pairs. This way you have top kicker in the Ace. If the Ace pairs and you get a lot of action, including a raise, you may be facing either two pairs headed by an Ace, or Aces with a better kicker, especially if there was a raise before the flop. Here's an example. You're in middle position, sixth to act. You hold Ace♥ Jack♥. The fourth player called, the fifth player raised, you call, and both blinds fold. The fourth player calls, Now it's three-way action.

It would be more dangerous for you if the fourth player raised, for the earlier the raise, generally the stronger the hand. The flop comes up:

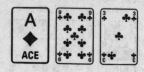

The fourth player checks, the fifth player, the original raiser, bets, and now it's up to you. You fear that he has an Ace with a bigger kicker. You can call and see the turn on this cheap street, hoping for the Jack. Or you can raise, and see if he really has the higher kicker. This might be a better option. If he reraises you, you might as well fold. But if he calls, he'll probably check to you on the turn and you'll see a free card if no Jack comes up.

So you raise. The fourth player folds, and the raiser calls you. On the turn the board comes out:

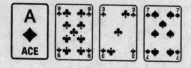

Your opponent checks and you check behind him. On the river, it looks like this:

Three clubs on the board! Your opponent checks, and you come out betting. He hesitates. Now you have him guessing. Was your reraise on the flop representing four clubs? Or an Ace-Queen? He hesitates, then calls, ready to muck his hand. But all you have is the Ace-Jack of hearts. He shows Ace♠ King♦, and wins.

You could have saved a bet, of course, but the only way to win is to bet. You didn't figure to be raised because of the clubs. If you were reraised, you could have mucked the cards. So you endangered one bet.

Sometimes in Hold 'Em the only way to win is to put in that final bet. I was once looking at a final board:

I'd been first to act from the outset, and been raised on the flop, so I merely called afterwards. Two players were in against me. I held Ace♦ 6♦ and had been the big blind. The pot had been raised by the button and I called the raise before the flop. When I had my two pairs, I was content, but I feared that at least one player had Ace-King or Ace-Jack.

On the river, I bet without hesitation. The first player to my left grimaced, peeked at his pocket cards, looked at the board, then mucked the cards. The second player showed me his Ace♠ King♠ before mucking them. I happily took the pot. If I had checked, there was no way I could have won. If they checked behind me, I would lose. If one of them bet, I couldn't call, fearing a flush in clubs or a better hand.

Moderately Strong Hands

Ace-Queen
Ace-10 s
Ace-Jack

King-Jack **s**
King-Queen
King-10 **s**

These hands play better from middle to late position, and if no one has raised before you, in late position, it's worth raising with any of these moderately strong hands. Unless someone is slowplaying a very strong Ace-King holding before you, for example, if an Ace or King comes up on the flop, and you pair with one of these big cards, you figure to have the best kicker.

A good flop for you holding Ace♠ Jack♦ would be:

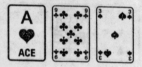

You don't figure anyone is holding two pairs, unless someone went in with Ace-9, but your raise was supposed to knock out stragglers with these types of hands. Now you're not too worried about a King or Queen coming up on the turn or on the river. If the board ended up

you're probably the winner. I say probably, because there always lurks the possibility of someone holding trips. But in Hold 'Em you can't constantly worry about this, otherwise you wouldn't play any hands.

Aces up with no one raising at any time should get you the money. With the hands headed by the King, you don't want to see the Ace show up on the board, because of all cards a player will hold, the Ace is most likely to be in his hand. Thus, with the King hands, if an Ace shows, and someone bets on the flop ahead of you despite your raise, you're in a bit of a bind. You can challenge them by reraising, but if the Ace is in your opponent's hand, you're a big dog here.

Let's assume you hold King♦ 10♦ and you raised from late position before the flop and got two callers, position four and position five. The flop comes up:

Position four checks, but position five bets into you. Most players holding an Ace with any kicker will bet in this situation. They reason that you could have raised with anything in late position. They hold the Ace. Do you? If you reraise, you're probably not going to get them out. Let's assume your opponent is holding Ace♠ 9♠. He'll go all the way to the river, hoping to pair up the 9. Even if you reraise on the flop, he's not going to be too intimidated. You might have Kings or King-Queen or Queen-Jack. He's boss with the Ace. On the turn, he'll check, and he'll check on the river, calling your bet. If you check behind him, you only give him more courage, and doom yourself. The question is, do you want to give up a whole bunch of checks to act macho? It's not worth it. Wait for a better situation, when you hold the Ace with the big kicker and flop an Ace.

Hands of Middling Strength
Ace-10
Queen-Jack **s**
King-Jack
Queen-10 **s**
Jack-10 **s**
King-10

Queen-Jack
Queen-10
Queen-9 **s**
Jack-9 **s**

There is only one Ace hand here, with a 10 kicker, not the best kind of holding, since any raise would indicate that there is a possible Ace out there among the opponents with a better kicker. The other hands are pretty much drawing hands, for they need help to win. If you play these hands from early position you might fall into a trap, getting raised before the flop, and sometimes having to face two raises before it's your turn to bet again. With any of these hands, no matter how pretty they look, I'd pass.

What you basically are drawing for with these hands is a straight. If there is a straight that's completed with your hand, assuming no flush draw is out and the board hasn't paired, you have the nut straight. That is, except for the Jack-9 **s**. A straight is preferable to a flush with any of these holdings, because you can develop a flush and end up being beaten with any of your suited hands. The point is, you don't have the Ace in any of these hands and you end up with a bad beat holding Queen♥ Jack♥ and seeing this board:

You are raised on the river, and call. One opponent shows you Ace♥ 3♥ and all you can do is float your cards to the dealer. You're beaten and beaten badly for a lot of checks.

Of all the holdings shown above, the weakest is the Jack-9 **s**. It rarely wins, and in middle position you'd be wise to muck it in early without jeopardizing any of your checks. In late position, it might be worth a call, but it won't withstand a raise. If you get a flush with it, you stand a good chance of being beaten, and if you get a straight, it's not a nut straight.

The Smaller Pairs

In this category we have the following pairs:

9-9	5-5
8-8	4-4
7-7	3-3
6-6	2-2

These pairs obviously weaken in strength the lower they go. A pair of 8s not only gives you the opportunity for trips, but also a bunch of ways to make a straight with the right board. A pair of deuces, on the other hand, is a very limited hand, and if you don't get trips it's pretty much a dead holding. Any other card showing on the board is a potential overpair.

If there has been no raise, any of these pairs can be played in late position, hoping for trips on the flop. If you don't get help with the flop, then they should be immediately mucked. There may be an exception with the 9s and 8s in late position. To create deception and to vary your game, you can put in a raise with these cards. If the flop doesn't help anyone, and it's checked to you, a bet can often win the pot right then and there.

For example, you hold 9♠ 9♣ and the flop comes up with a bunch of rags:

Two players remaining check to you, and you bet. One folds. If the next card is a rag, or one of the rags is paired, and it's checked to you, you'll probably win the pot if you bet. Let's assume that you bet and you're called. If the last card is a 10, and the board looks like this at the river:

and again, the opponent checks, you have to figure him for a holding of Ace with a big card kicker, or King-Queen or something like that. You can bet here, figuring that if he had a 10 he'd probably bet. He might call without a pair, hoping his Ace or King is the high card, and figuring you haven't gotten a pair yet from the board. After all, you raised, and probably either have a pair or, more likely, two big cards like him. He might pay you off, giving you an extra bet.

In early position I would play the 9s and 8s if the game was fairly tight and I didn't figure to get double-raised. If I was double-raised, it's no great loss to throw the hand away. The chances of getting trips on the flop are less than 11 percent, and there are no real outs here, unless you get a straight possibility. But even here you have to be careful. Holding 8s, if the flop is 9-10-Jack, you're on very dangerous ground. You have the low or ignorant end of a possible straight, the kind of hand that costs a ton of money in losses.

If you do see the flop and don't get trips and have no other outs, you must muck your pair unless there is no betting on the flop and you get a free ride. In middle position you can play the 9s, 8s, and 7s, and take one raise to see the flop. As to lower pairs, they're losers and you should play them only in late position if there have been no raises in front of you.

Now and then you see a player beat you with trips on the river, and your two pairs fall to a set of 4s. But you only see his cards when this kind of weak player wins. All the other times he held a low pair and took raises and reraises to see the river and mucked his pair; well, you don't see these losing cards. Let the weak players and losers play small pairs to the river, hoping against hope for trips. Muck them if you're not helped on the flop. That's as far as they should go.

Other Ace Holdings

By other Ace holdings, we mean suited or unsuited hands, with an Ace teamed up with a card lower than a 10.

Ace-9 to Ace-2 **s**
Ace-9 to Ace-2

Sometimes these will be referred to as Ace-x **s** or Ace-x (unsuited), x in this instance meaning any card from a 2 to 9. An Ace with another card of the same suit, such as Ace♣ 8♣, looks seductive. After all, if you get a flush with these cards, it will be the nut flush. If there is no other pair on board, and no chance for a straight or royal flush, then it will be the absolute nuts. Thus, holding those cards, if the board is:

you have the absolute nuts. You can't lose, nor can you be tied. You will win the pot by yourself. So why not, you might ask, always hold the Ace and another suited card, Ace-x **s**? There are a couple of reasons why you shouldn't always play this hand.

First of all, you will complete a flush holding any two suited cards only about 3 percent of the time, which means that 97 percent of the time you won't get a flush. The chances of course are the same whether you hold Ace-5 of clubs or 6-3 of hearts. But, you might ask, if you hold the Ace, then you have an out. You can get an Ace on board and win that way. That is so, as to the first part. You can certainly get another Ace, but what about your kicker? The most likely card any opponent will hold is an Ace, and if he or she has a better kicker, you're sucking air and going to lose some checks.

For example, suppose you start with Ace-6 of diamonds. The final board is:

With no pair out, and with an Ace and any card 5 or lower, or 10 or higher on the board before the river, there's always a chance of a straight developing. Here, if someone has a 4-2 he has a straight. Unlikely, but possible. But the biggest danger to you is that someone else is holding an Ace with a bigger kicker. If a player holds Ace-8 or Ace-7, you're beaten. Both of you have a pair of Aces, and the Queen and 9 play as well to form your hands. But the opponent's 8 is bigger than your 6, so you lose.

Many players automatically play Ace-x (with the x-standing for a 2-9) unsuited. It is a big money-loser for them. They constantly get outkickered. You hear the triumphant cries of winners at Hold 'Em raking in the pot yelling "kicker," as they show an Ace with a bigger sidecard than their losing opponent's.

If a large percentage of players play Ace-x unsuited, then Ace-x s excites them even more. They know they can get a nut flush, if only three more of that same suit show up on the board. They don't realize that they'll develop their flush only 3 percent of the time. Even if they have four to a flush on the flop, they're still only going to develop their flush about 35% of the time. And by the turn, they only have about a 20 percent chance of completing their flush.

However, if they don't get a flush, they have big, big problems. As we saw before, they can be outkickered by another player holding an Ace if an Ace shows up on board. Therefore, I would advise not falling in love with the Ace-x, suited or unsuited. If unsuited, I would pass this holding in any position. It's too much of a trap hand, even in late position. You'll save a ton of money automatically mucking the Ace-x unsuited hand.

As to Ace-x s, it could be played from a late position if there were no raises before you. In early to middle position I still think you save money not playing this holding. There may be times you'll regret it, with the fifth card of your flush showing on the river or turn, but most of the time you'll be saving money, much more than you'll get from the occasional flush that you'll make.

If you do play Ace-x s, then you'd prefer to hold an Ace with a card 5 or lower, so that you have the extra chance of getting a wheel if you see three other perfect low cards. But how often will you see this? It's a big long shot. In late position, if there were no raises before you, you can play this hand (Ace with a 2-5 sidecard suited) and even put in a raise at times if you are up against a couple of callers. But again, if you decide to muck the hand, there's no loss and a potential gain in the money you'll be saving.

Why raise occasionally? So that your opponents can't read you. You could be raising with anything in late position, and they have no way of knowing just what you're holding. If you're in early or middle position and put in a raise with these cards, and are re-raised, you're in deep trouble. You could be facing a holder of an Ace with a big kicker, and now you'll need a flush or straight to win the pot. You're a big underdog and it's going to cost you a lot of money to stick with this mediocre hand.

If you avoid the traps involved in playing the Ace-x, suited or unsuited, you'll end up saving a lot of checks. An occasional foray in late position, even a raise, will deceive your opponents, but other than that, I don't recommend playing an Ace-x unsuited. Ace-x **s** is stronger, and if played, you will prefer to have a hand that can form a straight, with the kicker a 2-5.

Suited Connected Cards
All the hands discussed in the following section will be suited, and will not involve a Jack or higher card. The strongest of the suited connectors is a holding of 10-9 **s**. The weakest is 3-2 **s**.

10-9 s	6-5 s
9-8 s	5-4 s
8-7 s	4-3 s
7-6 s	3-2 s

Suited connected cards are a favorite of world champion Doyle Brunson, who likes their hidden ability to break an opponent in no-limit Hold 'Em. A semiragged board hides them perfectly. For example, holding 6♦ 5♦ if the board shows:

you're going to get a lot of action from anyone holding Ace-Queen, Ace-King, or any opponent holding a set of 7s, 4s, or 3s. Better yet, if any opponent holds a pair of Aces or Queens as pocket cards, you're in clover. You have the absolute nuts and you're going to be raised and reraised. I like the suited connected cards for their deception as well as their ability to win a monster pot, even in limit poker.

Suited connectors are stronger than unsuited cards, such as 6♠ 5♦, which are unplayable except from late position with no raises before the holder of that hand acts. The suited connectors give you the added power to make a flush. If you make a flush, you can be beaten by a higher flush; therefore, you always prefer a straight over a flush. If you jam up the middle with your cards, such as seeing 9-6-5, when you hold 8-7, if there's no flush draw or pair on board, you've got the nuts.

But if you do get a straight, beware of having the ignorant end or lowest part of the straight. As we pointed out before, holding 6-5 and seeing 7-8-9, on board leads to leads to trouble and usually a big loss, as anyone with 10-Jack will reraise you till he runs out of checks. If you hold 6-5 and the flop comes up 7-8-9, it's best to bail out if there's serious betting action.

Since you want a straight, I wouldn't hold any suited connectors but 5-4 and higher. I prefer the 5-4 up to the 8-7, although I'll certainly play the 9-8 and 10-9. With the 9-8 and 10-9, you have to be careful with your straights, because the tendency of most players is to hold big cards. Thus, if you hold 9♠-8♠ and the board shows:

you have your straight with the 8, but a player holding King-Jack has the nut straight here. That's more likely to happen than if you hold 6♦ 5♦ and the board shows:

In this case, anyone holding 10-8 will have the nut straight, but that's more unlikely to be an opponent's hole cards. Your 5 should hold up here.

Why do I set the lower parameters at 5-4? Because of the possible straights you can make. There are three cards below the 4 that can form your straight. With a 4-3 there are only two cards, and with the 3-2, just one card, the Ace, can help you. Otherwise, if you hold 3-2 and there's a 4-5-6, you're once again looking at the ignorant end of a straight.

Since these suited connectors are pretty much pure drawing hands, you prefer to play them in multi-action pots, hoping for a solid flop. If you are hung out to dry with only one or two opponents pre-flop, I'd muck them. But if you can get four-or-more-way action, I'd see a raise pre-flop and play them. The later the position, the better you can judge the situation.

There's another aspect to these cards. If there is a lot of raising pre-flop, a few players are probably holding big cards and not the cards that you are looking for. If you hold a 10-9 s with a lot of action, I'd pass on these cards. If big cards, which you'll need, come up, it probably will help your opponents more than it will help you.

Not only can you get a straight or flush with the small connected cards, but a straight flush as well. I can recall a hand I held that made a ton of money and broke my opponent. I went in with a 7♥ 6♥ just to the right of the button in late position. There was a raise before it came to me, with three players already calling the raise, and so I called. The button reraised, and got four calls to his raise before I called as well. The flop came up:

I had a gutshot straight flush draw, as well as a straight and flush draw. The first raiser bet, got two calls; I called, and was raised by the button. The first raiser reraised and after I called, the betting was capped by the button (only three raises are allowed). I still had four other players in the pot.

Then came the turn:

Now I had the nut straight. The original raiser checked, and two players also checked to me. I bet, was raised by the button, and only the original raiser called. I reraised, was reraised, and I capped the bet. Three of us were in the pot.

Now I looked carefully at the board. I didn't want to see another heart, figuring someone had A-x of hearts, and I didn't want to see the board paired, figuring also that someone, probably the button, had trips. The button was an aggressive player, building up huge pots when he had any chance to win. So I said inwardly, no pair and no heart. But both my fears came true. The river card made the board look like this:

I took a long look at this board. I had a straight flush, and at the same time the board probably gave someone an Ace-high flush and someone else a full house. The original raiser checked, and I bet. I was raised by the button. The player checking called "time" and studied the board, playing with his checks. Then he mucked his hand. I reraised, and promptly was reraised! Now there were no limits to raises, not when only two players remained in the game.

I reraised, was reraised, and again I reraised, and

was raised. Finally my opponent ran out of checks and before I could show my hand, he triumphantly showed his hole cards—a pair of 5s!

"Send it over," he shouted to the dealer, a phrase used by players who win and want to rub it in. Or they say "Send it home," or "Send it down." But I turned over my hand. At first the shouter couldn't grasp its strength, thinking I had a flush, but when the dealer called "straight flush," he slumped in his chair and let out his breath, the way I guess a dying water buffalo must exhale his final spark of life.

Then he stood up and raced out of the club. The pyramid of checks in the middle of the table was pushed over to me. I was in a club that had no "bad beat" jackpot; otherwise, we'd both have had a big payoff from the casino. It was just a bad beat for my opponent.

Try and play these suited connectors from as late a position as possible and against at least three other players. The later your position, the more insulated you are from raises, and the better you see just how many other players are in against you. If there's no help on the flop, don't be stubborn. Give them up. But if you do get help, there's a possibility of big payoffs if you make your straight or flush.

Suited King Hands

In this section, I'm discussing King-x **s**, with the x standing for 2-9. Hands with King-10 and better have been discussed previously. The best of these hands are King-9, King-8, and King-7, all suited. After these holdings, the value of the hands drops off considerably.

What you're attempting to do with these hands is get a flush, or two pairs, led by the Kings. These aren't the strongest hands, and even a completed flush is not a nut flush, for someone may be holding Ace-x of the same suit, and all you have to show for your hand is a bad beat.

Therefore you have to play these hands carefully.

In middle or late position, with only one raise, it might pay to see the flop. In late position, without any raise before you, it might pay occasionally to raise. If you see a King on the flop, you probably have the best pair. If you see a King and two of your suit, you have it both ways, and can play very aggressively.

Since the most likely card against you is an Ace, the following is a flop you don't care for when you're holding King♥ 7♥:

You don't have any chance at a flush, and the Ace is an overcard that probably pairs someone against you. If there's a bet to you, you lose nothing by dumping the hand. If you lead the betting and are raised, again you can get rid of your hand. Play it cautiously. That's my best advice.

And remember, when you go in with two to a suit, your chances of filling in that flush are only about 3 percent. So you want at least two to the suit on the flop, or a pairing of the King, with no Ace out there to stay in the game.

Connected Nonsuited Cards
We're discussing hands that have no paint, so the highest of these is 10-9 and the lowest is 3-2, the same grouping that we showed in suited connectors. However, by not being suited, there's a big difference, and their value goes down considerably without the straight flush or flush possibility.

These hands are garbage and can't be played except in late position, and only if there hasn't been a raise, and there are at least four other players in the game. With certain of these hands you're hoping for a straight, and you need at least two to a straight to continue playing. For example, you're holding 9♠ 8♦ and the flop is:

You have a chance at the nut straight, providing no Ace or 9 shows on board, in which case you lose to a holding of Queen-Jack. And of course you don't want to see another diamond. An ideal final board would be:

With all these chances to lose, you can see how weak this holding is, and therefore play it only in late position against several opponents, and as cheaply as possible.

As with the suited connectors, don't play any holding less than 5-4, which gives you three small drawing cards (3-2-Ace) to complete your straight. Don't even think about playing a 4-3 or 3-2—they're really trash hands.

All Other Hands Are Not Playable

Sometimes we can be tempted by King-9 or Queen-8 s, but we should avoid even thinking about calling or putting out any sort of bet prior to the flop with these hole cards. For one thing, they are losers, and you will end up giving up checks and sometimes many checks with these cards.

Any hand that forms the top and bottom of a straight, other than the Ace-10, is a trap hand. If you have King-9 and see a board that holds 10-Jack-Queen, which completes your straight, then you are in dangerous waters. An Ace-King has the nut straight here. With a Queen-8, if you see 9-10-Jack, then a King-Queen has the nut straight. The same holds for Jack-7, 10-6, and so forth, all unplayable hands.

Many players will automatically play King-9, but it is a big mistake. You need to fill it in with three perfect cards to get a straight and even then you are in jeopardy. If an Ace shows on board, you're probably facing an overpair. If a King comes up, someone else can have Kings with a better kicker. There's not much really going for this holding.

Queen-8 suited down to Queen-2 suited are also poor choices to play. They are basically losers, though the higher the kicker the better the hand. In late position, you could call with a Queen-8 s if there were no raises, but this hand is best mucked in early and middle position. It forms the outside parameters of a straight, which is not good, and all you can basically hope for is a flush. Even there, you might be in trouble, with any player holding King or Ace-x of the same suit.

If Queen-x (8-2) s is a weak hand, then Queen-x unsuited is much worse. You need a Queen on the flop to give you any strength, and if another player also holds a Queen you are outkickered and a big underdog. It's best to release this hand.

Of course, there will be times you'll wish you had played your hole cards when you find a miracle flop occurring. For example, after mucking Queen♥ 3♥ the flop comes up:

But if you play enough Hold 'Em you're bound to kick yourself after discarding your hole cards. I had discarded the 4♠ 2♣ and watched the flop come up:

Then on the turn another 4 showed up, and on the river an Ace was dealt and there was a battle between two full houses, Aces full and Kings full, while I sat impotently by and couldn't do anything but grimace. But the bets were capped before the flop, by one player holding pocket Aces and the other holding pocket Kings, and how in the world could I call with 4-2 offsuit, one of the worst hands you can be dealt?

That's the nature of Hold 'Em. You can't read the future in this game, and there will be times you will sit burning up, as a big full house or four of a kind is dealt on board and you aren't participating in the pot. **Steaming** is the term the pros use, as in steam pouring out of both ears.

It happens to everyone. The only way to avoid this is to play every hand, and if you do so, hire a good bankruptcy lawyer to sit behind you. You can't play every holding. Occasionally you'll see someone try, either a drunk or a maniac or someone on a **rush** (winning hand after hand). But in the end, they'll get stung. I've seen players with five racks of checks go down to taking out cash from their pockets. They were playing everything, and winning out of sheer blind luck, but finally, the tables turned and the checks in front of them disappeared with frightening speed.

Hands to Play When Everyone Folds Except the Blinds

If you're the button or to the right of the button, then hand selection can go out the window, if every player has folded and it's only you and the blinds left in the game. Even then, you can't play every hand. For example, I wouldn't play any cards led by a 4, such as 4-3, and I wouldn't play cards separated by two cards, such as 7-4, but I would take a stab with 10-8, 9-7, 8-6, or 7-5, even unsuited. What you have to do is raise. You can't just call, because you want your raise to get the blinds out.

If the big blind calls, and you're head-to-head, what you want to see is a big card on the flop. If you're holding 8♥ 6♠ a flop of:

is not going to scare the big blind as much as a flop of:

If he checks to you with the latter flop and you bet, he'll probably figure you have a King and fold. In the first instance, he might check to you and then call. As a big blind he could have anything and might actually relish the three rags, which give him a pair of 9s or two pairs. You'll run across players who "protect" their big blind by calling a raise. They figure, "Well, I'm in for a bet, so I'll call another bet, and see the flop. It's only one other bet." And players with this mindset will see flop with practically anything, even 9-5 offsuit.

With the King out on the flop, this player will check and may see your bet, but if another big card falls on the turn and you bet, they'll not see the bigger street bet. But don't be stubborn. After all, you're just trying to steal the small and big blind bets—in a $10–$20 game, that's $15 ($5 and $10)—by raising to $20. If you're reraised by one of the blinds, give it up. Don't play like the fools who, once they try to bluff, are too embarrassed to muck their cards and end up going to the river with garbage.

Which brings us to the time when you're a small or big blind. There's nothing to protect just because you already have either half or a full bet out as a result of table position. Give it up when you have garbage. Even if you suspect that the late position bet is a bluff, give it up. Everyone at the table will be in the small or blind position every nine deals. If you have your $10 blind bet out in a $10-20 game, and every other player but the button has folded and he raises you $20, what's the point of trying to bluff him with a holding of Jack♣ 4♠? If you raise and are called, or worse, re-raised, now what do you do? Instead of merely losing the $10 you're forced to bet as a big blind, you find yourself putting out $30 or $40 on cards that are absolute junk.

You're much better off saving these checks for the times you have a legitimate hand and a chance to win a pot. Don't be stubborn and don't feel you have to protect anything, either your blind or your bluff.

The Flop

The structure of Hold 'Em gives you five cards to look at once the flop is dealt, and yet you're still on the first level of betting, preparing to make your second wager. In Seven-Card Stud, by the time you see five cards, you're on an expensive street, and have already made two bets.

By the time the flop comes, you should be aware of the following:

1. Who raised, if there were any raises?
2. Is the raiser behind you, or will he be acting before you?
3. How many players are in front of you and behind you?

4. How big is the pot?
5. What do you know about the players? Are they aggressive, passive, weak, or strong?

This sounds like a lot to know, but in reality, it isn't much. On any average hand, a player raises and is called by a couple of opponents. Or there is a reraise, again with a couple of opponents in the hand. Preferably, you should have been one of the raisers. If not, then you must make certain your hand is worth playing. Refer to our discussion of various playable hands, from the very best to those barely on the borderline.

Options on the Flop

You have various options on the flop. You can check, if other players have checked before you, or you can put in a bet. If there has been a bet, you can raise. If there has been a bet and a raise, you can reraise. Or you can fold if there has been any kind of betting action. It depends on your pocket cards and the flop. And what you perceive your opponents are holding.

For example, if either of the blinds or any early position player raised pre-flop, then, unless the player is a sucker, you have to expect him to hold a big pair or something like Ace-King or Ace-Queen, probably suited. An aggressive player might hold King-Queen s and raise in an attempt to drive out any hand consisting of an Ace and a weak kicker.

If a player has raised from a middle position, then he has a wider range of possible hands. He might have raised with a pair of 8s or 9s, or with any kind of Ace holding, such as Ace-10 or Ace-9 suited or unsuited, figuring that he will win if an Ace shows on board.

In late position, anything is possible. Players will take shots with all kinds of hands, hoping for a miracle flop, or a flop that is helpful. In late position, they have an edge and can be more aggressive than in early or middle position, or they can raise prior to the flop to see a free card if the flop doesn't help. If the game is young and you haven't yet gotten a fix on the opponents, then it's best to assume that early raisers have very strong hands, middle raisers moderately strong hands, and late position raisers can have anything.

The situation changes if there is a raise and reraise. Someone reraising from late position now must be accorded respect, especially if he raises one of the early position raisers. You're probably facing a big pair, Aces or Kings or possibly Queens.

But by the time you see the flop, you are playing a hand that has a chance to win. If your cards are not going to be competitive, then it's time to take an early exit before that flop is dealt.

Some Representative Hands

We'll assume you have a strong hand to start with, Ace♦ Queen♦. You were in middle position, and raised the big blind, and one player plus the big blind called your raise. The flop is:

This is the kind of flop you want. There's no real danger of a straight or flush with the flop, and you have the top pair.

But suppose the following is the flop you see:

The big blind checks, you bet, holding top pair plus the best kicker, and the player behind you raises. The big blind folds. What do you do? This is a common situation in Hold 'Em. You can't figure that the late position raiser saw your original raise with a 10-7. He might have had a pair of 10s or 7s, but if you are always worried about someone holding a set, it's hard to play this game. Don't always count on the worst; count on the most probable. In this instance, he either has paired a Queen, or he has two spades. If he has two spades, he wants you to check to him on the turn, so he can get a free card. He probably has big spades, otherwise why play against only two players pre-flop with just a pure drawing card? So you put him on King-10 or thereabouts.

Now you reraise. He calls, and here's the board on the turn:

You bet and he folds. If you hadn't reraised, and you checked to him on the turn, he'd get to see the river card for free. If you put a player on a drawing hand, you don't want him to ever get a free card. He must pay for each card, and as dearly as possible.

Holding the same Ace-Queen of diamonds, if the flop came up:

there's a good chance that someone is holding the other King. You have a chance for an inside straight if you get a Jack, but there's two clubs out as well, and someone may be drawing for a flush. Better to go for a flush than an inside straight. If the big blind checked, and you bet to test the waters and were raised behind you and the big blind called the raise, I would fold. Obviously, one of these players is going for a flush or straight, and the other may already have trip Kings. The big blind could have Queen-Jack unsuited or Ace-x of clubs, and he has a much better chance of winning than you have. Getting an Ace on the turn will help you, but might give one of your opponents a made straight.

The important thing is to stay alert and figure out just what the flop reveals and what the action of your opponents also reveals. In the above instance, an Ace on the turn might have helped you, but could have given one of your opponents the nuts.

Let's assume you've been dealt 9♥ 9♣. You're in middle position, and no one has raised before you, but the button raises, and there are four of you in the pot; the small blind, player in seat three, you, and the button.

The flop comes up:

The small blind checks, player three bets, and now it's up to you. What do you do? A Queen will give you a straight, but you'll have the small end of that straight, and any Ace will have the nut straight. So that's no good. If a 9 shows on the turn, it'll give you trips, but then anyone holding a Queen will have a straight, so that's no good either. Fold the 9s. In this instance, getting the card you're looking for might destroy your chances of winning.

Another situation that is seen in Hold 'Em is this: You're dealt Ace-King unsuited and raise pre-flop in late position, but still three players drag along to see the flop. The flop is:

An early position player bets, another player raises, and now it's your turn. What do you do? Well, you started with strong cards, but the 10-9 is of concern. Those are cards that players stay in with, especially if they're suited. The flop hasn't helped you at all, and now you may be facing two pairs. Give it up. It's easier to give up the Ace-King holding than the pair of Aces or pair of Kings. Figure that Aces or Kings are going to win only about 50 percent of the time anyway.

You are dealt black Kings and the flop comes up:

It's checked to you, and you bet. An aggressive player behind you raises, and is reraised by a tight, conservative player. Everyone folds and it's up to you. You had raised before the flop and were called by three players. What do you do?

Probably one player has an Ace. Bad news for you. And that tight player has either trips or an Ace with a big kicker. More bad news. Don't be stubborn here. Give it up. Again, what the flop and your opponents' actions reveal should guide your decision. Sometimes you'll be bluffed out. That's OK. That happens to everyone. But what you don't want is to see raises and reraises when you're beaten already. Get off at the cheap street station.

We're not being ultraconservative but realistic in our assessment of these hands. It doesn't matter how good your cards are; if they can't win, then don't bet them. The flop tells a lot; it's the key moment in Hold 'Em. A good rule of thumb is this: Unless you get help from the flop, don't stay in with any kind of action. Sometimes, playing this way, you'll see the card you need on the turn or on the river. That will happen. But most of the time, if you're not helped on the flop, you're sucking wind.

Flopping the Monster Hand

Now, there is various help that you can get on the flop. You can get, first of all, a monster hand. Let's assume you started with Queen♠ Jack♠ and the flop comes up:

You're in middle position, two players in front of you, and one behind, and the player behind you had raised before the flop. The first two players check. What do you do? From long experience, I would check. Too many times, in the beginning of my Hold 'Em career, I'd bet, and everyone would fold and I'd win a small pot with great cards. How many times can you flop a full boat? Rarely, believe me.

Even if the person behind me checks as well, I don't care. Now I want a good card to show. An ideal card would be an Ace.

Not having bet, everyone will assume that nobody is packing a Queen. A Jack, possibly. Or someone holds a Jack and was afraid of the Queens. Now, the first player checks, and the second bets. I'm hoping that the first player is ready to check-raise or that the player behind me will raise. But if they don't it won't matter that much, because, with this board, there may be Aces up or a made high straight, or perhaps someone is holding four to the club or diamond flush.

If I raise, I may drive out all the players but the bettor. So I call. I'm slowplaying now to get a big payoff on the river. After I call, the player behind me raises. Perfect. Both of the other players call the raise, and now, having trapped them, I reraise. All three players call the raise. The river comes up like this:

Now it's even better for me, because I figure someone has a flush, even an Ace-high flush, that they can't get away from. I'm proved right, as the first player comes to life and leads the betting. He's called by the second player and I raise. The player behind me hesitates, but the pot is so big, he calls. He probably missed his flush, but might have a big pair to go along with the Queens. I show the full house and collect the money.

If I had bet on the flop, I might have driven everyone out, or perhaps one player with four clubs would have stayed. If I bet on the turn, I'd lose him. The lesson is this—play the flop like a finely tuned instrument. Get the most out of it. To do this, slowplay a flop that gives you a monster hand, even if it means giving everyone a free card. Hell, let them have the free card. Give them a chance to try and catch up.

Whenever there is a big pair on board, and by big pair I mean Jacks and higher, and you hold the other card to the set, you can afford to slowplay. Even if there is a bet in front of you, merely call. Don't give away the strength of your hand till the first expensive street, on the turn. Thus, if you're dealt Ace♠ Jack♦ and the flop comes up:

I would check if everyone checked to me, and if someone bet, I would merely call. If there are a couple of callers, and a bet on the turn, it's then I would raise. You have trips and the top kicker. Players who see a big pair on the flop often try and steal the pot with a bet, figuring that if they represent trips everyone else will be too intimidated to call. This often happens, but sometimes everyone sees through this ploy. The more callers the better, as you get ready to lower the boom on the turn.

Catching a Strong Made Flop

Let's assume you started with King♠ Queen♠ and raised in middle position, and had three callers, two behind you as well as the small blind. The flop comes up:

Flopping the two best pair is very strong, and if there is a bet to you, you want to raise. Only trips have to be feared, and it's unlikely that someone is holding the 5s in the hole. Unlikely but always possible. However, you must play this hand fast. You must assume that you have the best cards at this point.

Another good situation is this: You were in late position holding 9-8 of hearts and a player in early position raised. The button also saw the raise. Often this raise doesn't mean the early position player has a high pair; more likely a hand like Ace-King. Either way, however, it shouldn't be a problem if you see a flop like this:

If the pre-flop raiser bets, you can safely raise here, figuring you have the best hand. Now let's assume that the button folds. If the board shows anything but a pair or paint, you can be pretty sure you have the winner. The original raiser, even if he holds a high pair, is not a threat to have a straight. So, if the final board is:

and it's checked to you, you can safely bet. It's unlikely that the original raiser is holding a 6. He's probably stuck with his high pair. If the river is the 7♦ and it is checked to you, just check. Your opponent might hold two high diamonds and might try to check-raise. If he bets instead of checking with the third diamond out, then you just have to pay him off. If he missed, then his only chance of winning is to bluff you out with a bet. You must call. One out of nine right decisions on the river and you're OK.

Catching a Good Flop

A good flop would be pairing one of your two cards and either holding the top pair or holding the top kicker. For example, you start with Ace♦ Jack♣ and the flop comes up:

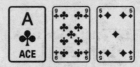

If you are first to bet and are raised, you probably have an opponent who has an Ace. The question is—what's his kicker? Hopefully, it isn't a 9 or a 5. That's when you have to analyze the situation. Before the flop, he just called. He's an aggressive player and might have gone in with Ace-x, or maybe he doesn't have an Ace and is representing one, not believing you.

I would just call here. However, there's another consideration. If he was holding something like King♣ 4♣, then his raise is an attempt to get a free card on the turn, and also thus see the river card for free, if both of you check on the turn. Let's assume now that it's just you and the raiser left. The turn comes up Queen♠. You should go ahead and bet. If you're raised again, you have a hard call to make. But I wouldn't be forced out. On the river, if no club shows, I'd simply check and call.

If you hold the same hand—that is, Ace♦ Jack♣—and the flop is:

You now have high pair with the best kicker. Again, if it's up to you to bet, bet. If it's bet to you, raise.

You're probably up against someone with two hearts, probably with the Ace or King of that suit. It's pretty unlikely that a person in early or middle position is in there with a 8-6. Players are more likely to hold the connected cards, like 8-7. Maybe he has Ace-8 and now figures the Jack didn't help you. In middle position you might have slowplayed your Ace-Jack suited.

After your raise, one other player behind you calls your raise, and the original bettor also calls. The turn is a 6♠. The first player checks and you bet, and they both fold. This is common in Hold 'Em. If you have raised before the turn and the turn pairs the board, it strikes fear in players. Now they figure you have trips and they're doomed. This doesn't always happen, but it happens enough to warrant your being an aggressor on the flop. It pays off in many ways; this being one.

Catching a Good Drawing Flop

An ideal flop here would be one that gives you not only a made hand but an excellent draw. For example, you started off with King♦ Queen♦ and raised in middle position, and got two callers, the big blind and a player behind you. The flop comes up:

Now you not only have the highest pair but a terrific flush draw. The only way you'll lose if your flush completes is if someone else is holding the Ace-x of diamonds. Possible but unlikely. You have to play as if you will win if a third diamond comes up, but don't be stubborn about it. I saw a player in $15–$30 Hold 'Em put in five raises holding King-Queen of clubs against an opponent who held Ace-four of clubs. It was head-to-head at this point, and the loser finally stopped raising when he ran out of checks. I knew he wasn't brain dead for he was able to correctly count out each raise, but what else was the matter with his brain? And this isn't the only time I've seen this kind of insane betting against a nut flush. I just don't know where these players are coming from. I want one of them to do this with me sometime.

Another ideal situation is to flop a possible straight flush. Let's say you're holding 8-7 of spades and the flop comes up:

There are five players in the hand. A player from the early position bets, and when it comes to you, two other players have seen the bet. You raise, and now the button reraises. The early position bettor calls the raise, the others fold, and now it's up to you. What could the button have? Most likely he went in with Ace-3 suited or unsuited. He has a made straight, and you are holding a four to a straight flush. Who's the favorite? You are. You have fourteen cards to complete a bigger straight or a flush and are about a 6 percent favorite over the holder of the wheel. You should go ahead and reraise here, and if there's a reraise, cap it. You have to assume he's not looking for a straight flush either, but merely has a straight. You can't always worry about straight flushes; you have to play your cards here as you see it. And as you see it, you're the favorite.

Most of the time, if you have a drawing hand, and the flop benefits you, it will give you four to a flush or straight. For example, you start with Jack♠ 10♣ in late position and see this flop:

You have four to a straight, and if you complete it, you'll have the nut straight. But that's pretty much your only out with this flop. What you're basically concerned with are the two spades. If another spade comes up, and there's action, you may be drawing dead for your straight, and it's best that you let it go if the turn is a King♠, for example. Drawing dead is a big trap in Hold 'Em because of the community cards on board, so you have to be aware of this at all times.

Dangerous Flops

I'm going to discuss a few situations here. First of all, if you go in with a hand like Ace♠ 10♠, calling a middle position raiser, and the flop comes up:

You have two pairs, headed by the Aces, but how good is your kicker? If you're up against another Ace, and that hand has a King, Queen, or Jack as a kicker, you're a humongous underdog. This is a classic instance where the kicker is boss.

Another tough situation is this: You go in with a 9-8 of clubs and the flop is:

You've flopped two pairs, but they're the bottom two pairs on board. You have to be really careful here. Suppose your opponent is holding Ace♠ Queen♠. Now, if an Ace comes up, you're pretty well dead, and if two running cards come up, such as 4♣ 4♥, you're also dead in the water. In fact, any other pair on board along with a big card and you must be very very careful. With action from your opponent, you're probably beaten.

Here's another situation to be aware of. If a player holds two overcards against you in his hand, such as Ace-King, and you are holding a pair of Queens, you're a favorite, but very slightly, just about 6-5. When an overcard comes up on the flop and there's action, it's not a crime to muck the Queens.

Take, for example, a flop like:

With an early bet or a bet and raise, you are probably facing a pair of either Aces or Kings and you have no real outs here. The same holds true if there's any Ace or King on board—you're probably beaten. Thus, a flop like:

and caution bells should be ringing in your ears. You now have to know your opponent who's betting. If he's an aggressive player, he might be representing a King and not have one. With a conservative player, you can be pretty sure he has the King in his hand.

Flops That Hurt You

There are a number of flops that will practically kill your chances of winning, even though you are slightly helped. For example, you go in with Queen♠ 9♠ in late position. The flop comes up:

All you have is the bottom pair, and there are two overcards against your Queen. With action on the flop I'd dump this hand, which in itself is just a borderline holding. It would be different if both the Ace and King were spades, for now you must go to the river with the possible nut flush.

Another example: You hold King♥ Jack♦ and the flop comes up:

Those three spades should be treated with caution. You have a pair of Jacks, but what about the Queen? A player against you may or may not have the Queen, but someone could already have flopped a flush. If there is a lot of action, it's not worth playing. You're praying that your Jacks hold up against a possible flush and a pair of Queens. And your King is not the best possible overcard. Suppose at the turn, the board looks like this:

Now you're looking at two overcards, a possible straight, and a possible flush. Too much to overcome.

Another tough situation is this: You raised from middle position with a pair of red tens. There are three callers. The flop comes up:

The big blind, who called your raise, comes out betting. Another player raises, and now it's your turn. Though the 9s made you two pairs, you're worried about the Ace, and the pair of 9s could have given someone trips. You basically have no outs here other than hoping for a third 10. Don't stay and guess as to what the early bet and raise meant. You've got to respect this action, especially when your two pairs look awfully weak here.

Any time there's three to a straight flush, to a straight, or to a flush on the flop and it hasn't helped you, you must be prepared to muck your hand against action involving a raise and reraise. It's hard to get away from a big pair like Aces or Kings, but if you hold King♦ King♣ and the flop is:

And you're up against three players who called your pre-flop raise, you're probably in a lot of trouble. That kind of flop is very unfavorable for you. A player holding a Jack-Queen has made a nut straight, while anyone holding two spades has a 35 percent chance of completing the flush. You have no part of the flush, and with two cards to go, you're hoping to see a King, and that might not be enough to win. Suppose in this instance, one player held the Jack♠ Queen♦, another Ace-3 of spades, and a third 10-9 of diamonds. You're running fourth here. You might face capped raises on the flop with three players holding these cards, and these raises are telling you something. You're pretty much doomed with your Kings.

Flops That Don't Help You

As you play more and more Hold 'Em, you're going to realize that most flops won't help you at all. If you clock your play, going in with fairly strong cards as an average, you'll be happy to win the pot 25 percent of the time. If you win more often, you're going to have a big day at the poker table; less than that, a hard day. But there are exceptions, of course. Sometimes, getting involved with one monster pot can make a big loser into a big winner. This happens when you have a big hand against another big hand and a big draw.

If you prevail, you'll see a lot of action and a pyramid of checks on the green felt table. Or you may have a big draw against other big draws, and win. I can think of one hand where I had the King-Jack of spades, and was at a table with a lot of aggressive wild players. I was able to hold my own, and after an hour's play was up about $50. The flop was:

By the time the bets came to me, there were three raises, capping the raises. Six players were in the hand, and there had been two raises before the flop. It was a $10–$20 game, and by now the pot held over $400. Suddenly, all the wild players were in at the same time. I had a chance at the nut straight if the Queen

came up, and I had a four-flush headed by the King.
My checks were melting rapidly, but the pot was too
big to drop out of.

The turn showed:

A complete rag on the turn, but this didn't stop the
bettors. They raised and reraised and capped the betting. There was about $900 in the pot, and I had an
open-ended shot at a straight, as well as those four
spades. I was thinking "Queen, Queen, Queen," and
sure enough the board looked like this when the river
card came.

This time I capped the raises, as two players folded.
One of the raisers turned over a Jack-10 and yelled
that the pot was going to be chopped up. To my
amazement, another player turned over Jack-9, and
the third Jack-10 as well. But my King-Jack was the
nuts. I took the pot, with four players getting a straight
with a Jack in the hole. I didn't count my checks,
but I knew I had won over $1,100. Just one pot, and
everything was rosy after an hour's frustration.

After that digression, let's get back to flops that
don't help. Most of the time, at least more than half
the time, the flop won't be of any use to you. For
example, you go in with a pair of red nines and the
flop comes up:

With those two overcards and action on the flop, your 9s are dead in the water.

Or you hold King♦ Queen♦ and the flop comes up:

And there is a raise and reraise on the flop.

Or you hold Jack-10 of diamonds and the flop comes up:

These kind of bad flops can go on **ad infinitum,** forever. What you do hope for is a helpful flop, but if you've paired a small card, you may be stuck in a trap situation. For example, going in with 9-8 of clubs, the flop is:

If you can get away cheaply, either with a free card, or one bet, you might want to see the turn. But against a bet and raise, I'd muck the hand. I don't like to just be a caller, and I certainly hate to be a chaser.

To me, the flop is the key moment in Hold 'Em,

and your decision to continue playing depends on what goes on when the flop is revealed. You should also be aware of what we discussed at the beginning of the section on the flop—who raised, where the raise came from, and so forth. The more you know, the better you can make correct decisions.

You basically want help on the flop. You want to have a strong made hand or a strong drawing hand. You're not always going to get this, so you have to calculate your chances of winning. You also have to know if a card that you're looking for on the turn or the river will end up destroying your chance of winning by giving another player the nut hand. A quick example: You hold 9♦ 9♣ and the flop is 10♠ Jack♠ Queen♥. If a 9 shows, it will probably give an opponent a high straight to the King, and even if an 8 comes up, someone might already hold King-Ace for the nut straight. And another spade, such as the 9, might complete someone's spade flush.

In playing Hold 'Em, not only do you want to win pots and money, but another goal is to not bleed away your checks by making foolish moves or by not examining just what is going on in a particular hand being played. If you save money by not making mistakes, it's as good as making money. Don't be a chaser and don't constantly be a caller. If you are one or both of these things, then either you're playing weaker cards than you should, or you didn't improve enough after seeing the flop.

Trying to Win the Pot
Without Improving on the Flop

The best way to do this is in late position, with a flop that looks scary and hasn't really helped anyone else. For example, you're last to act, and someone has raised pre-flop, and there are two other callers. You hold King♦ Queen♣ and the flop comes up:

Everyone checks to you. Since you're still on the cheap street, you can try and win the pot then and there by betting. You're representing a spade flush. If the original raiser stays in, he probably has a high pair, especially if he raised from an early position. But if he holds Ace-King to Ace-10, without a spade, he'll probably give it up. If he now check-raises, you're out of there. But it will be extremely difficult for him to raise unless he holds the Ace of spades. He fears the spades. He might just throw his cards away rather than guess. If he calls and then checks on the turn, which is a 5♥, you have to decide—do you check also, or make a bet? Betting would be your only chance to win the pot now.

Sometimes in early position you might put in a bet with a scary flop, and hope for the best. For example, as the big blind you hold Ace-Queen of diamonds and the flop comes up:

Being the big blind has its advantages in this situation. Other players might think you called a late raise just to protect your blind, and now the 8s have given you trips. If they haven't improved, they may just give you the pot.

To steal the pot on the flop, you have to pick your spots. In the last position, you have an ideal chance if everyone has checked to you. If an early position player has bet, a raise by you will probably not drive him out, and may subject you to a reraise. You don't want to put in too much money just to steal. Respect the early bettor. Wait till you have a valid hand to raise on.

Fourth Street Play—The Turn

Fourth Street will give you fewer problems than the decisions you have to make on the flop. By this time, you either have a made hand of some sort or a drawing hand. You've analyzed the other players and seen what they've done on the flop. You still have to be alert, for there are players who will slowplay strong hands on the flop, waiting for the more expensive streets to reveal the strength of their cards.

Always be aware of who is betting aggressively, and his or her position at the table. If it's a strong, tight player, then you need cards to beat him. If it's an aggressive player who will occasionally bluff and try to steal pots, then you decide hand against hand. Your hand against his hand—which will win? You can't always be sure of your decision, but at least you're making it intelligently; not guessing and not playing hunches.

Here's an example. You've started in middle position with Jack♥ 10♦. The big blind raised and was called by you and another player behind you. At least you're behind the raiser, an advantage. On the flop, you see:

The big blind bets right out. You have the high pair on board, and can't really be sure if the bettor has a bigger pair in the hole. You call, and the third player folds.

On the turn, the board looks like this:

Nothing but a rag has come out. Now the big blind checks. You can be fairly certain that he started with an Ace and a big card, and has gotten no help from the board so far. Or is he ready to check-raise? Not likely. If you check behind him, you're giving him a free card.

I have a general rule that I follow. When I'm checked to by a player in an earlier position, I generally bet. So I'd bet now. He calls. He still is looking for that big card. On the river, the board looks like this:

Now he bets. At this point, you can almost read his cards as though his hand was open. He's holding Ace-Jack. If he had a pair of Jacks, he'd have check-raised you on the turn. He would have had the biggest possible pair and would have wanted you to put more money in the pot. It's unlikely that you'd have two pairs—how could you have started with 10-3 or 5-3 and faced a raise before the flop? Now you can raise him. He's not going to reraise with a pair of Jacks. Now he figures you for two pairs, beating him. He guesses that you have Jack-10.

Sometimes players with Ace-x x being a big card, King, Queen, or Jack, will play aggressively right to the river, even if they've not been helped by the flop or turn. You must gauge their strength and qualities as a player. Most of the time, a raise pre-flop doesn't mean that the raiser has a big pair—they don't come that often. He probably has that Ace-x we've been discussing.

If you have a pair as a result of the flop, and you figure that the raiser is still on the come, you can see him all the way. Don't raise unless you get two pairs or trips, but see him right to the end. You won't always win, but you'll win enough times to make it worthwhile. But if the turn shows a big card, bigger than your pair, and he bets out, you can muck the hand.

For example, you started with Queen♦ Jack♦ against an early raiser. There are two other players in with you, as well as the raiser. The flop comes up:

The raiser bets, the others fold, and you call. You're putting him on Ace-x (a big card). Hopefully, the x doesn't stand for a Jack. On the turn, the board looks like this:

The raiser bets again. Now you're in trouble. You can muck your hand before you have to pay out two expensive bets. Sure, he might have missed and is holding Ace-Queen, but that's a real guess. If he has the King or Jack with the Ace, you're pretty well washed up here.

Sometimes, if you have gotten past the flop cheaply, the turn gives you new life. Suppose you begin with 9♥ 8♥ in late position. There was a raise just before you, but after you call the raise, so do three other players. The flop comes up:

This pile of garbage doesn't suit anyone, but after everyone checks, the player in front of you bets. You call, figuring no one is going to raise on the mess out on the board. No one does, though one player folds. Now four of you are left in. You want help on the turn, and up pops a 10♥. The board now looks like this:

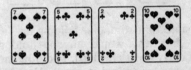

Your hand has come back to life. You have four to an open-ended straight, and it's well hidden. If a Jack or 6 comes up, you have the nut straight. But having just a drawing hand without any other possibilities, you try and get in to see the river as cheaply as possible, and check to the bettor. If a 9 had showed on the turn, then you'd have to make a decision. Does the bettor have a bigger pair? Even if you assume he does, you call. You have the top pair on board, plus the chance to make a gutshot straight. There are enough cards to help you—the four 6s, two 9s, and three 8s—to give you sufficient reasons to see the river.

In the above example, you're a little more than a 4-1 underdog to improve, and the pot is giving you more than that, good pot odds. So you call the player's bet.

If you had the lead on the flop and the turn comes up with a rag, by all means bet out. For example, you are holding Ace♠ Queen♦ and raised from an early position before the flop. You had three callers. The flop showed:

You bet and got two callers. Now the turn looks like this:

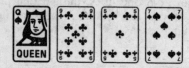

It's possible that someone holding an 8-6 has made a straight, but why would anyone hold those cards against an early raise pre-flop? You'd be more worried if the turn was an 8; then it's more possible for someone to hold 7-6 suited and still play, especially if they held two clubs. If you, being the first to act, check and worry about an 8-6, you're playing into the hands of anyone holding drawing cards. They get a free card here and then they see the river for free. That's bad poker on your part. You must make them pay.

If you get called, you're on pretty safe ground so far. One player may be holding two clubs and the other a pair lower than the Queens. If you're raised after betting on the turn, then you may be facing trips or two pair. You might as well call the raise, see the river, and check on the river, unless you get an Ace or Queen. I would still bet out with either of these cards, unless I saw another club. Even an Ace or Queen of clubs. Then I'd check and call.

It's awfully hard for another player to raise, if an Ace or Queen, neither of them clubs, came up. If he does raise, then you see the raise. You can't afford to be intimidated. He might have two pairs and you'll win. If he has trips, then you pay him off. It's just a blip to your bankroll; but your table image is important here. You don't want to get a reputation of someone who can be run over by a late raise.

If, on the other hand, you flopped a set and slow-played them, now is the time to make your move, when you see the turn. For example, you held 5♣ 5♥ and called a raise from late position. There are two other players competing for the pot. The flop was:

There was a bet and one other call. You called, deciding to slowplay the trips, waiting for that more expensive fourth street.

On the turn, the board looks like this:

The turn was good for you. No one has made a flush or straight with that rag of a 6. Again, the first bettor puts in his checks, he's called, and now you raise. You'll likely be called. On the river, you don't want to see a diamond or club unless it pairs the board. In that case, you'd have a full boat without any real worries.

If an odd card falls on the river, like a 2♠, they'll both check to you and you can bet, hoping for them both to call. The name of the game in poker is to win as many checks as possible, and if you can get them both to pay you off, fine. If one calls, that's OK. If they fold, well, you won the pot after getting some good action on the turn.

If the river card were a 2♦ and both checked to you, I'd merely turn over my cards and hope the pot is mine. Making a bet might put you in jeopardy of being check-raised, and giving up a lot of checks when you could have played safe. Even if they both missed, you'd probably get no action anyway. Don't be cautious, but don't be foolhardy either. With two diamonds and two clubs out there, someone may have a flush draw. And that third diamond on board should raise a red flag in your brain.

When you hold drawing hands, it's essential that you calculate the odds the pot is offering you against what the true odds are of completing your hand. For example, as a quick rule, you can calculate that with a four-flush or four to a straight, it's about 4:1 to make your hand. Is the pot offering you those odds? If it is giving you more than 4:1, make the bet. If it's less than that, fold.

If you're going for an inside straight, the odds are approximately 10.5:1 against you. There's only one card that can help you. Again, you're in a $10–$20 game going head-to-head against a tough player. Your only hope is the straight. The pot holds $120. You have to bet $20, getting 6:1. It's not worth betting.

Calculate and study the pot before betting on a hand that you must draw two to win. That's the sane and smart way to play any form of poker, especially Hold 'Em.

Fifth Street Play—The River

Now you're on the river, that treacherous running river, where dreams are often washed up, or, conversely, are made. I can't recall the number of times I've heard a triumphant player turn over his cards and yell "River!" As you gain experience in Hold 'Em, you'll understand the dangers of the river. When you're ahead, let's stay with trip 9s, but there are two diamonds on board, you want to see anything but a diamond. Anything! And of course, a diamond shows, and some tense player is shoving out checks as fast as he can, and you can only shake your head and curse the river.

Or you have a made flush, but you know someone is there with trips, and you don't want the board to pair up, because then a full house will beat you, and you see a 5♥ being turned over, pairing another 5, and you know you're finished as the checks fly out of a player's hand.

Or worse yet, you have a made flush on the turn, and you're holding Jack-10 of spades and praying that a red card shows on the river, any red card, but here comes another spade, and a player who's been laying low suddenly comes to life. You know he's holding that Ace and been trailing you all game, and now he's boss.

There are a lot of sad tales players can tell you about the river. Some may be exaggerated. I was playing next to a terrible player who was cashing $100 bills as fast as he could take them out of his pocket, and explaining to a pretty woman next to him that he was "killed, absolutely killed" the previous day at a $15–$30 Hold 'Em game when "four players in a row made inside straights against me." Sure. This was the kind of player who would call with anything. I figured if there were three Aces on board and someone accidently exposed the fourth Ace while betting, he'd see the bet. He was a pleasure to play against because he'd always be paying you off at the river, mucking his hand in disgust when you showed Aces and Jacks. Well, what did he expect when the flop held an Ace and Jack, and you were leading all the way?

Often, you'll find yourself at the river with a drawing hand, needing that extra flush card of a 10 to complete your straight, only to see some rag of the wrong suit or just some rag show up. It's frustrating, especially if the checks in the center are sky high, and all you need is that heart.

Let's say you hold Ace♥ 10♥ and the board on the turn shows:

You know someone has a made straight and someone else, the original raiser before the flop, might have a set of Queens, but if you get that heart, other than the Jack of hearts, that pot is all yours. You'll have what are called the **living nuts,** the absolute best. And the dealer burns the top card and then turns over a red card, but it's the 9♦ and it's *"sayonara, baby."* It's all over. A $600 pot out of your grasp.

On the other hand, the river is not just a muddy water filled with woe that drowns Hold 'Em players. It will reward them as well. As we said, when you have the best hand on the turn, you want a garbage card to show on the river, but when you are drawing, you want that certain card, that heart or 10 or whatever. And sometimes you're in luck.

A hand I well remember had me starting with King–8 of spades. I had won the previous hand and was ahead quite a bit. There was a raise before the flop and I had four other players in there against me. The flop came up:

The original raiser opened, and had two callers. I put in a raise, being in last position, and was reraised by the original raiser. I called and now there were four of us, with one player dropping out. Another spade wouldn't give me the nut flush, but I liked my King's chances here. And I had a pair.

On the turn, the board looked like this:

The original raiser bet, and the two players before me folded. I called. It was easy to calculate that the original raiser had either a pair higher than Queens, or trip Queens, or Ace-Queen, or maybe Ace–10. Maybe even a pair of 10s in the hole. He was an aggressive player and I had seen him raise with all kinds of hands in early position; any pair or King-Queen, suited or unsuited.

In any event, I still had a big out, and that was getting a spade. The river card was dealt:

Where'd that 8 come from? I was looking for a spade and here I had trips. My opponent bet, and I immediately raised. I figured, if he was trip Queens or trip 10s, I'm doomed. But I had a gut feeling he was in with Ace-Queen or Ace–10 at the best. If he had been a tight player I'd have merely called, but I wanted that extra bet. Instead of raising, he looked closely at the board and at me. I looked him square in the eye, an intimidating gesture—a tell indicating that I had nothing. He called. I showed the trip 8s and he folded.

"I figured you on spade draw," he said, "and I figured you missed." Well, he was right about that, but he didn't count on the set of 8s.

One of the big decisions to make on the river, is whether or not to call an opponent's final bet when you have something, but not much. For example, you are holding 10♠ 9♠ and the final board looks like this:

The other player has been leading from the start, raising before the flop. You weren't that worried about the Jack, figuring him for an Ace-King, but that Queen on the river now worries you. There were originally four players in the pot, but now it's head-to-head. Do you call his bet?

A general rule to follow is this: If you are right only one out of eight or nine times, you'll make money calling on the river with any sort of hand. Think back to your own play. If you held Ace-King and kept hammering at the pot by betting, unless someone held a Jack or 10 or maybe even a 3 at the flop, he or she would have folded.

Then, after getting all but one player out, if you checked on the river with your Ace-King, you'd lose to any pair. But if you bet, representing Queens or a high pair (higher than the Jack) or perhaps Jacks with an Ace, you put your opponent on a hard call. If you're leading all the way, you might as well lead on the river against someone who hasn't raised you.

In this case, the other player had Ace-Queen. He won because of that river Queen.

Another river situation is this: Do you bet when it's checked to you on the river? A good general rule: Bet. As Doyle Brunson so succinctly said, "If you bet in this situation, you have a 2:1 chance of winning. First of all, you might have the best hand. Secondly, you might not get called. So bet." Those words from a world champion make a lot of sense.

If there are two players in against you at the river, and both check, then what do you do? With one, it's almost an automatic bet. Now you have to understand whom you're up against. If a player is tight and conservative, he probably has something and won't want to be bluffed. A strong player can be bluffed. I found that many women tend to play conservatively, and they'll call that last wager with anything decent. But with weak players, you're going to have to show them a hand to win. They'll call with anything, unlike conservative players.

Therefore, you should make a decision based on your opponents. The board here is secondary. Obviously, no one has really benefited from the board in any major way. But will both checkers fold if you bet?

Let's say you are holding King♥ Jack♠ and the board looks like this:

Both players now check to you. You've held four to a straight from the flop on, and nothing is there for you. One player is fairly conservative, but that second 10 might scare him off. The other player is aggressive and from being a big loser, has come back and is ahead. In this situation, you want to get rid of the conservative player first. He might fold, leaving it up to the aggressive player to call your bet. So you bet, and sure enough, the conservative player folds. The aggressive player fools around with his checks and slides his cards back and forth. He looks to you. It's best to look away, for that is nonthreatening and seen as a sign that you are anxious for him to call you. In the end, he shakes his head and mucks his hand.

You won a pot that you couldn't win without that final bet. And that final bet is often the difference between winning or losing the pot. You can't be scared then or play passively. Aggression is the name of the game in poker, and especially in Hold 'Em, where your opponents' cards are hidden, and there are community cards on board. You must retain that strong table image; otherwise, players will run all over you when they see you play passively, when they see you are nothing but a calling station. Don't let them do that. Play aggressively. Do the betting. Let them do the guessing.

As you play Hold 'Em you'll see that when everyone checks on the turn, and a rag comes up on the river, the first person to bet usually wins the pot, as everyone folds. This last bet is sometimes more effective from an earlier position, for when it comes in later position or in the last position, sometimes someone will call, feeling that the bettor wanted to steal the pot.

If you're leading all the way with the betting, especially against one player, the best move is to bet on the river, no matter what the river card is. That's often the way to win, even if you've missed many times in this situation, you're up against a player with a drawing hand, hoping to complete a flush or straight. If nothing scary comes on the river, then bet, no matter what you have. Usually, a player who's been checking and calling or simply calling, will fold. Sometimes they'll call, and very occasionally, they'll raise. If you've missed completely and are raised, or check-raised, don't be stubborn. Give it up.

But if you have any kind of hand, then you are back in the situation of deciding whom you're up against—and then calling most of the time. I've seen situations where the board looked like this at the river:

One player bet and the other raised immediately. Now, this is a scary board, with four diamonds out there, plus three to a straight. All sorts of made hands can come from that board. What happened was this: The raise was called, and the raiser sheepishly said "I missed," and turned over a King-Jack of hearts. And what did the other player have? A pair of 6s! With all that potential trouble out on the board, neither player could get a flush or straight.

When an opponent says "I missed," that's what you want to hear. Another wonderful phrase is, "It's yours." Even better, the other player simply mucks his cards after making a bet. I was watching a real sucker playing. At the river, he raised and when called, simply threw away his cards. What was he thinking? The player he raised had some sort of hand, and had raised before the flop, and there was a King and Ace on the board.

When you're going for the flush or straight and miss, and there's one or more bets out when it's your turn to act, you're not going to fool anyone with a raise. It's just thrown-away money. When there's a bet and raise, then it's suicide to try and steal the pot. Give it up. Wait for the time when you have the strongest hand and can put in a legitimate raise and gain a few extra bets.

Some Final Thoughts

I've discussed Hold 'Em more than any other game in this book for a good reason. It's by far the most popular game in casinos and clubs, and one can play it on any level, from $1–$2 all the way up to no-limit. The most popular games seem to be the $6–$12 and $9–$18 ones, where there is a lot of action and a great deal of money changes hands. It's not impossible to win $1,000 or more in a $9–$18 game, or $600–700 in $6–$12 Hold 'Em.

The game has pretty much the same structure no

matter at what level you play. I covered the blinds at the beginning of the section, showing how most are tiered so that the small blind is one-half the big blind, which in itself is one-half the maximum bet. Thus, in a $10–$20 game, the small blind is $5, the big blind $10. There are exceptions to this. In a typical $6–$12 game, the small blind is $2 and the big blind $6, and the $9–$18 games have a small blind of $3 and a big blind of $9. Another exception is the $15–$30 game, where the small blind is $10 and the big blind $15.

But other than these vagaries, the structure of the game, as I have written, is always the same. If you master this fascinating and complex game, you can move up from smaller to bigger games, depending on your skill factor and your bankroll. To start, I'd suggest playing at least a $5–$10 game or a $6–$12 one. The reason is simple. If you play a smaller game, such as $1–$2 to $3–$6, you'll find players going in with everything. After all, why not see the flop for a measly $2. Anything can happen. You can't hone your skill in these games, nor learn the essentials of reading players and their moves. In the very small games, you can't really be sure what anyone is holding. It could be a 6–4 offsuit or a pair of Kings. They'll want to see that flop, no matter what.

When you're playing serious Hold 'Em, and follow the principles outlined in this book, you should be a winner. However, the game is such that bad beats are inevitable, and there may be times you take losses at the table. But don't be discouraged by one or two losses. Sometimes the cards run badly and you find yourself with good cards, only to be beaten by better cards. It happens.

The important thing is to be patient. Patience, patience, patience is like location, location, location in real estate. It's essential for financial well-being. Don't start playing mediocre hands; don't start gambling. Play the big cards for the most part. Play according to your position at the table—that is, tight in the front and loose in the back. Study your opponents and get a fix on their game. See which players are in on every hand and punish them when you get the good cards. Respect early raises by good players.

Above all, play aggressively. Play so that the other players are always guessing the value of your hand. You do this by raising. Don't be that calling station I'm always disparaging in these pages.

As you improve, as you move up to bigger games, you'll find the main difference is the speed of play. In bigger games, there'll be more raising before the flop. There'll rarely be free cards allowed by everyone checking on any round of betting. If you find that this fast play is too much for you, and you can't beat a bigger game, go back to a smaller game, where you're more comfortable. Plenty of money can be made in a $6–$12 or $9–$18 game where the play is slower, and the raises fewer, especially before and on the flop. But if you keep winning and can handle the action at bigger games, by all means move up. A lot of money can be made in this very popular game.

X

Omaha—Eight or Better Hi-Lo

Omaha is an offshoot of **Texas Hold 'Em,** and the two games share some characteristics. However, there are a number of important differences, so that the games cannot really be played with the same strategies. For one thing, Omaha is a high-low game, in which the low hand, if it is eight or better, shares the pot with the high hand.

In Omaha, players receive four hole cards instead of the two in Hold 'Em, but a player must use two cards from his hand to form the best high hand, along with three card from the board. In addition, he must also use only two cards from his hand to form the best low hand, if he has one, along with three cards from the board. In Hold 'Em, a player may use two, one, or no cards from his hand to form his best holding. Not so in Omaha. In Omaha, two cards *must be used from the hand.*

Novices often get mixed up in this game when they have to show their best hand. For example, suppose a player holds Ace♥ King♣ 2♥ 5♣, a good starting hand. The board on the river shows:

At first glance, it seems as though this player has a solid low, but he has no low at all. His 5, 2, and Ace were duplicated—or **counterfeited,** in Omaha parlance—and he can't produce two cards from his hand to form a low. OK, but what about a high? Those Aces up would be a strong hand in Hold 'Em, but with a lot of action on the river, they're not worth a bet. Why?

First of all, there are three spades on board, and any player holding two spades has a made flush. Even if no flush is out there, any player with a 4 and another **wheel card** (a card that can form a wheel—Ace-2-3-4-5) has the nuts as far as low. Let's say another player is holding 4-3. If he shows these cards, he combines his 4-3 with the board's Ace-2-5 for his wheel. That's a nut low hand, and it will be high as well if no one has the spade flush or a 6-4.

That's the problem with this game. It is in reality a nine-card game, with a bunch of possibilities or outs, and it's a game with wide swings in the fortunes of the players. A lot of luck is involved even after you have good cards to start with. In no other game does the river (last card on board) play such an important role. Here's an example of this. You start with Ace♠ 2♠ 3♥ 4♠—an outstanding group of cards, with the possibility of a nut flush and a nut low. The flop comes up:

You have two flop cards to your low, and you have two cards to your spade flush. You have a good chance to scoop the pot (win the whole pot). All you need is another low card, any low card, and a spade. Preferably a low spade.

The turn looks like this:

Well, you didn't get a low card but you did make the nut flush. And you still have a powerful drawing hand for low and the whole enchilada. The river comes up like this:

You missed your low, but you still have a spade flush, but is it the nuts? Not really. The pair of 5s can give someone a full house if he or she is holding a pair of 9s, Kings, or 6s in the hole, or, even better, four of a kind if he has a pair of 5s.

Now let's assume that this is a $6–$12 game, a common game of Omaha played in clubs or casinos, and the turn and river were bet till the bets were capped. That means on the first expensive street it cost you $48 and if you felt your flush would hold up, another $48. But you probably would be gone with any sense at all on the river. The hand is strictly a high one and from the action, your flush is a weak sister here. If you want to bet, bet that you're beaten.

These examples give you an idea of the pitfalls of this game. For the most part it's a drawing game, and it's not enough that the flop helps you somewhat. The board has to give you big help, a nut hand if possible, for you to have any confidence in your cards.

Another thing that differentiates Omaha from Hold 'Em is the **kill** feature. In a game where kills are in use, if anyone scoops the pot, the next hand is played for double the previous stakes. Thus, a $6–$12 game turns into a $12–$24 game, and this can involve a lot of money in a game like Omaha. Ask if there is a kill before you sit down to play this game. It's an important consideration and you want to make sure you have a sufficient bankroll in case there is a kill.

How the Game Is Played

The game is played similarly to Hold 'Em. There is a button signifying the imaginary dealer, who thus acts last. There are two blinds—in a $6–$12 game, the small blind is $2 and the big blind, $6. The blinds are live and can raise when it is their turn again to bet.

Each player is dealt four cards at the outset and keeps all four to determine his or her best possible hands. After each player has received four cards, the player to the left of the big blind must match the $6 bet or fold. Or he can raise. Only three raises are permitted on any round, unless just two players remain in the game, in which case the raises can be unlimited.

After the betting is finished, the dealer burns the top card and deals out three open cards, the flop. The betting level is the same as pre-flop—$6 and increments of $6. When that betting round is finished, another card is burned and the fourth street or turn card is dealt out. Now the betting is at the higher level of $12 and increments of that amount. When that round is finished, the next card is burned and the river card put out. Betting is again at the higher level. After all the bets are completed, the players turn over their cards to determine who has won low (if there's an 8 or better) and who has won high. If there are two winners, the pot is equally divided between them.

Sometimes the pot is divided among more than two players. If there are three players and two have tied for low, then the winner of the high hand gets one-half the pot, and the other two divide the low pot. They are said to have been **quartered,** since each gets one-quarter of the pot. And at times, the division can run deeper. If one player wins the high hand and shares the low hand with two other players, he gets half the pot for high and one-third of the low pot, leaving the two others with only one-sixth shares.

That's another factor in this game—you can win a share of the pot and yet lose money. If you get quartered, you barely win some money. If two players are going for low and both have the nuts, and constantly raise and reraise each other, all they're doing is making money for the high hand in with them. These factors must be considered when putting in raises.

To facilitate the division of the pot, as the rounds are played and bets are made, the dealer will constantly stack the checks in equal piles, especially if there is going to be a low on board. After the payments are made, the button is moved to the player to the left of the previous button, and a new deal commences.

Before the Flop

Position

As in Hold 'Em, position is important in Omaha. Because of the nine-card nature of the game, a player can't use position the way he can in Hold 'Em—that is, representing a big hand in late position and pounding and pounding till he drives out the other players. Sometimes this may work in Omaha, when there's only a one-way high hand, but when players are competing for low as well, it's awfully tough to bluff anyone out, especially if they feel they have the nuts or close to the nuts.

As with Hold 'Em, we'll divide the positions into three groups. The first is early position, the blinds and the player next to the big blind. Middle position consists of the next three players to the left, and then late position is the remaining three players, including the button, who is in the best and last position.

Playable Hands

Even more important than position is the quality of the starting or playable hands. As you shall see, the best starting hands are generally the low hands. High hands can only win one way (unless there's no low), but low hands have the power to win both ways, especially with a wheel. For purposes of our discussion, we'll call the 2-3-4-5 wheel cards.

The Nuts

Before we deal with the starting hands, let's say something about the nuts, the best possible hand. Unlike Hold 'Em, where the nut hand at the river will take the whole pot, and where it's possible to have an unbeatable full house, flush, straight, or even trips, nut hands, especially low hands, are often split. And it's rather difficult to know just when you have the best high hand. There will be rare times when this is apparent, but there are four hidden cards in each opponent's hand, and that makes the idea of a nut high hand guesswork at times, or intuition at other times.

For example, whenever there's a pair on board, a full house is possible and sometimes even four-of-a-kind hands, known as **quads**. If there is a flush draw out there and you hold King-x of that suit, you have to fear the Ace-x of the same suit. Aces are extremely powerful and desired in Omaha, because of their low and high values. They must be respected when held by other players.

About the only time you can know you have the nuts is holding Ace-2 with a low completely formed and without the Ace or 2 being counterfeited. But you may have to split the low end of the pot with another Ace-2. As to high hands, you have to hope you have enough power to overwhelm your opposition.

Starting Playable Hands

The Best Hands to Play

When discussing the best hands to play, as well as all starting hands, we're going to look at the four cards held by the player in terms of their ability to make various types of hands, including wheels, and other kinds of nut hands, such as flushes, straights and lows. We do this because of the unique nature of Omaha, where we are dealt four cards at the outset, but must use two of these cards for high and two for low. It thus becomes important for the player to know exactly what possibilities various holdings offer him before deciding to play any particular hand.

These hands can be played from any position. Because of their strength, you don't necessarily want to force anyone out with an early raise, for they don't go down in value with multiway hands, the way Aces do in Hold 'Em.

Ace-2-3-4. The Ace should be suited with one or more wheel cards. This hand has the potential to make a wheel, a nut flush, or a nut low.

Ace-Ace-2-3. One of the Aces should be suited with the 2 or 3. This hand can make Aces full, a nut flush, and a wheel.

Ace-King-2-3. The Ace should be suited with a wheel card, and better still, the King should be suited with the Ace, 2, or 3. The power of this hand is that it can make a wheel, a nut flush, and a nut straight, and there is a possibility of holding the two top pairs.

Ace-King-2-5. The Ace should be suited with a wheel card. The hand can make a wheel, a nut flush, and a nut straight.

Ace-Queen-2-4, The same situation.

Ace-Jack-2-3. The same situation.

Ace-2-3-x The x stands for any card 9 or above. The Ace here should be suited with any one of the other cards. The hand has the potential to make a wheel, a nut low, and a nut flush.

Strong Hands

These hands can be played in any position, but in early position I'd merely call a raise. In middle position or late position I'd raise with them if mine would be the first raise.

Ace-2 with a pair. The Ace should be suited with the deuce. This hand gives us a possible nut low, a nut flush, and chances for trips or a full house.

Ace-2 with two other low cards, such as Ace-2-6-7, with the Ace suited with another card. This hand gives us the chance for a nut low, a nut flush, and a wheel.

Ace-3 with any other cards, but the Ace is suited with another card. Without the deuce, we hope for a deuce on the flop to give us a nut low. A nut flush is a possibility here.

2-3 with two other low cards. We are looking for the Ace on the flop; otherwise it is dangerous to continue playing. With an Ace that may counterfeit another player's hand, we have a good shot at the wheel and nut low.

Aces and Kings, suited, as well as Kings and Queens and Kings and Jacks, also suited. We have a good shot at a full house here and a nut flush and straight with the Ace holding. The other pairs give us a full house potential and a chance to make the second best straight or flush, unless an Ace comes on board. Then we have the top straight and/or flush possibilities.

Ace-King-Queen-Jack, Ace-King-Queen-10, Ace-King-Jack-10, and Ace-Queen-Jack-10, with the Ace and another card suited. We have possibilities of nut straights and flushes with these hands.

Borderline Hands

These hands should be played only in late position and against only a single raise. If the pot has been double-raised, muck them.

King with three wheel cards, where the King is suited with a wheel card, such as King-2-3-4 (best) or King-2-4-5. There is a flush possibility here (second best) and a low straight. An Ace is needed on the flop to continue for low.

A hand with four cards lower than a 7, but where there is no Ace-2 or 2-3, such as 2-4-5-6. Without the nut low, this is a dangerous holding.

A big pair, such as King-King, with big cards, such as Queen-Jack and Queen-10, where the King is suited to another card. There is no Ace in this hand, and thus there can't be a nut straight or flush without an Ace on board.

I have left out Ace-2 unsuited with two odd cards that can't help. Often the Ace or 2 is counterfeited, (duplicated on the board) and without any other low card, the nut low is gone. There is also no outs for high in a hand like Ace♠ 2♦ 9♦ Jack♥.

I realize that it is difficult to memorize all these playable hands, and so I suggest that when you are dealt a hand in Omaha, see how the four cards mesh. Omaha, because of the nine-card factor, is a game where you should be looking for the nuts. If your starting hand will give you second- or third-best low, or second- or third-best high hand of whatever kind, then it pays to pass. You'll end up saving money in the long run. You must be patient and play only the strong cards suggested. With four cards in your hand, it will be tempting at times to look at a 6♦ 6♥ 10♣ 8♦ and figure that you have two to a low and a pair of sixes that might give you trips or a full house, but your low is awful, and the 6s are weak cards.

If you get a straight with this hand, it will probably

be a second- or third-best straight. Just how many checks will you put out to see if somehow you have the best straight? Let's assume you see a board with straight possibilities:

And although you flopped the nut straight, by the river you have to worry about a full house or flush. With a lot of action on the river, you'll just be melting down your checks seeing the raises.

To familiarize yourself with playable starting hands, I suggest you practice at home by dealing out nine hands and playing them open, looking at an open board. See which hands do well; see why others consistently fail to bring home the bacon. After a while, instead of memorizing hands, you'll get a feel for those hands which work together, and those hands that are alive when it comes to scooping the pot.

The Flop

The flop will often determine what course you should take. If it doesn't help you, then you should muck your hand. Don't count on miracle Fourth and Fifth Street cards to carry you along to victory. Much more often than not, you'll get one good turn card and then be buried on the river. By the time you see the flop, you should have a good determination as to whether or not you have any chances to succeed and win either half or the whole pot.

Ideally, you want a flop that dovetails with your hand. A flop that doesn't is big trouble to you and your bankroll. You can start with great cards, but if the flop isn't a good fit, muck your cards. I can't repeat this advice often enough.

Now let's look at the various flops that can come up.

A High Flop

This flop will contain two or three cards 9 or above, such as:

If you're holding a low hand, such as Ace(s) 2(d) 3(s) 7(h), this flop doesn't fit in at all. You can't count on two running low cards, let alone two that will not counterfeit your cards. You have to muck your hand. The hand above is going to help someone holding a pair of Kings, Jacks, or 6s, or someone holding King-Jack or Queen-10. An Ace-Queen holding has only one card, the 10, that can give him the nut straight. Too much of an underdog here.

High Flop—Flush Possibilities

If there are two to any suit on the flop, there are flush possibilities. With three to a suit, there is a good probability that someone has flopped a flush.

A typical flop might be:

With this flop, you can easily muck a hand going for low, and any hand that would give you an inside straight possibility, such as 10♠ Jack♦ 4♦ 2♦. Let's assume you came in late with this hand with no pre-flop raise. It's a hand that can get you into trouble, because you don't have any big cards for a nut flush, and you need a 3-Ace to complete the low—that is, if you see two more low cards.

A good hand to hold would be Ace-x of spades, or two Kings or two 9s. With two 3s, you have two over-cards to worry about for trips, and if either the King or 9 pair, that's more trouble for you.

High Flop—Straight Possibilities

With a flop containing two or three to a straight, you don't want, as in Hold 'Em, to have the ignorant or low end of the straight. Let's assume that the flop comes up:

You hold 8♣ 7♣ 4♣ Ace♦. With your hand, you've flopped a straight, but how good is it? A player with the King-Queen has a nut straight at this point, and anyone holding a Queen has an open-ended draw at the straight and will also beat you. With any real action, you're probably sucking wind here and can let your cards go.

It would be different if you held King-Queen, of course, for then you have the nut straight and can bet aggressively on the flop. The whole idea of Omaha is having the nuts. Middling cards won't give you the nuts; that's why the Jack, 10, 9, 8, and 7 are cards you don't want to see in your hand when you're in the pot.

A Low Flop

A low flop is defined as any flop in which two of three cards are 8 or lower, such as:

To take advantage of the low part of this flop, ideally you should be holding the 3-Ace. If they're both clubs, your hand has the potential for not only a nut low but a nut flush. Another ideal holding would be 3-Ace together with a pair of Kings. You have the potential for a nut full house if the board pairs, and then it won't matter if there's a low or not.

If the final board is:

your full house is boss unless someone is holding four 4s, but you can't really worry about that. What will help you here is someone making a smaller full house or the nut club flush. Then you should get plenty of high action. If there is a player with a low, he can only get one-quarter of the pot, even if he has 3-Ace. Any other low holding on his part and you scoop the pot.

Players starting with a smaller pair than Kings are in trouble with the flop above. At best they'll have a hand like Queens up. The 4s are real roadblocks for their winning the pot.

Low Flop—Flush Possibilities

With this flop, two or three cards are 8 or lower, plus two of them, at least, are of the same suit. For example, this would be a representative flop:

Ideally, you should be holding the Ace-2 of hearts, which gives you not only the nut low draw, but the nut flush draw as well. A King-x holding in hearts will give you only a shot at the high end, unless the remaining two cards are above 9 and one is a heart. For you to be beaten, another player will have to have an Ace and another heart.

If you started with no hearts and don't have a low draw, with a hand such as Ace♠ King♠ 8♣ 8♦ your chances are slim to none of winning either way. You can muck this hand.

Low Flop—Straight Possibilities
With these kinds of flops, a wheel is usually the strongest possibility. For example, with a flop like:

it is best to figure on someone possibly holding a wheel. A player holding 6-3 is in an excellent spot, having flopped a straight that will beat a wheel for high. Even better would be 6-3-Ace, with the nut low and nut high straight. If you held 4♦ 2♠ 7♠ King♠, you have a shot at the spade flush, but you'll be second best against anyone holding Ace-x of spades. It will get expensive going after a flush that might not be the nuts. I'd wait for another hand. Your other hope is getting a 4 or 2 on the turn or river, but you'll have a low full house that also can be beaten. And you're over a 5:1 underdog to see a 4 or 2 in the next two cards.

A Pair on the Flop
Whenever a pair shows on the flop, players going for flushes and straights have to be aware that they're in jeopardy because of the possibility of a full house. A pair can also destroy the chances of any low hands,

no matter how low the pair is. For example, a flop like:

And you should be gone if you just have a low hand. Because players hold low cards for the most part, it's entirely possible that someone is holding the third 3, and already has trips. If you're holding a pair and it's not a 9, you have to proceed with caution here. This flop hasn't helped anyone going for a straight either. There's a flush draw in spades as a result of the flop, but that pair is awfully scary.

Other Flop Considerations

Once you see the flop, you have to decide whether to continue or not. *First of all, you should see if the flop meshes with your hand.* If it doesn't, then there is no reason to continue. If you are going for low, and it's a high flop, give up your hand. If you hold a pair of Queens and the flop shows a pair of Kings or Aces, give it up. If you're going for high and it looks as if a wheel is probable and you can't beat it, muck your cards.

The second consideration is—will you have the nuts? I have tried to stress the importance of having the nuts in Omaha. Coming in second or third best is going to put a big dent in your bankroll. If you're going for a flush, try and go for the Ace-high flush. If you're going for a straight, make sure it's the nut straight. If there's a pair on board and you have a full house, try and be going for the nut full house.

You won't always need the nuts, but you should be aware of the action at the table and who's in against you. Try and analyze the situation, just as you have to do in a game like Hold 'Em. Who's been raising, and from what position? Is the raiser aggressive or conservative? Be aware of what is happening in the game, be alert, and watch the action even when you're not contending for the pot.

After a while, you should be able to get a feeling as to which players will automatically raise with a Ace-2, and which will only raise with high hands. Keep watching the action at all times. Because of the nine-card aspect of Omaha, it's essential that you get some kind of fix on your opposition.

The third consideration is—are you going for half the pot or the whole thing? If you have a chance to scoop the pot, then you stay in, see the raises, and go to the river. It's a different situation if you can only win half the pot. Then you have to see if it's worth it, going all the way to the river, with two expensive streets coming up, to possibly win half the pot. To figure this out, you must again carefully review the betting, and try and put players on hands. Judging from the position and what the flop shows, is it likely someone or more than one player is going the same way as you? Or are they going the other way?

If you're going high, for example, and hold a pair of black Kings as well as 4♦ 2♥, and you see the following flop:

and there's a lot of action, you're probably looking at a made straight or wheel. Where are your Kings going? Even if you end up with trip Kings, you probably have a loser.

Finally, count the money in the pot. If it's a small pot and you don't have the nuts, what's the use of continuing? Or, if you have to draw out to win half a pot, with a chance of losing the whole thing, is it really worth staying in? Suppose you're heads-up in a $6–$12 game and there's $36 in the pot after the flop. You have a chance at half the pot, the high side.

Your opponent, you figure, is probably going for a low. He's raised before the flop, and you know him to raise if he has a chance at the nut low. There's an Ace out on the flop, and you have a pair of Queens. If the other player has an Ace, he'll have top pair even if he misses the low. Why stay in? Even if you check and call the remaining two bets, that's $24 you're putting into a pot to collect $42. It's just not worth it.

If you win pots, at least win big pots. Go in trying to scoop the pot, not limping in, checking and calling, with a vague hope of winning half a small pot. That's bad decision making and bad poker.

The Turn

On the turn, the fourth card on board will give you a better idea of your chances, especially if you have a pure drawing hand. You have to make an important decision here—whether to go all the way to the river. It depends not only on your cards but on your position at the table. If you're in late position, you have a distinct advantage, because now, on the first expensive street, players who have slowplayed powerful hands will try and get some real money into the pot.

If you have a couple of players behind you in a four-way game, and you're still drawing or uncertain as to whether you have the nut high or low, you leave yourself open to being raised and possibly reraised, so that you have to put in three bets to see the river. Before you do this, you should be pretty certain that you have a chance at the nuts, high or low, or possibly both ways.

For example, suppose you hand is:

You're in middle position, and there was no raise before the flop. Your best chance, you felt, was a nut diamond flush. You also have a good chance at a nut straight. The flop was:

You paired your 9 and now, with two diamonds out there, you have a good shot at the nut diamond flush. There is some action on the flop, and a player behind you raises. You and two other players see the raise. The turn looks like this:

An early position player bets, you and another player call, and the raiser on the flop raises again, and is promptly reraised by the first bettor. There is a call and now it's your turn. You assess the situation. You have a chance at a nut flush, and nine cards will do it for you. That would give you half the pot. However, you're troubled by the fourth player, who's been seeing the raises. What does he have? You put him on trips or two pairs, probably trips, looking for the board to pair up.

This means that you don't want to see a 3♦ or a 9♦. That gives you seven shots at the nut flush. And you have a nut straight working. A Queen or 7 does it for you. But that's only six more ways, because of the Queen♦ and 7♦. You have thirteen ways to get the nuts. There are forty-four cards that are unseen. You're just a little more than a 2:1 dog to win half the pot. As the bets are capped, assuming this to be a $6–$12 game, you calculate that there was $78 before the turn on the table, and your $48 would win half of a $270 pot if you had the nuts now.

And if you get the nuts on the river, then you'll make even more. You'll get two bets at least from the two players going for low. So it's a good bet, well worth seeing all those raises. A very aggressive player might even put in a raise. But you have no other outs, so you're content to let the others raise. Now you don't want the board to pair, but you want an odd diamond, a Queen, or a 7.

Calculating this way is calculating correctly. You put the players on hands, judging their holdings by their bets and raises. You figured that one player is also going for high. With trips he isn't raising, because he fears that you might already have a straight, and his cards aren't vying for the diamond flush. He needs that board paired. You also recognize what the nut draws are—your diamonds, Queen, or 7, and for your opponent, a pairing of the board.

The fact that an early player bet into the raiser tells you he probably has the nut low, as does the final raiser. Maybe one of them has another out, such as a low straight draw, holding Ace-2-7-4. Or maybe the final raiser has the Ace-2-7-5 and that's why he's been raising. He has a shot at the nut low and already has a straight.

Now the river card comes up.

That's an excellent card for you. It gives you the nut straight without its looking obvious. If it were a dia-

mond, then it would be apparent that you have a diamond flush. The player with trips is trapped now. The
holder of a straight and the nut low thinks he's getting
three-quarters of the pot. The bets are capped again.
You show your hand—you get half of a big pot.

The early position player held:

He ended up with trip Queens and figured he could
win three-quarters of the pot with his high and nut
low.

The player whom you feared had trips turns over:

Unless the board paired up, he was doomed. He
wasn't worried about the Queen that much, figuring
only a diamond would beat him. But he ended up
third for high—far off the pace after putting $114 into
the pot.

The final player turns over just what you put him
on:

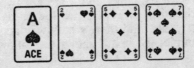

His straight gets him nothing for high. He gets quartered, tying for the nut low, and must share the low
payoff with the first player.

The first player, raising and reraising only to win

half of half a pot, should have let well enough alone when the 3♣ fell. He should have figured that there was another nut low out there. The last player, holding the straight as well as the nut low, had every right to raise and reraise. It was just bad luck for him that the Queen fell on the river.

You can see that Omaha, with all its complex possibilities, is a thinking man's game. If you want to play this game seriously, you must calculate. The weaker players, the losers, go in without making these computations. They'll stay in and take a few raises with hands that won't be the nuts even if they get what they want on the river. A few of these second-best losses are tough to make up. Sometimes, the best of players will come in second best, or won't draw out on the river. That's the nature of poker. But, if you intend to stay to the river, at least make sure you have a solid chance to win half the pot. Better still, try and play hands that can scoop.

You're in the driver's seat when you have the nut hand, especially the high hand, and you know the other players are either going for low or can't win high. In this situation you must get as many bets as you can in, building up the pot. No one is going out—they're stuck waiting for the river card or with a nut low, and will put more money into the pot. That's the way to build up a monster pot for yourself.

You can also play aggressively when you have chances to win both high and low if you get the right card on the river. Get your bets in if you hold an Ace-2 of hearts, for example, and there are two hearts on board at the turn, as well as two low cards that don't counterfeit yours, and there's multiway action.

For example, the board shows the following at the turn:

Someone may have a straight already, but if another heart shows, you have the nut flush. And if a small card, other than an Ace or deuce comes up, you have the nut low. If it's a 7-5-4-3 of hearts, there's a good chance that you can scoop the pot. These are the times to be aggressive.

The River

Because of the high-low nature of Omaha, the river is of extreme importance, because the board up to this point may be very seductive, offering scoop possibilities or a big payoff even if only half the pot is won. You can get stranded on its banks with nut-drawing possibilities, having to see that river card because the pot is so big and your cards are so promising. An example is Ace-2 suited with chances for a nut high and nut low, with two cards of the same suit out on the board, as well as two low uncounterfeited cards, as we saw in that last example on the turn. If some blank or rag comes up or the board pairs and your suit isn't on the river, you just have to take your beating.

If you've got the nut high on the river, and are in early position, against two players you figure are going low, don't try anything fancy like check-raising, especially if there are three low cards on board. Your opponents may be shrewd enough to figure that they both have the nut low, and they may check behind you, not wanting to lose money by having to bet and then having to call your raise. Go ahead and bet and force them to put money into the pot. You might get lucky and be raised by someone who isn't thinking clearly and figures his nut low won't be sliced up. Then you've got the other players where you want them.

On the other hand, if you have the nut low and are in late position, and an early position player has bet, you have to figure out the situation. If he came alive only after a third flush or straight card came out, you've got to put him on a high hand. If the other players in the game just call, and they are players who would stay in through hell and high water with the second-best low, then you should raise. You won't always know that you have the low locked up, but by this time you should have analyzed both the play of the hand and the opposition.

If you are last to act and there's been a bet and a raise, you may be stuck in there with someone else holding the nut low, and there's nothing you can do but call and see two more raises. And hope that both are going for high or that you don't have to split the nut low. If you have the wheel in addition to the nut low, then you should go ahead and raise. You may be sharing the nut high and nut low here, for half the pot, especially if no other high seems possible.

The important thing is to look over the board and see just what it holds. What is the nut high that is possible? What about the low? Is there a low? Just who woke up on the river and came out betting? What can he have? Pause a moment and look over the situation. Take your time. You don't want to make a quick foolish bet and then find yourself facing three raises because you didn't notice that the river card could have given someone a nut straight beating yours.

Sometimes the river card can make your hand by ruining your opposition's hands. Suppose you hold 3-Ace and the river is a 2. For those players counting on their nut low of Ace-2, this can be a devastating card, counterfeiting their deuce and destroying their low. When one or two players have been betting and raising and then suddenly stop on the river when that 2 shows up, your Ace-3 becomes boss.

Bluffing at the River

It's hard to bluff all the players out at the river, because they may feel that you're going in the opposite direction and their weak low or high will claim half the pot. Even if everyone checks to you, unless you have a chance at the pot, you don't want to bet and find yourself called by two opponents and end up feeding each of them half of your last bet.

Sometimes head-to-head against a tight player you can throw in a bet if a scare card comes on the river and he checks to you. For example, the board shows:

You've put him on a straight from the flop on. You end up with Jacks and 10s for the paired 9 didn't help you at all. Not only was it the third spade but it made your opponent think of the possibility of a full house in your hand. If you check after him, you're giving up the whole pot. You know he's tight and he's been betting till that spade 9 showed. Here I'd throw in a bet and put it to him. He has to make a decision, and he may just fold. This won't work against a weak loose player who will want to see your cards and hates to be bluffed.

And bluffing, as we mentioned before, is difficult against two players on the river. One of them may figure he's going in the opposite direction and will see your bet, hoping he guessed right. Bluffing works best against tight and tough players, who will respect your bet when they're head-to-head with you.

Since most players have a tendency to play low hands, there are situations where you can steal the pot against a player when the river card is a high card and you put him on a low hand all the way. For example, the board looks like this at the river:

You are in last position, behind the other player. You've put him on a low hand, possibly the nut low, holding Ace-2 all the way. He's bet on the flop and turn and you've called. You are also going for a low with Ace♦ 3♦ 4♠ 6♠, plus an outside shot at a spade flush with your 6-4.

Now your opponent checks to you. If you figured right, he's missed his low. You have nothing but Ace high, and would have to show your Ace-6 for high. If your opponent paired up or holds an Ace-7, you're beaten. So you go ahead and bet as though you're going high and can now claim the whole pot since your opponent missed his low. Many players just see their one-way hand miss and lose interest in the pot. In this situation, if your opponent has Ace-2-3-7, he'll probably muck his cards.

A Final Word

Omaha is a game that is basically played at limits of $3–$6, $4–8, and $6–$12. There are bigger games available, mostly in casinos like the Mirage in Las Vegas, where you can find games up to $20–$40. In a California club like the Commerce Club or Bicycle Club, there are usually one or two games going. It doesn't have anything near the popularity of Hold 'Em, for several reasons. First, many players don't like split-pot games. And it's a game where the restriction on using two cards from your hand makes it complicated, at times, to determine the eventual winner of the high and low hands.

Finally, even if you become quite good at the game, you will have trouble finding bigger games, unlike Hold 'Em where you can keep moving up as your skill improves. If you want to test your skills in this game, I'd suggest a smaller game, such as $3–$6 or $4–$8. Play only good cards and be patient. This is not a game for loose players holding weak cards. If you do find your niche in this game, it's a good money-maker, with a lot of action and many multiway pots, especially in the smaller games.

It's also a game with big swings in players' fortunes, in the course of an evening's play. Be sure that you have not only the bankroll but also the temperament to play Omaha–8 or Better.

XI

Crazy Pineapple—8 or Better Hi-Lo

Crazy Pineapple, or **Pineapple** as it is commonly called, is an offshoot of **Hold 'Em**. It is played for the most part in poker clubs, and the rules are slightly different from jurisdiction to jurisdiction. The rules we'll discuss are the standard in the California clubs.

The popularity of the game seems to be on the increase, and for the most part, the game is played for smaller stakes, such as $3–6, $4–$8, and $6–12. It is much closer to Hold 'Em than is **Omaha,** for, like Hold 'Em, a player may use both the cards from his hand or one card from his hand or can merely play the board to determine his best hand.

The main difference from Hold 'Em is that it's a high-low game, in which a hand must form five cards 8 or lower—thus the term "8 or better." In order for this to happen, at least three cards from the board must be 8 or better. All the other rules of Hold 'Em apply, as we shall see.

How the Game Is Played

The most common form of **Pineapple** is a nine-handed game, with a house dealer shuffling, cutting, and dealing the cards. A **button** signifies the imaginary dealer, and in the clubs, especially the Southern California clubs, the person holding the button antes for the table. In $3–$6 game, the ante would be $3.

There are two blinds in that same game; a $1, or

small blind and a $3, or **big blind**. If we assume a nine-handed game, and the small blind is to the left of the dealer in seat one, then the button would be in seat nine, to the right of the dealer. After the blinds put out their **checks**, the dealer shuffles the cards, cuts them himself, and then deals the first card to the small blind and continues dealing around the table till he has dealt a card to everyone at the table, including the button.

Then a second card is dealt in the same manner, then a third. Each player will have three cards at the outset, but one of these cards must be discarded or **mucked** after the **flop** is seen. But before this happens, there is a first round of betting. The player to the left of the big blind acts first, and must either match the $3 big blind, raise it, or fold. No one can check on the first round of betting.

Three raises are allowed on this round and on every subsequent round of play, except when only two players remain in the game. Then unlimited raises are permitted. The blinds are live—that is, when it is their turn to bet, they can raise or call any raises. Or they can fold.

Let's assume that seats three, four, and five folded, seat six raised to $6 (all raises at this time are in $3 increments and check and raise is allowed), and seat seven called the $6 raise as did seat eight and the button. The small blind folded and the big blind saw the raise also. Now we have five players remaining in the game.

The dealer burns a card and puts out three cards at once, face up. This is the flop, just as in Hold 'Em and Omaha. After this is put out, the big blind will act first. He can now check. In Pineapple, as in Hold 'Em, player's positions don't change throughout the course of betting in any round.

Let's assume the big blind checks, and player six bets and is called by players seven and the button, as well as the big blind. Now four players remain. At this point, each player mucks a card from his or her hand, leaving them each with two pocket cards.

The dealer again burns the top card off the deck, and deals the fourth card to the board. This is Fourth Street or the turn. Another round of betting ensues in the same order, but at double the previous bet. Now the betting and raising is in increments of $6. After this is completed, the dealer again burns a card and deals out the final or river card. The board is now complete.

The players now make their final bets. After these are complete, the participants turn over their cards to determine whether or not they've won high or low, or have scooped the pot and won high and low. Although the rules vary from club to club, there is a **kill** feature when the pot is scooped. In a $3–$6 game, if more than $40 was in the pot and one player won, he puts out $6 as a blind in addition to the small and big blinds in the next game, and it is played at $6–$12.

As the cards are dealt forming the board, if it appears that the pot will be split, the dealer stacks the checks evenly, preparing to give half to the best high hand and half to the best low hand.

As mentioned before, a player can use any combination of his hole cards and the board to form his best hand, either high or low or both, or he can play the board and not use any of his pocket cards at all. An instance of using the board would be the unusual one of:

In this case, nobody can have a low and no one can beat the board for high. Those players remaining for the showdown will split the pot evenly.

A more common situation with the same result would be a board like this:

Again, no one can beat the board, and the pot would be split evenly.

Before the Flop

Pineapple is similar to Hold 'Em in terms of the importance of position at the table. Since position never changes throughout the course of each game, where a player sits is sometimes of vital importance in terms of the cards he'll play or whether or not he'll get involved. The big difference between the two games is, of course, the three cards each player receives and the fact that a low of 8 or better is entitled to half the pot.

Since a pot may be split, it's important that you play for at least half the pot with cards that can win. The game gets too punishing if you contribute to pot after pot and don't collect. In order to avoid this, think of the nuts and where your hand is in relation to the nuts. To do this, you must analyze your cards in relation to the board, as well as the actions and skill factors of your opponents. Questions such as "Who raised?" "From what position did they raise?" "Is the raiser a tight or loose player?" and so forth should always be in your mind. Like Hold 'Em, an early raise in Pineapple from a strong, tight player is a warning signal. You need strong cards to overcome that player and you don't want to have weaker cards than he has.

For example, if you know the early raiser will only raise with a big pair or Ace-King, if you hold King-

10 unsuited, it doesn't pay to get involved. Even if a King shows on the flop, his Ace kicker may leave you sucking wind all the way. On the other hand, if you figure the early raiser is a loose, aggressive player, he could have a pair of 9s or 8s and push through that extra bet. In that case, your King-10 unsuited is worth holding to see the flop.

Position

For purposes of our discussion, we'll divide position into three distinct groups, early, middle, and late. The two blinds and the player to the immediate left of the big blind—that's early position. The fourth, fifth, and sixth players—middle position. The seventh and eighth players to act, plus the button—late position. Some hands that can be played from late position should be mucked from early or middle position. In late position, you have a good idea of the actions of four players plus the blinds. You can assume that the blinds don't have powerful hands. Sometimes they will, and will surprise you with a raise, but a random deal will usually give them garbage.

Playable Hands

Because of the 8-or-better low factor, hands that were just mediocre in Hold 'Em are rather strong in Pineapple. A good example would be Ace-2 s (s = suited). Not only can it give the holder the best low, the absolute nuts if not counterfeited (duplicated on board), but there's a chance for a nut high flush and a lesser probability of a wheel. In Hold 'Em it's a playable hand as well, but usually from a later position and without taking more than one raise. You don't lose much in Hold 'Em letting it go if there's a ton of action pre-flop.

So, to start our discussion of Pineapple, let's discuss playable hands, starting with the low hands.

Low Playable Hands

Low Hands with an Ace

The ideal hands to start with for low in Pineapple have at least an Ace. But an Ace, of course, is not sufficient. The best low hand would be: Ace-2-3 with at least the 2 or 3 suited with the Ace.

With this hand, and the right board, you are a big favorite for the nut low. You have three cards to the ideal low, and a possibility for the nut flush and a wheel. The value of three low cards is that it's going to be difficult for all three to be counterfeited. Even if one is counterfeited, you've got the other two working.

Suppose you hold Ace♦ 2♦ 3♣ and the flop is:

You simply muck the 2♦, with your Ace-3 giving you a shot at the nut low. Any 4, 5, 7, or 8 coming up and you've got the nut low. You don't want to see the 3 or Ace counterfeited, but even if the Ace shows, that gives you Aces and a chance for high.

Also quite strong is the Ace-2 with either a 4, 5, or 6 attached, with the Ace suited with one of the other cards. This gives you the nut low shot, as well as the nut flush, a wheel, and with the 6, the best high as well as low with the right board. For example, holding Ace♠ 2♣ 6♠ the flop comes up:

You muck the 2♣.

And then the board completes with:

You're going to share the nut low with another Ace, but that 6 will probably give you the nut high. With that kind of board, you push the action on the river as much as you can. Players won't be able to get away from their hands holding the Ace. You should win three-quarters of the pot unless someone is holding 6-7, a very unlikely starting hand in Pineapple.

The next low holding of Ace-2-3, none of them suited, severely restricts your high potential for it limits your chance for a high hand to the wheel, without a flush chance, unless by some miracle four cards of the Ace's suit show. You're not going to count on that, but on a low and possibly a wheel here. The fact that you hold the three lowest cards is a good protection against being counterfeited by the board.

An Ace-3 s as well as an Ace-4 s and Ace-5 s is weaker than the Ace-2 s but is stronger than the Ace-2 unsuited, because of the nut flush possibilities. We're assuming that the above hands come with a high card-x, that has no real value, such as Ace♠ 3♠ 9♦. Weaker is the Ace-3 to Ace-5 non-suited, because of the non-high factor as well as the weaker low potential. Of course, the Ace-3 is better than the Ace-4, which in turn is better than Ace-5.

To summarize the Ace situation: Ace-2 s with another wheel card is the best low hand to see the flop with, followed by the Ace-2 s by itself. Then comes the Ace-3 s and Ace-4 s. These last two holdings are best with another wheel card. The Ace-5 s is next best. These hands can be played from any position, and can be aggressively played. Ace-3 unsuited is better than the Ace-4 unsuited, which is probably not going to make any money for you. These hands can be played from middle position cheaply or from late position, taking one raise. Ace-5 unsuited is marginal at best and can be passed.

Low Hands Without an Ace

The best of these non-Ace hands would be 2-3-4, with at least two of the cards suited. Going for a flush with these cards, even if two of the same suit show on the flop, is a pretty fruitless venture. You're still a 2:1 dog at this point, and if you do get your flush, any other two-card holding of the same suit will beat you. So you can forget about the flush possibilities here.

A better chance would be a low straight, but then you need a flop that fits in well with your cards. For example, with the 2-3 of spades and 4♦ the flop is:

Using your 3-4, you have a wheel. Of course, with your holding, you wanted to see an Ace on the flop. Without the Ace, you're pretty much dead for a low.

Let's assume, with your same hand, you see the following flop:

Well, you have a low, but anyone with an Ace-2 or Ace-4 is going to beat you. And you can be pretty certain that someone is holding those cards, especially if there was any kind of raising action before the flop, and more raising on the flop.

Since it's extremely unlikely that you're going to hold 2-3 and 4 at one time, more logically, you'll have a 2-3-x or 2-4-x or 3-4-x. How strong are these cards for low? Again, the specter of a missing Ace hangs over these hands. I wouldn't play the 3-4 at all. The 2-4 is marginal at best. I'd come with the 2-3 in late position if I could see the flop cheaply. Then I'd want to see an Ace. If there's no Ace, I'm gone.

If there is an Ace and no counterfeited card, such as a flop of:

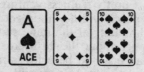

I've got a nut low, with a chance for a wheel. I'm in an excellent spot here.

But I must see the Ace on that flop.

Other low possibilities without the Ace showing will end up costing me a lot of money. I can't afford to go for low without an Ace, and there's no sense in hoping it'll show up on the turn or river, especially if I have to see a raise or two on the flop and may already be facing one or two players who are holding the nut low.

A lot of action on the flop with two low cards out there suggests that one or more players is holding an Ace. That means my chances of seeing an Ace on the turn or the river are greatly reduced.

As to any other holding, such as 2-5, 2-6, 3-5, 3-6, forget about them, suited or unsuited. Just as in Hold 'Em, they're just junk, and all you end up doing with them is throwing checks into the pot in a fruitless endeavor to win something. Unless you get a miracle flop, you're wasting your time and money.

High Playable Hands

Aces with a Wheel Card
Holding a pair of Aces along with a wheel card (2-5) gives you the best of all possible worlds in Pineap-

ple. You have a shot at high and a chance for a nut low, especially if you're holding Ace-Ace-2. Your hand gets even stronger if one of the Aces is suited with the deuce. Now, for high, you've got a chance with the Aces or with a nut flush. Plus you are in the running for the nut low. Of course, the lower the sidecard, the better your shot at low. A 2 is much better than a 5 in this situation.

Suppose you're holding Ace♦ Ace♣ 2♣ and the flop comes up:

This is a no-brainer. You muck the Ace♦, giving yourself a shot at the nut low and nut flush. You might as well play as aggressively as possible on the flop. You have a shot at the whole pot, becoming a "hogger," as they say.

On the other hand, if the flop came up:

you muck the deuce, and go with your Aces. You can still play aggressively here, with a good shot at the high hand. If you raise and are reraised, you might be looking at trips, and then you have to analyze the opponent before proceeding. It's awfully hard to get away from Aces—Doyle Brunson commented that he either won a small pot with them or lost a big pot with the same Aces.

With Aces you must try and thin out the field at the beginning and put in as many raises as you can pre-flop, particularly if the sidecard is a 4 or 5. With a 2 or 3, you might want to keep as many players in with you, given that you have two good shots at half the pot with a shot at the whole thing. Of course, you play these hands from any position and raise from any position.

As a general rule, with two small cards on the flop, you discard one of the Aces. With only one small card or none on the flop, or if your small card is counterfeited, you retain the Aces. Once you're going for high alone, your Aces become vulnerable to flushes, straights, and two-pair hands, especially if the board doesn't pair. An example of this kind of board, where you hold Ace♦ Ace♠, would be:

You're vulnerable to a heart flush and a straight and possibly two pairs, since players will hold Queen-Jack as a good straight possibility. The hearts are a long shot, since only one showed on the flop, but if there's a lot of action on the flop continuing to the river, you're probably beaten.

What you really want to see on the flop is two of the same suit as your suited Ace-3 for the nut flush shot, or an odd pair with only one low card to give your Aces their best chance. Or better still, two or three low cards, with two of them being in the same suit as your Ace-3.

High Pairs

High pairs are Aces down to Queens. With Aces, the sidecard, if not a wheel card, is not that important, although the higher the better, for sometimes a different hand than the one you're after can develop. For example, suppose you start with Ace♦ Ace♥ 10♠ and see the following flop:

You naturally discard one of the Aces (which one is immaterial) and start with a set of 10s. Naturally you'd like to hold all of your cards, for you have a full boat, but one Ace must go. Of course, any sidecard that gives you trips on the flop is a big fat bonus.

With Aces and a high sidecard (9-King), you naturally want to narrow the field, for Aces work best against few players. It may be hard to do with a few players going for low, but if you put in a raise or two, you should reduce the opposition. After all, the two Aces you hold limit the remaining Aces to just two floating around. If players are going for low with hands like 3-4 or 3-5, God bless them. They'll probably miss their low and open the way to just a high board, with you having the best chance to scoop the pot.

When you see the flop, you wouldn't mind a middling pair showing, such as 8s, 9s, or 10s, for few players will play middle cards and stand a raise or two to see the flop. They don't have a shot at the nut low and their high may be based on a straight. Other flops may hurt you, even an innocuous 5-3, for it may give someone two pairs, and if they guess that you have a big pair, they know they have a good shot at winning high unless the board pairs up.

In Hold 'Em it's common for players who flop two pairs, no matter how small, to raise on the flop and pray that the board doesn't pair with the cards they don't hold. For example, if the flop came up:

and a player held 6-7, he would immediately raise on the flop against what he perceives as a big pair, figuring that an early raiser held them or held something like Ace-King or Ace-Queen. So the flop helps him and not the raiser. But if the turn shows another 10, then he's in big trouble. Now he faces two pairs led by either Queens, Kings, or Aces. Of course, if a weak player checks to him or checks behind him, then he can put the opponent on Ace-King to Ace-Jack.

Kings are another strong pair, with only one overcard to fear, and that is the Ace on board. So your best King-King holding includes the Ace sidecard. King-King-Ace is formidable in that it takes away an Ace from the other players and makes the chances of someone holding two Aces against you something like like 15:1.

With King-King x (x = any card but an Ace or King) you still have a very strong hand, and Kings in Hold 'Em is an automatic raise from any position. I would also raise them in Pineapple from any position. The one card you fear is the Ace, and though it will come up on the flop about 20 percent of the time, four-fifths of the time it will not show.

As long as the flop looks safe, keep betting and keep raising. Such a flop might be:

And you hold King♠ King♥. There is an outside chance of a spade flush developing, and if two running spades come up you probably have the nut flush. But besides that, there are no straight chances and even if someone flops a pair of Queens, you can't figure him to hold Queen-9 or Queen-5, not after there's been one or two raises.

A dangerous flop would be two high consecutive

cards, such as Jack-Queen. Now you don't want to see another King, for it might give someone a high straight. You also don't want to see 2-4-5, for a wheel may already be in play. When there's been a lot of raising on the flop and you can't figure why, you might be facing a set. Again, you have to understand who's doing the raising. A loose player may be betting on the come, hoping for the flush or straight card to hit. A tight conservative player has his set. It's no crime to dump your hand in light of this player's bets if you don't get help on the turn. This is more true if two of the cards are low, for then you are only competing for half a pot. For example, with a flop like the following:

if a tight player raises you it probably means he has trips, probably a set of 10s. You can't put him on a straight, for he wouldn't go in with 7-9, and he's not the sort of player to raise with Ace-2. For one thing, he doesn't have the low completed, and for another, if another low card shows, he wants as many players in the pot as possible, so he wouldn't raise.

What I would do is call his raise, and see the turn. If I don't improve, I'm out of there. I wouldn't call an expensive bet hoping for a miracle on the river. You've got to study your opposition and study their moves and the board. In that way you won't be going to the river doomed to lose.

Queens are strong but the two overcards, Aces and Kings, lurk there in the shadows of the flop. The ideal holding when you have Queens is to have either an Ace or King to go along with them, and even better, to have a Queen suited with the big kicker. In middle or late position, if there has been no raise before me, I'd put in a raise pre-flop.

On the flop I don't care if there's an overcard if I'm holding the Queens with either a King or Ace. For example, if my hand is Queen♦ Queen♠ King♦ and the flop is:

I muck the Queen♠ and now have the Kings with a Queen kicker. Of course, if an Ace came on the flop with the same hand, I'd have to proceed cautiously and would probably muck the Queens if I don't get help on the turn. Depending on the opposition, I wouldn't wait to see the bets capped. If that happens, I'll give up the hand right there and then.

If there are no overcards and the flop seems innocuous enough, I'll lead in the betting or raise if there's been a previous bet. Such a flop would be:

If I'm holding a pair of Queens with x (x = any card lower than a Queen), I'd prefer a Jack or 10, for the straight possibility. With any card lower than a 10, I'm probably in for a rough ride to the river hoping my Queens hold up. If the flop shows an Ace or King, I won't like it, but I fear the Ace more than the King because of the low power of the Ace, which players will hold to see the flop, along with any other wheel card.

If there is three to a straight on the flop, I'd prefer a 7-8-9 to a 3-4-5, figuring players aren't going to hold 5-6 or 10-Jack as much as they will hold Ace-2. If there is a lot of raising on the flop with the 3-4-5 out,

I'll give up the Queens. I don't want to get trapped into putting out a lot of checks for a so-so high that can win only half the pot.

Medium Pairs

I would classify medium pairs as Jacks, 10s, and 9s. They are dangerous cards to play because the possibility of an overcard on the flop is so great, and even if you don't see the overcard there, you still have to run the gamut of the turn and river. The Ace is especially dangerous, for it probably gives one of your opponents Aces.

When holding these medium pairs, it's best to have an Ace as your kicker, and the Ace should be suited to one of the pairs you hold. If you have this combination, then you can see the flop from middle or late position and take a raise, hoping that the flop either gives you a set or shows you four to your flush. Having a King sidecard, I'd play the hand from late position only, taking one raise. Anything below a King, and I'd play these medium pairs only from late position, trying to get in as cheaply as possible.

In that situation, what you're basically looking for is trips. If you don't get them, except for certain hands, then you muck your pairs. An example would be staying with your black 10s, for example, if the flop shows:

There is no low and you have two ways to get your straight. Very few players will play a naked 10 to see the flop, so you have a good shot at taking the whole pot. Of course, it's not a nut straight if a Queen or even a 7 comes up on the turn or river, but it's worth going after.

The best hand to get a straight with, assuming a

terrific flop, is Jack-Jack-Queen. Then if you see the following flop:

you muck one of the Jacks and go for the straight. If you get it, whether with the King or the 8, it will be the nut straight. But when holding the medium pairs, with an indifferent sidecard, such as a wheel or low card, you're basically going for the trips. In this situation, get in cheaply from late position or release your cards.

The Smaller Pairs

Eights through 2s are the smaller pairs. They're pretty well useless in Hold 'Em unless a set develops on the flop. In Pineapple, unless there's an Ace kicker with the smaller pairs from 5s on down, there's no real chance for low and precious little chance for a high. You might want to see the flop in late position only, assuming you don't have an Ace kicker. If there is any action, including a raise, you are not losing anything by dumping these small pairs.

The Suited Connectors

These have some value in Hold 'Em, particularly in late position, but in Pineapple, I wouldn't play them unless I had an Ace kicker and an out for the nut flush. For example, 6♥ 7♥ Ace♥ is playable without too much action pre-flop, but 6♦ 7♦ 10♠ is pretty much a worthless hand. A 2-3 suited in late position is playable, but the Ace has to show on the flop to continue. Getting rid of the 2♠ 3♠ is not a mistake against a lot of action pre-flop. In middle position, if you feel that you can get in cheaply, knowing there are conservative players behind you, you can take a shot with these cards.

With the bigger suited connectors, from 10-Jack to Queen-King (we'll discuss Ace-King **s** in another section), you have a chance for a straight or a flush. If the sidecard is one rank higher, then you have a much better starting hand. For example, 10♠ Jack♠ Queen♥ gives you much more leverage than the 10 and Jack alone.

Suppose you see this flop:

Even though the 10 was counterfeited, you can throw it away and go for the nut straight here. You're about a 2.3:1 dog to get it, and so you want as much multiway action as you can get. You want to go all the way with this hand, because there is no other danger, unless the board pairs up, or two running spades, hearts, or diamonds show.

With the big suited connectors, you have flush and straight possibilities, but you will always prefer the straight, since it gives you the nuts. The flush will be strong, but the Ace of that suit won't be in your hand, and that is the nut card.

Ace-King, Ace-Queen, Ace-Jack, and Ace-10 Hands

The best of these hands is the Ace-King **s**. If your sidecard is a 2 or 3, that makes the hand so much better and gives you leeway on the flop. For example, suppose you're in late position, and a player raised from early position. You know this player to be tight. He probably has a big pair—Aces or Kings—or maybe he has the same hand you have, Ace-King **s**. The flop reveals:

What do you discard, if the raiser comes out betting? He might have trip Queens, or perhaps Queens with an Ace kicker. That's one less Ace for you to get. Here I'd switch to a low hand, and dump the King. Your best shot is to get the nut low.

But suppose with the Ace♦ King♦ your kicker is a 10♠. Then you missed the flop and should muck your cards if you have to face two raises. Even though you have two overcards to the Queen, you have no other outs. It would be different if two diamonds showed on the flop. Then you should go all the way to the river for the nut flush, and hope, if an Ace or King comes up, that you have top pair for high as well.

If the final board shows:

and there's no action at all, in late position, with your Ace-King, you can throw in a bet if you're aggressive. You probably have the high locked up.

With an Ace-King, suited or unsuited, and an indifferent sidecard, you're looking for high pair on the flop, just as in Hold 'Em. In Hold 'Em this holding is a good raise from any position, for it usually drives out other Ace-x hole cards, such as Ace-3 unsuited, but not in Pineapple. No one's throwing those cards away before seeing the flop. Since an early raise isn't knocking out the Ace-wheel card holdings, I'd raise only if I had Ace-King with a 2-5 kicker, suited with the Ace or King, preferably with the Ace. With an ordinary Ace-King, suited or unsuited, I'd call a raise from any position, and if there was little action, such as two callers of the big blind, I'd put in a raise with any Ace-King holding from late position.

What you're looking for with this holding is help on the flop in the way of the top pair, with the top kicker. For example, if you get Kings, you have the Ace kicker, and if you have Aces, you have the King kicker. With Ace♦ King♣ you'd rather see this flop:

than this:

With both flops, low players are going to stay in. With the latter flop, someone probably has made his or her low, and you'll definitely be splitting the pot with a low. But it's more likely that anyone holding a low containing an Ace has already flopped two pairs. Suppose someone is holding Ace♥ 2♣ Jack♥. The logical muck card is the Jack♥. Someone else, with two low cards, has a shot at a wheel. Just having the Aces isn't going to do you much good if you face a lot of action on the flop.

Again, if you're not helped on the flop with your Ace-King, suited or unsuited, muck your hole cards. If you go for the pair on the turn after seeing a flop like:

you have only six ways to get a King or Ace and forty-six cards to do it with. That's over 6.6:1 against you.

And it's 3.3:1 against your getting it on the river as well as the turn. And if a King does come up with the above flop, you may be looking at a completed nut straight, so in essence, you might be drawing dead. That you never want to do in any poker game.

Suppose you come in with Ace-King **s** in clubs, and raise in late position. The flop comes up:

There are three players in the pot; seat one, seat five, and yourself on the button. They both check to you and you bet. Seat one calls and seat five now comes in with a check-raise. What do you do? Well, you should analyze the situation before acting. Obviously no one has made a low yet. You have seen the player in seat five play solidly and aggressively. He must know you probably made top pair and yet he's check-raising you. You could put in another raise, representing trip Kings, and give him a hard call.

But if you had a set, why reraise back now? Why not wait for the turn, when, if he raises, you put in a reraise? Or if he checked, you'd bet. But you have to put him on either trips or two pairs here. And he won't be releasing them if the board gets two rags. In this case, I wouldn't be stubborn. I'd fold the hand.

With an Ace-Queen, suited or unsuited, we'd want to see a wheel card as the kicker before the flop comes. Then we have a choice of high or low, especially if the wheel card (2-5) is suited to the Ace. Otherwise, with an indifferent card x, such as Ace♠ Queen♥ 8♣, we don't have much of a starting hand. In Hold 'Em, many players from middle and late position will raise with the Ace-Queen to "protect their ace." But in Pineapple, with its split pots, this holding isn't that strong. You only get a flush about 3 percent of the time, and the flop, even though it may help you slightly, may be a brewing pot for big trouble.

Let's assume you hold Ace♦ Queen♣ 6♦ and see the following flop:

You may be up against a formed straight already, and there are two spades out there as well. Against a lot of action on the flop, you have to consider dumping your hand. The King will give you the nut straight, but that's only four chances out of forty-six cards. You won't be getting that amount in the pot for your bet, and certainly, as the raises come in, they punish you even more for your desperate try.

With Ace-Queen, suited or unsuited, I would play them in a tight game from any position, but in a wild, aggressive game, I'd only play them from late position, again cheaply, just to see the flop. If I miss, or the flop looks too scary, I muck the hand. Needless to say, I'm not in love with these cards in Pineapple. I'd take one raise and that's it from late position. If I can get in that way, I see the flop. If not, I pass these cards into the muck pile.

The Ace-Jack, suited or unsuited, with a wheel card is playable, like the other Ace hands from any position. But if the kicker is an indifferent card such as a 9, then you want to see the flop as cheaply as you can, and the only way to guarantee this is to play the hand from late position. There's not much future with an Ace-Jack if there's been an early raise. Then you have to worry about someone holding Ace-King or Aces or Kings, and your hand has turned to garbage at that point.

I would try and play the Ace-Jack s only from late

position, taking but one raise. And I have to be helped on the flop to continue. I wouldn't mind a flop like:

I still have the high kicker, and hope that someone in with an Ace counterfeits one of his low cards so that, if an Ace comes up on the turn or river, he has Aces up, but I have the bigger second pair. For example, an opponent with Ace♦ 3♥ is going all the way for low. An Ace comes up on the turn. He is staying in for his low, and figures his Aces will give him an out for high. The river card is a 3♠ and now he'll stay in for high with Aces up and end up paying you off.

Ace-10, suited or unsuited, is weaker than the Ace-Jack, and much weaker than the Ace-King. One of the raps against this holding is that it forms both ends of a straight, the way a King-9 does. On the other hand, the straight will be the nuts.

If you flop an Ace, you are in danger of being out-kickered by another Ace holding with the Jack, Queen, or King. And if you are dealt a 10 on the flop, three-quarters of the time you'll be beaten by a higher pair, lose to a straight, or be looking at a bigger overcard by the time you see the river.

What you want to do with this holding is come in from a late position with the Ace-10 suited. Nonsuited, with any raise I'd let it go. Therefore, it's best playable from a late position to deter the chances of being raised. If you only play the Ace-10 s from late position, and hope to get a great flop, such as an Ace and 10, or trips, or two more of the suit, you're in good shape with this holding.

Otherwise, even if you pair the 10 or the Ace alone, proceed with caution. There are too many ways to get beaten with these cards. And you're fighting, in essence, much of the time for only half the pot.

Other Possible Playing Hands

Because of the high-low nature of Pineapple and the dangers of being whiplashed by raises from potential nut highs and lows (or worse still, completed nut highs and lows), you should be supercareful about playing hands that you might try in Hold 'Em, such as Queen-10 or Jack 9 suited or unsuited. These are basically losers, and you don't want to risk money on them unless you get in from late position without any raises. With an early raise, you might be facing the kinds of hands that will make bigger flushes or bigger straights.

King-Queen, Queen-Jack, and Jack-10, all unsuited, have some value for a straight and a possible high pair, but you want to get in with no more than one raise to see the flop. Maybe two raises with the King-Queen, but the other hands aren't worth two raises. They're best played cheaply from late position. 10-9 unsuited I'd muck every time I saw them in the hole. We're assuming that the kicker is an indifferent card like a 6.

The best situation is to have three consecutive cards to see the flop with—for example, King-Queen-Jack or Queen-Jack-10, even unsuited, though if two were suited, they'd be that much stronger. Then I'd come in from any position to see the flop. Any flop in the same range and I have a lot of leverage. For example, let's say with King♠ Queen♠ Jack♠ I see a flop like:

I have a flush draw and a shot at a straight. I wouldn't raise here, for I want as many players as possible in with me. If someone holds the Ace-x of spades I won't get them out anyway. What I want is a straight rather than a flush. An 8 on the turn would be perfect, because someone with Ace-2 might stay in for the nut low. Thus, on the turn and the river I can pound in the raises.

King-Jack s is a playable hand late without much action, as is King-Jack unsuited. But you must get in cheaply with these hands. An early raise might doom your hand even if you get help on the flop. For example, if you hold King♥ Jack♥ and the flop is:

and the raiser from an early position bets into the flop, he probably has paired the Kings as you did, but his kicker is going to be higher than yours, and you'll be chasing all the way. That's why you have to get in cheaply with these hands from a middle, and better yet, a late position so that you can be somewhat secure if the King flops. Of course, if the Jack flops, then you have to fear the Ace, which you can bet one or more players is holding. The Queen is a card you don't want to see either, but it's not as scary as the Ace.

If the flop is:

and there's a lot of action on the flop, if you're holding King-Jack of diamonds, you can continue, having the best pair on board. If a small card comes up on the turn or river, you'd prefer an 8 or 7, to negate the possibility of a wheel beating you for high. The Jacks might very well hold up to the end if there is no straight or flush out there, or the board paired with 8s or 7s.

King-10 **s** is a borderline hand, and I wouldn't bother with King-10 unless I wanted to gamble in late position without a raise. If I pair the 10 on the board, I still have to worry about a bunch of overcards, as well as a straight showing up and I have to sweat the hand out to the river. Better to play stronger cards at a different time.

Queen-9, suited or unsuited, can be passed. The trouble with hands like this is the low nature of Pineapple, which encourages players to hold onto an Ace for low, and makes the possibility of someone pairing the Ace that much more likely. And with any of the hands mentioned in this section, where there's a shot at a straight as well as high pair, if the board pairs on the flop, and there's a lot of action, be aware that you may be facing trips. Some opponent who came in with Ace-3-8 might get lucky if he sees a flop like:

And you're sucking wind with your Queen-Jack of clubs.

The Flop

The flop is going to determine the course of your future play of the hand. Sometimes it will help you, other times it will end your hopes of winning any part of the pot then and there. And sometimes it will force you to make a decision; whether or not to go low or high.

Let's suppose you start off with the following hand: Ace♠ 3♣ 10♦. You have a shot at low and want to see the deuce on the flop, along with another low card. Instead you see:

You simply muck your hand. Only a sucker goes for two running low cards, especially if the 2 hasn't shown up on the flop. Even with a 2, you are nowhere. Continuing to play is a sure way to destroy your cache of checks.

Or you hold King♦ King♣ Queen♥ and see the following flop:

Well, you have the nut club flush if two running clubs come up on the turn and river. But you have to be self-destructive to hope for that. The Ace has probably paired someone, so you'll be chasing all the way with your Kings. In essence, you have no real shot at high, and low was never an option. Muck your hand against action on the flop.

Let's assume you hold: Ace♣ 3♣ 7♦ and the flop comes up:

Now you have the shot at a nut low and a nut flush. You muck the 7♦ and play aggressively all the way. If a low club comes up on the turn or river, you have the whole thing. This is the time to build a big pot for yourself.

But suppose that you are holding Ace♣ 3♦ 7♣ and you see this flop:

Do you go for the nut flush or for the low? There are nine clubs out of forty-six unseen cards. If any one of them shows on the turn or the river, you have the nut flush. Of course, if a 4♣ shows and pairs the board, it might give someone a full house.

Now, what about the low? There are eighteen cards that will give you a low. That's four 2s, four 5s, four 6s, three 7s, and three 8s. But unless a deuce comes on board, you won't have the nut low, just the second best, or **second nut**. If another small card, other than the 2, completes your low, and an opponent is holding Ace-2, you're essentially drawing dead.

Still, you're almost even money to get the low at this point, and 2.5:1 against getting the nut flush. In this case, I'd take a deep breath and get rid of the 7♣. I'd play the percentages and hope that my low is the nuts. It's not like I'm counting on an Ace-4 or Ace-5—I'll have the second nut, the Ace-3. Of course, if I had to get rid of a card before seeing the flop, it would be a no-brainer—the 7♣ gets mucked immediately.

Any time I'd have a two-way hand, contending for high and low, I'd play aggressively on the flop and raise or reraise. If I had a high hand, such as high pair, with help from the flop, and outside possibilities of straights or flushes out on the flop, I'd again play aggressively. I want to make it expensive for my opponents to draw to their hand. If there's a raise to me and I reraise, it might discourage someone from a **cold call** (calling two bets without having previously bet).

However, if I had no help from the flop, I'd be more careful, even if I went in with a big pair. Suppose I started with King♠ King♦. I raised from middle position and there were three callers, one in front of me and two behind. The flop comes up:

An early position player bets, the previous caller folds, and now it's up to me. My Kings are still the high pair, but that 8-7 might mean that someone behind me has a 6-5 and is going after a straight. Or someone behind me has a 9-10, and saw the flop with a holding like 9♠ 10♠ Ace♠. Now he'll muck the Ace because he has little chance of completing the flush, while his four-straight is alive and well.

But what about the early bettor? If he has a nut low, he wouldn't want to scare out anyone else going for the low. Let's assume he's a tough player. What could he have started with in early position? Perhaps he had an Ace-3, or perhaps an Ace-8-8, with one of the 8s suited to the Ace. Or the same situation with the 7s. Or perhaps he has Ace-2, and figured I'd started with Ace-King or Ace-Queen and put in a raise with those cards.

I miss on the flop. My Kings are still boss, but do I want to reraise now, with the intention of forcing out the players behind me, and face another raise from someone holding trips? And what if I raise and am reraised behind me? Then I might as well muck the cards. I'm not going to see the raises capped without any help from a flop that seems to have helped two other players.

I'm showing a difficult situation for a player. It's always tough when an early position player bets on the flop or check-raises on the flop. His early bet here may have come with trips, figuring that, if he checked, I wouldn't have been helped by the flop and might check behind him, and everyone would get a free card.

Since I wasn't helped by the flop, I'll call the bet, but if there's a raise behind me, and then the original bettor reraises, I muck my cards. I don't want to be trapped between two raisers. My chances of improving the

Kings are 6.6:1 on the turn. If the board pairs, I might be looking at a full house. If even a 4 or Jack comes on the turn, someone might have completed a straight. My high pair is hanging in the wind here. I'd rather go out after analyzing the situation and have it be a mistake than stubbornly hang in there, only to wind up second or third best after expending a ton of checks.

In Hold 'Em you either have a made hand or a big draw if you're helped by the flop. If you get action, you weigh your options. Is it worth staying in for the flush? Are enough players in? Is there sufficient money in the pot? Everyone is going the same way, for high. In Pineapple, there are other considerations. Who represents a low hand and who a high hand? And how strong is my hand against a lot of action? Have I been helped sufficiently by the flop to stay in against a bunch of raisers? And finally, which card do I muck in certain situations? Do I go for high or for low?

Sometimes the answers to these questions are not easy. That's when you have to analyze just what is happening. You won't always be right, but it's better not to chase or be trapped. Get out cheaply if you're unsure of the strength of your cards relative to the other players' holdings.

The Turn

By Fourth Street, you have a much better feel for your hand, judging by your hole cards and the action before and on the flop. Generally speaking, if no low can be completed by what the flop shows, the raises have probably come from those players holding a high hand, or players having a big draw with the possibilities of going high and low. Players with a nut low potential generally don't show their strength till they are able to complete their low or on the expensive streets, the turn being the first of these streets.

You've mucked your odd card by the end of betting on the flop, and now are playing the two cards you selected. The turn, like the flop, can give you a pleasant or unpleasant surprise. Or it can be neutral. By this time you have a shot at either the low or high, or both ways. Otherwise, why are you staying in the pot?

Because of your cards and the potential for the nuts, you may be forced to see the river even though you don't yet have a complete hand. Either you'll win an enormous pot or you'll be contributing to the monster pot. For example, you are holding Ace♠ 2♠ and the board on the turn shows:

You have a shot at both the nut low and the nut flush. Any odd low card that doesn't counterfeit yours will give you the nut low; any spade that doesn't pair the board will guarantee you the nut high, and a low spade gives you the whole pot.

Many times the game comes down to the river. You want to stay in when you have an absolute shot at the nuts, either high, low, or the whole hog. On the other hand, you don't want to stay in for miracles if the pot odds don't warrant it. Count the money in the pot, calculate your odds of winning, and how much of the pot you will win. If it all doesn't add up in your favor, muck the cards. You're now on the expensive street, and it's here, where players are more certain of their hands, that they'll bleed you dry with raises and reraises.

The River

The river card will give you complete information on what you have, and should also give you some information on whether or not your opponents have benefited from the final board. For example, let's say you are holding Ace♠ King♠, and the board looks like this at the river:

You're in late position and two players have checked to you. The low didn't complete, falling one short. The two possible flushes didn't complete either. The 8s pairing on the river isn't that much of a threat to you, because that's not a card players will retain, unless they have a pair in the hole. There hasn't been much action except for your bets on the turn, and calls by two other players. If someone had trip 8s, you would have been check-raised on the turn. And if someone held an 8 in the hole, you would have heard from them on the river. After all, with trip 8s, a player would like to get a call by weaker high hands.

So you can bet in this situation. Your Kings should hold up. The two players in against you might think that an Ace will hold up for high, and one of them might call. That's an extra bet for you. And one of your opponents may be stubborn enough to call with anything, figuring you missed as well. Extra bets add up.

If the river presents a scare card against you, then you have to think about saving bets yourself. For example, say you are holding the Ace♦ King♦ in late position against two players and the board looks like this:

An early position player who bet on the turn comes out betting on the river. You figure him for a completed low. The middle player, who's been calling all the way, suddenly puts in a raise. You have top pair, but that Queen♣ is a very disturbing card for you. It could have given the raiser a flush, and less likely, a straight. Or perhaps trip Queens, but that might be unlikely, with the Ace on board. Why chase with a pair of pocket Queens?

All you have are Aces. Maybe you can be bluffed out here. In Hold 'Em, with only a high hand winning, you'd probably see only one raise, but now you're faced with three raises, boxed in as you are between a high and a low hand. It's wise to give up your hand. You aren't going to win with just Aces after that third club showed its ugly head.

A Final Word

Pineapple is becoming more and more popular and has attracted a large number of players who feel that it is more exciting than Hold 'Em, with much more action and bigger pots. Although pots are split a great deal of the time, when a player can grab the whole thing either by winning high when there is no low, or winning high and low, the checks he wins can be considerable.

I've watched a number of games in the clubs and noticed that most players didn't really know how to play the game correctly. Their most glaring fault was twofold; Starting with hands that were weak, and lingering in pots where it became apparent from the board and betting that they were going to come in second or third. And many didn't understand the power of a hand that could go both ways.

If you start with the strong hands I have recommended, play aggressively when you can trap other players into staying in and when you have a decent shot at the whole pot. And finally, when you analyze the individual game you're in so that you either save checks by mucking your cards in hopeless situations or get in extra bets when you have the lead, you'll find this a fertile game in which to make some serious money.

XII

Draw Poker Loball—Ace to 5 (Loball Draw)

Draw poker used to be the main staple of the California clubs when Gardenia was in full bloom in Southern California. The games were either loball or high, all played with a **joker** or **bug.** And all the games were dealt by the players themselves. The reason for this was simple—California law mandated that only draw poker games were to be played, and that no dealers were permitted. The clubs were there for the players, and the players ran their own games. The clubs charged rental fees and that's how they existed.

Then the law changed, and all forms of poker were permitted, and no longer could players deal their own cards. The clubs hired professional dealers, and the stud games, and particularly **Texas Hold 'Em,** took hold and flourished. One would be hard-pressed to find a draw poker game anymore, though there are casinos which feature one or two games, basically **Loball—Ace to 5**. From now on, we'll refer to this game as **Loball Draw**.

Unlike the games we've discussed previously, there are only two betting rounds in Loball Draw. There is a bet before the draw, and one after the draw, at double the previous bets. For example, in a $3–$6 game, the betting and raising prior to the draw is in increments of $3; after the draw, it's in increments of $6. Players can draw cards after the initial round of betting. A player must discard a card or cards to draw an equal number of cards. For example, if a player discards one card, he is dealt one; if he discards two, he gets two, and so forth.

The object in this game is to have the lowest possible hand, which wins the pot. Straights and flushes do not penalize the low, and thus a hand like

is merely a 7-5 low. Low hands are called according to the two highest cards in the hand. Another example would be:

which is a 6-5 low. If another player also holds a 6-5, then the third card is examined, and if it's a tie, the fourth, and so on. Thus, a hand like:

will beat the above 6-5, because the Ace in the second hand is lower than the deuce in the first.

The game is played with a joker, known as a bug, which is the fifty-third card in the deck. The bug is used by any player holding it as his best possible low card. For example, if you hold:

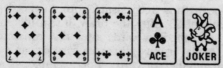

the joker is considered a 2, the lowest possible odd card in your hand. The joker is extremely valuable in this game, because not only is it the lowest odd card in your hand, but it can't duplicate any other odd card. And of course, if you hold the bug, no one else possesses it.

The joker, though important, is not stronger than any other card. Thus, if one player holds:

and another player has:

the two players tie for low, each with an 8-5.

Low hands can be smooth or rough. When describing a holding, a player may refer to a **smooth 7**. Such a hand would be 7-4-3-2-Ace, which could also be called **the smoothest 7,** since no one else holding a 7-high can beat it. It can be tied, but not beaten. On the other hand, a **rough 7** would be 7-6-5-3-2.

The best possible low is a wheel, the 5-4-3-2-Ace. In this game, an Ace is always the lowest card. When determining who wins in any showdown, the highest card is first looked at, then the next highest, if there's a tie, and so forth. Any five odd cards will beat any pair. For example, a hand like this:

will beat

It's easy to see what happened here. Both players drew one card, and each got a rag, but the King hand stayed odd and the 6 hand paired up. To continue this, a pair will beat two pairs, and two pairs will beat three-of-a-kind, and so forth.

How the Game Is Played

Position is very important in Loball Draw, so a button, signifying an imaginary dealer, is moved around the table in a clockwise fashion. The person on the button bets and acts last. The player to the left of the button gets the first card and then the cards are dealt, one at a time, again in clockwise fashion, till all the players have five cards. This game is best played with eight players, but not more, because of the fact that each player will receive five cards and then have the right to draw for more cards. There just aren't enough cards in the deck, even with the joker, to accommodate more than eight players.

Before the Draw

Each player will receive five cards before the draw. In a $3–$6 game, the person to the left of the button will be the small blind, and the player to his left, the big blind. In some games there is an ante, but when there isn't, there is usually a collection put in by the button, which is taken as the house's cut. In a $3–$6 game, the small blind is $1; the big blind, $3. These are live blinds, giving the blinds a chance to raise when the betting gets around to them.

After each player has gotten his or her five cards, the betting begins. The player to the left of the $3 blind acts first. He or she must match or raise that amount or fold. No checking is permitted on this round of betting.

The Draw

After all the bets are in, players *discard* whatever card or cards they don't want to play, and then the dealer burns the top card and, bending forward, is careful to slide a card or cards from the top of the deck to each player in turn. This is done beginning with the player to the left of the button and going around the table till each of the players now has five cards again.

After the Draw

A player may announce how many cards he wants or be obvious in discarding a card or two, so it is clear to the dealer. Any player can discard as many cards as he desires, up to five. If a player doesn't want to draw any cards, he is said to **"stand pat"** or **"rap pat."**

Another round of betting now ensues, again beginning with the player just to the left of the button. In the first round no checking is permitted. On this round of betting, *check and raise is not allowed, but checking is permitted*.

The Showdown

After all these bets are made, there is a showdown. The cards are turned over by the players remaining in the pot, and the lowest hand wins. If there is a tie for low, the pot is split.

At the showdown, cards speak—that is, whatever your cards reveal is your low, to be called by the dealer. Players sometimes declare their hand out loud but as we shall see, there is a danger in this, particularly if a player calls a holding he doesn't really have by mistake. Our best advice is to simply put your hand down with all five cards showing openly and let the dealer sort it all out.

Kill Pots

In some clubs and casinos, there is a **kill** feature, which means that if a player has won two consecutive pots, the player winning those pots gets a kill button. He must put up double the big blind, and all bets prior to and after the draw are doubled. If he has won one game, then he is said to have completed "one leg up" of the kill. If the player who is one leg up next wins a split pot, he still is considered to be one leg up. In order to win two consecutive pots, a player must win at least one full bet, besides the blinds.

There may be other rules governing kill pots. Check with the dealer or floorman before playing, so you'll be aware of them and comfortable with the game. For example, in some clubs, a new player may request a kill pot in order to be dealt cards immediately. The other players may have to agree to this.

Other Rules That May Apply

Declaring Incorrectly

I mentioned before that cards speak, and suggested that you simply place your open cards on the table and let the dealer call your hand. In some casinos or clubs, if you call your hand, your oral declaration is binding, no matter what you hold. For instance, suppose you call a "7" low against one other player in the pot, but don't have it. Rather you have an 8 low. If your call caused your opponent to muck his hand, your hand is dead and the other player wins. If he didn't **muck** or **foul his hand** (the same thing), then the lowest hand wins. But if you miscall your hand in a multiway pot, your hand is dead and the lowest remaining hand wins. Therefore, I repeat again, don't call your hand, let the cards speak. And keep your cards; don't muck them prematurely in a multiway pot.

The rule is more stringent with pairs. If you have a pair, you must call it, or you will lose the pot if you caused someone to muck his hand. For example, you don't announce that you have a pair, and your only opponent mucks his cards. The dealer sees your pair. You lose the pot. If there were more than two other players remaining in the pot, and at least two players keep their cards intact, the best hand wins, even if another player has mucked his hand. This rule is flexible, however. In some clubs, the remaining players, even the one who mucked his cards, split the pot.

Exposed Cards

Before the draw, an accidentally exposed card dealt by the dealer must be taken if it is a 7 or lower. If it is higher, then it will be replaced after all the other players receive their initial five cards. After the draw, an exposed card can't be taken. That's why dealers generally bend forward and carefully slide draw cards to players after the draw.

Responding to Another Player

After the draw, another active player can ask you how many cards you drew. If there has been no betting after the draw, you or the dealer must respond to the question. If there has been action, then you're not required to respond.

Raises

Before sitting down to play, check on how many raises are allowed. In most clubs and casinos, the limit is three, unless only two players remain in the game; ·then it is unlimited. Limits on raises are to prevent collusion. If two players are left, there can be no entrapment of a player between two confederates, who raise and reraise to the sky.

In the $15–$30 Loball Draw game at the Commerce Club, six raises are permitted. Therefore, again, I urge you to find out exactly what rules are in force before playing.

Playable Hands

Playable hands depend upon not only what you are holding, but also your position at the table. The later the position, the more loosely you can play. This holds true for any game in which position plays a key role. One other factor presents itself in Loball Draw, and that's the joker. If you're holding it, you have much more flexibility than if it's not in your hand.

First, let's examine position. We'll assume two blinds, then there's third and fourth—the early positions. Fifth and sixth—the middle positions. Then there's seventh and eighth—the late positions. Now we'll further assume that no matter what our position is, no other player has entered the fray. So in each of the hands we're going to examine, we're the first to act behind the blinds.

In early position, since we are **under the gun** (the first to act), the highest card in our hand, assuming we have a **pat hand** (one that we're not going to draw to), should be a 9. Without a joker, we want to play a hand no higher than 9-7; with a joker, a 9-8. The reason for this difference is that the joker can't be in anyone else's hand, and thus they may have weaker hands. By weaker, in this game we mean higher hands.

If we don't have a pat hand, then we should play any 7-5 or lower assuming we don't have the joker. A 7-5-4-3 would be a good starting hand here. With the joker, we can play a rougher 7, or even an 8, such as 8-6-5-2.

In middle position, we can play the roughest of 9s, a 9-8, as a pat hand, and even venture in with a 10-9 if we have the joker. Without the joker, a drawing hand should be no more than an 8-6, while with the joker, we can go up to 8-7.

Note that when we say drawing hand, we assume four cards to a low. We don't fool around with two-card draws; that's for suckers. There may be a time when we can draw two cards, as we shall see, but those times are rare.

In late position, we can play a 10-9 as a pat hand without the joker, and the same hand with the joker. As far as I'm concerned, we don't play **paint** as a pat hand. By paint, I mean a Jack, Queen, or King. Without a pat hand, we can draw to a 9, no matter how rough, if we don't have a joker. With a joker, we can even draw to a rough 10, but we would have to be in last position.

When should we take a two-card draw? In late position, if we're holding cards like 3-2-Ace and there's been no raises before us. If you hold the joker, you can come in with a 4-3-Joker or even a 5-4-Joker.

With all the hands mentioned above, facing only the blinds, whether in early, middle, or late positions, we should raise with our hands. Being aggressive has its rewards. First of all, it will knock out later players with marginal hands, pat or otherwise, who might be afraid of our raise. Second, especially in middle or late position, unless someone in front of us has gotten a 7, they'll probably check to us after the draw. Our bet may force them out right then and there.

As in all poker games, it doesn't pay to be a **calling station**, rarely showing any aggression. As is often said in poker, "To get action, you have to give action." Let's assume you're aggressive with a 10-9 pat hand in late position and get called and lose. All right, you can't win them all. But more importantly, your table image has been enhanced. Other players will take note that you aggressively played a 10-9. Next time you could have a 7 smooth or better and get tons of action, and win a really big pot.

After that win, opponents will be guessing as to the strength of your raising hands. You aren't a **rock** (a player who only plays the very best hands, ones that stand a small chance of losing), and so you'll get action on future hands. That's what you want; that's the key to big wins.

Action Before the Draw

You won't always be involved with the pot with only the blinds. More often than not, you'll find yourself facing a raise. If there is a raise, then you have to figure out what cards the raiser is betting with, and then, if you can match that hand, you call. If you can beat it, then raise.

You won't always be correct, of course, but it will give you a good idea of what is going on.

For example, if an early position player raises, you can put him on a pat hand of 9, even a rough 9. Or he may have a drawing hand. If you don't have the joker, he might, and can even play an 8 here. If you have the joker, then he probably has a draw to a 7. Suppose in this situation you have a pat 8 and are on the button. No one else has called. You can raise here.

But with the pat 8, if an early position player raised, the player to his left called, and then another player in middle position reraised, you can throw away your 8. It is up against a call and a reraise after a raise. You're probably beaten in this situation.

As you play more of this game, you'll get to understand your opposition better. It's imperative that you see and study the hands at the showdown, even if you aren't involved in the pot. You've got to see how players handle their position and hands. As a general rule, you'll probably notice that a call after a raise by a player in early or middle position means he's drawing, not standing pat. If he had a superior hand to the early raiser, he'd reraise. After all, there are only two betting rounds, and precious little time to get your bets in. This is not a game for the cautious caller.

When you have a monster draw, you should call a raise in earlier position with other players behind you yet to act, and if in late position, you want to put in a reraise. For example, suppose you hold:

If you hit perfectly here with a 4 or a 2, you've got a wheel. Even a 6 gives you a superpowerful hand. And best of all, you've got the joker. By calling in position four, for example, you want others to trail in and build the pot for you if you do hit.

When you're in late position after a raise and two callers, for example, go ahead and reraise. You've got the callers trapped in the middle. If reraised, you can put in another raise. The thing is, you don't want to play head-to-head against an early raiser with these cards. You hope he draws one, rather than stands pat, if you end up head-to-head.

With a pat 8, no matter how rough, when you're in middle position, if there has been an early raise and no other action, put in a raise. You want to eliminate players behind you and get this kind of hand head-to-head. If you are in late position and there's no one between you and the raiser, reraise. Judging by early raising hands, you probably have the raiser beat. If he reraises, you're in a bind. I'd call the reraise. If he draws one card, you're in a much better position. If he raps pat (taps with his hand or knuckles to indicate he doesn't want to draw), you just hope your 8 holds up after you also rap pat. Being in late position may force him to check to you on the second round of betting.

The Power of a Pat 7

A pat 7, though it can be beaten by any 6 or lower hand, is an extremely strong holding. To get even a rough 7 or better pat hand, you're bucking odds greater than 90:1. To get a smooth 7 or better pat hand, it's over 200:1. Therefore, you want to play this pat 7 very aggressively. You can cap the raises before the draw with it, especially with a smooth 7.

When You're the Blind Against One Raiser

The first rule is this: When you have a garbage hand, don't get involved to "protect your blind." You're better off protecting your bankroll. If you're only in against one player, and you have a pat 9 or better and the pot has been raised, you can put in a reraise. If you just call, you put yourself in a tough position after the draw.

Suppose you just call, and the raiser behind you raps pat. He's putting you in a difficult situation. You're going to have to check to him, and if he bets, you hope you win in the showdown, and that's he's bluffing because of his position. But it will cause others to look at you as a meek player. Better to reraise. Now, if he draws one card, you can bet into him and make his call a tough one. You've taken command.

If you don't have a pat hand, but have a one-card draw to an 8 without a joker, or a 9 with a joker, you can call a single raiser. The later his position, the better off you are. If you feel that the button or player to the right of the button is trying to steal, you can call his raise with a 9 without a joker. But if this player is a rock, muck your cards and save a couple of bets.

If there's a raiser and a caller remaining in the pot when it comes to you, you want to be able to draw to a 7, with or without the joker. With a joker, if you have a smooth 8, you have a borderline call, and you should gauge your opponents and what they're likely to raise and call with. Again, you probably can expect the caller to draw a card and the raiser to stand pat.

Standing Pat Against One Opponent

If you're in head-to-head and in later position than your opponent, if *he* draws one card, you should stand pat with any 10 or 9 hand, particularly if you feel that your draw is worse than his. If you figure he's going for an 8, there's no point in getting rid of your biggest card. By drawing, you don't expect to improve much, and there are so many ways the other player can destroy his hand. That's the best move in this situation—no move. Stand pat.

After the Draw

Since there are a limited number of small cards available to the players, and only one joker, it is rare to have multiway action in Loball Draw, even in limit games. Usually it comes down to head-to-head play or three-way action. Other than having a terrific low, the best thing is to be in late or last position after the draw. Then you can make some moves that aren't available if you're first to act. For example, if your opponent drew one card and checks to you, bet if you stood pat, even with a 10. If you drew one card and caught good, bet, even if it's a rough 8. Obviously, your opponent doesn't like the look of his hand.

By doing this, you can force out players. Sometimes, against a good player, you can bluff by betting into him after he stood pat and you drew one card. This move will throw him off, and he might not want to pay you off with his 8-5, for instance.

When deciding whether to check, bet, or raise, review what has happened before the draw, and play accordingly. Also, after a while, you should have a good read on the players, and know which play loose, which are rocks, and which are tough and strong. Against a rock who bets in early position after the draw, be extra careful about raising. These rocks will sometimes only play a 7-5 and there's no reason to either pay them off, or worse, raise and throw in a couple more bets to feed their hungry pile of checks.

Checking a Seven

In a number of clubs, there is a rule prohibiting the checking of a 7 after the draw. If it is the best hand, all action after the draw is void, and the player checking the 7 cannot win any money on subsequent bets. The player can win whatever money was in the pot before the draw if he has the best hand at the showdown. Of course, if the 7 is checked and is beaten by a better hand, the player holding the 7 loses the pot and any additional calls he might make.

Make certain that you inquire about this rule before playing in any Loball Draw game.

A Final Word

Since Loball Draw is no longer the game of choice in clubs and casinos, you will find just a few games available. In the casinos, it's rarely played, but the clubs may have games of varying limits, such as $3-$6, $15–$30, and $20–$40 or even bigger games. If you're new to the game, play in the smaller-limit games and get a feel for Loball Draw. If you feel comfortable at the game and find that you're making money, try a bigger game, but only if you have the finances and the temperament for it.

Try and play in games that are loose. But to play loosely yourself is almost suicidal. When you see players in early position, or any position for that matter, drawing two cards without the joker or without a 6, 7, or 8 in their hand, you know they are suckers. That's what you want in the game, not rocks who will grind out a living, often at your expense.

If the table is full of older men who know each other and only raise or play hands when they've extremely powerful holdings, then that's not the game for you. Often they'll sit there glumly and brighten only when you sit down, a potential pigeon for them. Rather than tighten your game to the nth degree, don't bother staying. Look for another game, where everyone is kidding around, where you see some guys reading The *Racing Form* or looking over the point spread in the local papers. That's who you want to play against—dyed-in-the-wool gamblers.

And when you sit down, give the impression to these guys that you're one of them. You're in there just to "have fun," to lose a bunch of checks and leave saying "Easy come, easy go." But whatever your demeanor, play smart. Play cards that can win. Let the others take their two-card draws and let them call with a small pair at the showdown. Don't you go along with them in their loose-cannon play. With this in mind, you can make some money at this game.

XIII

Bad Beat Jackpots

What is a **bad beat**? It's a term familiar to anyone who has played poker seriously in the clubs or casinos. Basically, it's losing a hand that you expected to win, that was a sure thing. For example, in **Seven-Card Stud** you have Aces–full and the guy in against you, on your last bet, puts in a raise. You reraise and get reraised, and you look at his exposed cards. He's holding:

Well, what can he have? He could have a straight, or maybe a flush in spades, but not a straight flush; the stretch between the 3 and 8 is too great. So you pop him again, and again he reraises you. Now you start to feel a bit cold, it's just a feeling that somehow you're going to lose, so you just call, and he turns over rolled-down 5s, three of them in the hole. And you just sit there, steaming, while the checks are pushed over to him.

That's a bad beat. My friend Jack, who plays serious stud poker in Las Vegas, told me he'd like to write a book called "Bad Beats." He'd be on volume 7, page 1149 by this time. When you're counting your winnings, when you see a pyramid of checks out in the center of the table and are waiting for them to be pushed over to you, and at the last instant the fool you're playing against gets that impossible card, that one in fifty or one in thirty or whatever card to beat you, that's a bad beat.

When you see a straight flush wheel go down the tubes to a 6-high straight flush after you bet every check you had on the hand, that's a bad beat. And we could go on and on. Volume 8, rev it up! What can we do about these bad beats but bemoan our fate? There is certainly something we can do, and that is cash in on the bad beat jackpot.

Here's how it works. In many casinos and clubs, in the lower level games, usually below $10–$20, such as $1–$2, $2–4, and up to $9–$18, if you're the victim of a bad beat, you're entitled to a bad beat jackpot. In games like Seven-Card Stud you must have either a four-of-a-kind hand beaten by a bigger quad hand (the same thing) or a straight flush. Or have a straight flush beaten by a bigger straight flush or royal flush.

In other casinos and clubs, all you need is an Aces-full hand beaten by a bigger hand (not another Aces-full) to qualify. That is much easier to get than the quad hand. In games like **Omaha Hi-Lo, Hold 'Em,** and **Pineapple,** the same rules apply, with one exception. The winning and losing hand must each utilize both hole cards to form the best hands.

Let me give you an example. The game is Hold 'Em. You are holding Ace♦ 7♠. Your opponent is holding 10♠ 10♥. The final board shows:

You have Aces-full and are beaten by four 10s. Bad beat. But you think, so what, I qualify for the jackpot. But whoa! You don't qualify because you can't use your two hole cards to form your best hand. The 7♠ isn't in play. And so you don't share the jackpot. All you have is a bad beat. Notch one more for Volume 8.

At one time, bad beat jackpots were prevalent throughout the California club system, sanctioned by state law, which permitted the clubs to charge a small collection fee on each pot to pay for it. Then the state legislature decided to outlaw it. And boom, they were gone, only to creep back with individual clubs offering them once more, in smaller amounts. How can they do this? By not charging a collection fee for them.

It's not only California clubs that offer them. A number of clubs and casinos around the country and casinos in Las Vegas have these bad beat jackpots.

Just what is the jackpot? They can run $30,000 or more and are divided between the two players who qualify, usually on a 75 percent to 25 percent basis, with the loser of the hand getting the lion's share of the jackpot. In some clubs and casinos, some of the money from the jackpot goes to each player at the table where the jackpot took place.

If you're in a club or casino, ask about the jackpot, and see if there is one. If you have two clubs to play in close to one another, by all means play where the jackpot is offered. Usually it's posted on a board in full view of the casino or club. It's a sweet extra that you don't need skill for; all you need is the right sort of luck. Lightning can strike.

A few years ago, while I was working on a book early in the morning, I felt my eyes blue as I stared at the computer and thought to myself—enough. I'm getting some fresh air. It was about 9:30 A.M. on a weekday. I got into my car, and thought of driving to a local park, then thought—I hadn't played poker in a while, why not get into a game? So, since I lived in Studio City, in Southern California, I drove to the 101 Freeway, and then took it to the 5, and twenty minutes later I was parking my car with valet parking at the Commerce Casino. At that time bad beat jackpots were legal, and I had seen some reach $60,000, for on certain weekday nights, they tripled the jackpot after a certain hour.

Needless to say, on those nights you couldn't find a seat in the club and there were huge waiting lines for games. As long as the triple jackpot was in force, no one was leaving their spot at the tables. But on this particular sunny morning, the club was fairly empty. I hesitated, thinking of what game of Texas Hold 'Em to play. As I hesitated, one of the dealers yelled "Player, table 27."

That meant a seat was open at table 27, which was a $6–$12 Hold 'Em game. There was no board, no one waiting for a seat. I waved my arm and told the floorman to "lock it up." It was seat five, directly opposite the dealer. As I sat down, I saw that the seat to my right was empty, though checks were stacked in that spot. Also seat number one held no player, though a few checks were in that spot. I sat down, and gave $200 to a runner to get me checks.

As the checks were delivered in a rack, the button had moved to the player in seat two. The player in seat four returned and took the big blind. I decided to wait for the button to pass me, so I could avoid two blinds and a collection, and simply put in a position blind of $6 and have good position. The button was at seat number four, so I didn't have long to wait. After that game was over, the button moved past me to seat number six, and I put in my position blind of $6.

My cards were 8-3 offsuit. There was a raise, and I mucked the hand. My next hole cards were 7♥ 4♦. I was getting good doubling down cards for blackjack, but absolute garbage for Hold 'Em. I mucked the cards quickly. Someone won a small pot. As the dealer was shuffling the cards, the player in seat number one ran to his seat and yelled "Deal me in."

I point this out because whatever was fated to happen, happened because of this player returning to his seat. The button was now at seat number eight. I was in late middle position, not bad at all. The cards were dealt. I slowly peeked at my cards. The first was an Ace♠. The second, Ace♣. All right! After the trash I had been dealt, this was more like it. There were four callers of the big blind, and I raised. I ended up with five callers of my raise, including the player to my right.

The dealer put out the flop:

I had Aces full. Everyone checked to me and I bet. Everyone folded except the fellow to my right, A Chinese guy in his thirties, wearing a white shirt and black pants. He called. The turn came up:

No problem there. He checked, I bet and he check-raised me! I looked at the board, and promptly re-raised him, and was popped. I reraised, and was popped again. I thought of reraising, but simply called.

The river came up:

There was now a heart draw out on the board, but that was no problem with my Aces full. My opponent bet, I raised just to clear the air one more time, and was reraised. I stubbornly reraised and was reraised.

So I called. He said gleefully "You lose," and turned over two Kings from his hand. I had indeed lost, but before I could even think about it, everyone at the table yelled "Jackpot" when they saw my two hole Aces. A floorman materialized out of nowhere.

Now that I was involved in a jackpot, I looked up at the jackpot board looming on one wall of the club. Next to 6–12HE, it read $10,300. I was entitled to 75 percent of that and my companion in arms, 25 percent. That amounted to $7,725 for me. I had played three hands, mucking two of them, I had been at the table a total of eight minutes. I got up, grabbed my checks, and followed the floorman and the Chinese guy to a nearby table to fill out W-2g forms. I showed my social security number and driver's license number for proper ID, and in fifteen minutes was given seven packets of crisp $1,000 bills, plus seven $100 bills, and the rest in smaller bills, I went over and toked the dealer, went out and got my car, and went first to my bank and then home. Not a bad morning's work.

Bad beat jackpots. Try and win one yourself. All it takes is a bit of good luck and some good karma.

XIV

Home and Private Games

The intent of this book was to give the reader the necessary tools to compete successfully in casino and club poker games. However, the same principles of sound poker strategy apply to private and home games. If you play aggressively, start with good hands, study your opposition carefully, you should have winning sessions no matter what game you find yourself in.

Home games tend to be wilder, and luck plays a bigger role than in the casino or club games we've covered. But luck can only go so far; it cannot replace skill as the chief ingredient of winning poker. The losers always point out how unlucky they are; the winners know that luck often moves to the skillful player. He has the cards that can improve enough to win pots. The weak poker player, starting with losing and unprofitable hands, needs miracles to win. Sometimes he gets them, but more often than not, those weak hands cost him oodles and oodles of money.

Private Game Factors
and How to Handle Them

Dealer's Choice

When you're playing in a casino or club, you're involved with one game alone, and you can study how your opposition plays, whether they're weak or strong, aggressive or meek, or various combinations of these factors. Most private and home games do not concentrate on one particular poker game. It's usually **dealer's choice,** meaning that the dealer chooses the game to be played.

In a recent private session I was involved in, I counted seven different games that were played. Some players had their favorites; other players shrewdly played a game in which position was an important factor, such as **Loball Draw** or **Omaha**. But most of the players simply wanted variety. I found that the losers played games in which big pots could be won, and these games were less skillful than most, with many more betting rounds and more chances to improve a hand.

My best advice is this: If you're playing dealer's choice, then choose a game where position is an important factor, where the chance to act last gives you a big advantage. Avoid **Seven-Card Stud** and concentrate on draw games, as well as games like **Hold 'Em** and Omaha.

Of course, if you feel that the other players don't have a clue about playing a game like Seven-Card Stud or **Hi-Lo Split,** then play those games. If you get solid cards, play aggressively and punish your opponents. If you get nonplayable cards, then simply muck them.

Wild Cards and Spits

Since most players have limited skills, the only way they can win a lot of money is to be lucky in games where big pots are artificially created. One way to do this is to have **wild cards**. A wild card designated in advance by the dealer can be used by any player to improve his hand by having that card become any card he wishes. For example, if deuces are wild, then a Seven-Card Stud hand like the following becomes a monster Royal Flush.

The two deuces convert into the Queen and Jack of spades, and thus, instead of having a garbage hand whose high is a pair of 2s, the player now has the absolute nuts, the best possible hand in high poker. If another player holds two deuces, or even if two other players have a deuce apiece, they can dramatically improve their hands, and wild action usually follows.

Another way to create big pots is **spits**. A **spit card** is a common card, dealt face up, which remains open to the end, and can be used by each player to improve his or her hand. Thus, a Seven-Card Stud game becomes an eight–card game, and if there are two spits, then it turns into a nine-card game.

Generally, there are no more than two spits, but if the dealer decides to have more before the deal, the game can be crazy. You have to turn your hands up a notch or two to win with spit cards. With wild cards, if you don't get a wild card, then get out unless you have a monster hand despite not having one of the wild cards.

Roll Your Own

In many home games, players are allowed to choose which card to show as their **doorcard**. For example, in Seven-Card Stud, each player receives three cards face down, and must determine which card to use as a doorcard. Of course, this is an advantage, and should be used as such, yet I've seen players willy-nilly turn over one of their cards without even looking. Oops, an Ace! If you get a hand like King♠ King♦ 3♥, you simply put up the trey.

Declaring in High-Low Games

In casino and club high-low games, the players show their hands and let the dealer sort out who has the best low and the best high, or who scoops the pot. This is done basically to move the game along and prevent endless disputes. The cards speak. Whatever cards one has determines his hand, high or low, or high-low.

In most private and home high-low games, the players declare which way they're going—high, low, or high-low. They do this usually with chips hidden in the palm of the hand. One chip is low, two is high, and three is high-low or **pig**. All the players put up one hand at the same time, and at the same time open their fists. They are bound by their declaration. Declaring adds a bit of deception to the game, and hands that look high are declared low, and so forth. Usually the rule as to declaring high-low is this: You must win both ways. If you win one way and tie the other, you forfeit the complete pot.

Let's say you went high-low and tied for low. One player went high and one low. They split the pot, even though you could have beaten the high hand. If you went high-low and lose the high but beat the low, and three players against you only went high and one low, the low declarer wins half the pot, and the best high hand wins the other half of the pot. Of course, if you go high only and tie with one other player going high, and another player goes low, you and the other high caller split half the pot.

The ideal situation when declaring is to have a hand that looks one way, while in reality you have the nuts the other way. For example, in Hi-Lo Split, your hand is as follows:

From the outset you looked low, and were drawing to either a full house or a smooth 7 at the river. Getting the Ace♠ gave you a full house. If you had been betting aggressively, everyone against you will put you on a low, and if they had mediocre lows or no lows at all, they'll naturally go high. And the whole pot is yours.

Buying and Exchanging Cards

In many home games, to add to the luck factor, players, after they receive their five or seven cards and form their hands, are allowed to improve still further by buying another card or two. This works as follows: A player gets rid of a card, either an open or hole card, and replaces it with a new card from the deck. He usually pays for this privilege. Now he uses his new card to improve his hand. Or he might have the right to exchange again, by buying an additional card. In some games, if you exchange an open card, you get another open card. Exchanging a closed card gives you a closed card. In other games, you can flip-flop and get the new card open or closed, as your choice. This is done before you see the dealt card.

With two exchanges and a spit, a Seven-Card Stud game turns into a Ten-Card Stud game. Forget about straights or flushes now; a full house is probably going to be the winning hand. And for low, it's probably at least a 6-5. A 7-low in this kind of game is usually trash.

If you play in games like this and are uncomfortable with the never-ending buys and exchanges, plus the spit, just avoid them. When it's your time to deal, play a game that calls for skill and gives you the edge in position. Or go to a club or casino nearby, if that's possible. Or find another home game where skill plays more of a part.

Other Poker Games

Poker game variations have been stretched to the limit. There are two-card and three–card poker games, where players keep exchanging up to three or four cards, with betting rounds in between. There are criss-cross games, where five cards are put out face down, while each player has three to five cards of his own, and these criss-cross cards are turned over one at a time. And there's a bet before they get turned over, and one bet for each turned–over card, usually escalating for the last two or three cards.

And players keep making up new games all the time. What most of them have in common is this—exchanges and complications. The idea is to get away from skill and let blind luck predominate. Again, my advice is to avoid these games, or if caught up in them, have superstrong cards at the outset. Don't count on luck. That's what losers do.

Glossary of Poker Terms

Ace-High: Any hand in which the Ace is the highest–ranking card, such as an Ace-high flush.

All-In: To have bet all the money you have on the table in any particular game.

Ante: Money or chips put into the pot before the deal to build up the pot.

Ante Structure: The relationship of the ante to the minimum bets in a game such as **Seven-Card-Stud**.

Baby: A small card, usually a 6 or lower.

Back Door: Making a hand you weren't originally going for.

Bad Beat: Losing with a powerful hand that was expected to win.

Bicycle: See **Wheel**.

Big Blind: The largest of the blinds in a game like **Texas Hold 'Em.** (See **Small Blind**.)

Blank: A card dealt or drawn that adds no value to the hand.

Bluff: Forcing out a player with a hand inferior to yours.

Board: Cards that are open or face-up in a poker game and thus seen by all the participants.

Bring It In: The forced initial bet initiating the action in the first round of betting.

Bug: Also known as the **Joker**. In **Loball Draw,** a card that stands for the lowest-ranked card in the hand.

Burn Card: The top card of the deck, which is removed by the dealer and placed out of play prior to a round of dealing.

Button: A marker put in front of a player's seat to signify he or she is the theoretical dealer.

Buy-In: The minimum amount of chips or money a player needs to get a seat at a game.

Call: To make a bet equal to a previous player's bet.

Calling Station: A derogatory term for a player who always calls a previous bet.

Cap the Bets: Making the maximum number of raises on any particular round of betting.

Cards Speak: Allowing the value of the cards themselves, rather than a declaration of their value, to determine the winner of the pot.

Case Card: The final card of the particular rank remaining in the deck, such as the case 9.

Catch Good: Getting a card that really helps your hand.

Chase: Playing against a hand that is obviously better than yours in the hope of beating it.

Check: To forgo a bet on any round of play when it is your turn to act.

Check and Raise: Also called **Check-raising**. Raising a previous bet after you originally checked your hand.

Checks: Also known as **Chips**. The professional term for small disks or counters that represent money at the poker table.

Chop: A slang term for splitting the pot.

Cold Call: Calling a bet plus a raise without having bet previously on any round of play.

Counterfeit: A card duplicating the rank of a player's card appearing on the board in a game like **Omaha—8 or Better** or **Pineapple**.

Cracked: A slang term to indicate that a player lost a hand. "My two pairs were cracked by his trips."

Crying Call: A weak call, made reluctantly.

Dead Money: A player's money left in the pot after he's folded his cards.

Dealer's Choice: In home games, where the dealer decides which game of poker he will deal.

Declare: A player, announcing whether he is going high, low, or high-low by placing chips in his hand to designate his choice.

Dog: Also **Underdog.** A player who is not the favorite to win.

Doorcard: The first card dealt face up in a game like **Seven-Card Stud**.

Double Raise: A raise after an initial raise.

Draw: To receive a card after a round of betting.

Drawing Dead: Trying to improve a hand that will be beaten even if improved.

Drop Box: A container in a casino or club table where cash and chips are dropped by the dealer.

Early Position: Usually the first three players to act in a nine-handed game.

8 or Better: Designation of a low hand headed by a ranked card no higher than an 8, the minimum holding in **Omaha, Hi-Lo Split** and **Pineapple** in order to win low.

Family Pot: A pot in which most of the players are involved.

Fastplay: Betting and raising aggressively.

Fifth Street: In stud poker, the third round of betting. In **Texas Hold 'Em** and similiar games, the last card on the board.

Floorman: A supervisory employee of a club or casino who, among other duties, settles disputes at the table.

Flop: The first three exposed cards dealt at the same time in games like **Texas Hold 'Em**.

Flush: A hand in which all five cards are of the same suit. Ace♥ 10♥ 7♥ 5♥ 2♥.

Fold: Also known as **Mucking Your Cards**. To get rid of your cards and no longer get involved in trying to win the pot. You're out of the game.

Foul A Hand: Disobeying certain rules of the casino or club and thus making your hand worthless and out of play.

Four of a Kind: Also called **Quads**. Four cards of

the same rank which make up a player's hand, such as four 6s.

Fourth Street: Also known as **The Turn**. In **Seven-Card Stud,** the fourth card dealt to a player. In **Texas Hold 'Em** and similar games, the fourth card on board.

Free Card: Getting another card or seeing another card without having to bet on the previous round.

Freerolling: Generally used in games in which high and low hands each win half the pot. When a player is assured of half the pot and has a shot at the whole pot, he is said to be freerolling.

Full House: Also known as **Full Boat**. A hand consisting of three cards of the same rank together with a pair. For example, 7-7-7-3-3.

Garbarge Hand: Also known as **Trash Hand**. A holding not worth investing money in or playing.

Gutshot Draw: Also known as an **Inside Straight Draw**. Drawing to a straight where only one card can help you, such as drawing for an 8 with a 10-9-7-6 hand.

Hand: also known as **Holding**. The cards a poker player bets on in order to win the pot.

Hard Rock: See **Rock**.

Heads-Up: Playing against only one opponent, head-to-head.

High-Low Poker: Also known as **Hi-Lo**. Poker games where the pot is split between the holders of the best high hand and the best low hand.

Hole Cards: Also known as **Pocket Cards.** The cards a player holds that are not seen by the other players.

Ignorant End of a Straight: Holding cards that form the lowest end of a straight. For example, holding 4-5 to a flop of 6-7-8.

Inside Straight Draw: See **Gutshot Draw**.

Jamming a Pot: A great many raises and reraises.

Joker: See **Bug.**

Kicker: The odd card in a holding. For example, a player holding a pair of Aces and a 9, has the 9 as his kicker.

Kill: Doubling the stakes in certain high-low games after a player has scooped the previous pot.

Late Position: Usually the last three positions in a nine-man game.

Limp In: To be able to call a previous bet, without having to call one or more raises.

Live Blind: A blind that still has the option to act or raise when it is his turn to bet.

Live Card: A card that can still be dealt to a player to improve his hand, that has not been seen in another player's hand or on the board.

Living Nuts: A strong hand that cannot lose.

Loball: A variation of poker in which the lowest hand wins.

Middle Position: Usually the fourth to sixth positions at the table in a nine-man game.

Miss the Flop: Where there's no help for a player's hand on the flop.

Muck Your Cards: See **Fold**.

Muck Pile: That section of the table in front of the dealer where burned cards and discarded cards are placed.

No Board: In a club or casino, an indication that there is no waiting list for a particular game.

Nuts: Either the best hand at any round of play in a game, or the absolute best hand.

Offsuit: A hand in which the cards are of different suits.

On Tilt: When a player gets so angry that his emotions take over and dictate his play at the table.

One Pair: A hand containing two cards of the same rank, plus three odd cards, such as 8-8-Jack-Queen-King.

Open-Ended Straight: A hand that can be completed into a straight by drawing a card at either end, such as 5-6-7-8.

Outs: Having the possibility of making several different hands from the cards held. For example, holding Ace♦ 10♦ 8♣ 4♦ 8♠ even if you miss the diamond flush, you can get Aces up or trip 8s.

Overcard: A card in your hand that is of higher rank than any card on the board or, conversely, a card on board higher in rank than any card in your hand.

Pair the Board: In games like **Texas Hold 'Em,** card dealt is of the same rank as a previously dealt board card. Example: 6-9-3-9.

Paint: Also known as **Face Cards**. The cards with the pictures—Jack, Queen, or King.

Pat Hand: In draw poker, a holding that does not have to be drawn to. A player holding this kind of hand is said to be standing pat.

Play the Board: In games like **Texas Hold 'Em,** where a player elects to play all five cards on the board as his best hand.

Pocket Cards: See **Hole Cards**.

Pocket Pair: Starting out with a pair as your pocket cards.

Pop: A slang term for a raise.

Position: Where a player is relative to the other players as far as the betting sequence goes at the table.

Position Blind: Being obliged to make a bet equal to the big blind when entering the game as a new player.

Position Raise: When a player raises because he is in last position and uses this as leverage.

Pot: The total amount already bet by all the players after any particular round of play. Also the total amount bet by all the players after all betting rounds are over.

Quads: See **Four of a Kind**.

Quartered: In high-low games, when two players share half the pot for either high or low.

Rabbit Hunting: Attempting to know the next card off the deck after the game is over. Usually done by a player who has folded.

Rack: A plastic container which holds one hundred chips of any denomination.

Rag: A useless card for high, such as a 5 or 6.

Ragged Board: A board in a game like **Hold 'Em,** with all rags.

Raise: To increase a previous player's bet by putting more chips into the pot.

Rake: The fee for running the game, removed from each pot by the casino or club.

Rap Pat: A player tapping the table to indicate that he doesn't wish to draw cards in a game like **Loball Draw**.

River: The last card or betting round in a poker game such as **Seven-Card Stud** or **Pineapple**.

Rock: A tight player who will only play strong cards.

Rolled-Down Cards: Three cards all of the same rank, held as hole cards by a player, such as 10-10-10.

Rolled-Up Cards: Three of a kind dealt as the first three cards in a game like **Seven-Card Stud,** such as Jack-Jack-Jack.

Roll Your Own: In home games, the option of a player to turn over any card he wishes to from his first dealt cards as his doorcard.

Rough Low: A low hand where one or more cards is close to the highest card of the low, such as 8-7-5-4-3.

Round of Play: See **Streets**.

Royal Flush: The best possible hand in high poker, without the use of a joker. It is an Ace-high straight flush, Ace-King-Queen-Jack-10, all of the same suit.

Running Cards: Two cards that fall consecutively on the board, such as a Queen on Fourth and another on Fifth Street.

Rush: Winning a number of consecutive hands.

Sandbag: Trapping a player into believing he has the best possible hand, and thus getting him to bet, so you can raise.

Scare Card: An open card that appears to greatly benefit a player's hand.

Scared Money: Money that is insufficient for the game being played. Being undercapitalized for any game of poker.

Scoop, Scoop the Pot: To win the entire pot in a high-low game.

Second Nut: Holding cards that are the second-best possible hand.

Set: Also called **Trips**. A designation for three cards of the same rank held by a player. For example, 4-4-4, a set of 4s.

Set Up: New decks of cards given to a dealer, to replace the ones he's been dealing.

Seventh Street: See **River**.

Showdown: Cards displayed openly by the players to determine who has won the pot or a portion of the pot. This is done after all action is over.

Sidecard: See **Kicker**.

Sixth Street: The next-to-last round of betting in **Stud** games played with seven cards.

Slowplay: Playing a strong hand without betting or raising, so that you disguise its strength.

Small Blind: Designating the player putting in the smallest forced bet prior to the dealing of the cards.

Smooth Low: A low hand where the cards after the highest-ranking card are much smaller. For example, a smooth 7: 7-4-3-2-Ace.

Spit Card: In home games, an open card which all the players can use to improve their individual hands.

Splashing: When a player aggressively throws chips into the pot while betting.

Split Pair: In a game like **Seven-Card Stud,** where the pair held by the player at the outset of play is split, one card open and one closed, or in the hole. For example, 7(in hole)-Queen-7(open).

Split Pot: When two or more players share the pot. Also known as **Chopping**.

Stand Pat: See **Rap Pat**.

Steal the Antes: Betting aggressively on the first round to win whatever antes are in the pot.

Steaming: Displaying anger at the table after losing a pot or several pots.

Straight: A holding of five cards in consecutive order, but not of the same suit, such as 5♣ 6♦ 7♣ 8♥ 9♠.

Straight Flush: A hand consisting of a straight and

flush combined, with five cards in consecutive order, all of the same suit, such as Queen-Jack-10-9-8 of spades.

Streets: A designation of the individual betting rounds in a poker game, or number of cards dealt to each player.

String Bet: An illegal way to bet in which a player first puts in one amount and then adds to that amount without doing it in one continuous motion.

Stuck: A slang term used by a player to indicate that he is losing. Example: "I'm stuck $200."

Suited: In games like **Texas Hold 'Em,** a term to indicate that the two pocket cards a player holds are of the same suit.

Suited Connectors: In a game like **Texas Hold 'Em,** pocket cards, usually of low or middle rank, that are of the same suit and also in sequence, such as 7♥-8♥.

Table Stakes: A player is limited to betting only what he or she has on the table in chips and money in a poker game.

Tells: Mannerisms of a player, either conscious or unconscious, that reveal the strength of his or her hand.

Third Street: In a game like **Seven-Card Stud,** the point when the first round of betting takes place after each player is dealt three cards.

Tip: See **Toke**.

Toke: The term professionals use when referring to a tip.

Top Kicker: The highest sidecard, when two or more players have identical hands at the showdown. For example, with 5-5-Ace against 5-5-King, the Ace is the top kicker and will win the pot.

Top Pair: In a game like **Texas Hold 'Em,** when a player has paired one of his pocket cards with the highest card on board.

Trap: To play a hand that cannot win, and thus be subject to a number of raises and reraises.

Trips: See **Set**.

Turn, the Turn: See **Fourth Street**.

Two Pairs: A poker holding of two separate pairs plus an odd card. For example, 2-2-3-3-King.

Underdog: See **Dog**.

Under the Gun: The player who must act first in any round of poker.

Up in the Air: Designating a pair that forms on the board. Example: "He has 9s up in the air."

Wheel: Also known as **Bicycle**. A holding consisting of the Ace-2-3-4-5, the lowest possible straight and the best possible low hand in most forms of high-low poker.

Wheel Card: The 2-3-4 or 5, any of which will be useful in forming a wheel.

Wild Card: In home games, a card that can be used by a player to improve his hand by giving the card any value he wishes.